✿✿✿✿✿✿✿✿✿✿✿✿✿✿✿✿✿✿✿✿✿✿✿✿

Assessment
of Lives

Personality Evaluation
in a Bureaucratic Society

✿✿✿✿✿✿✿✿✿✿✿✿✿✿✿✿✿✿✿✿✿✿✿

✫✫✫✫✫✫✫✫✫✫✫✫✫✫✫✫✫✫✫✫✫✫✫✫✫✫✫

Charles A. Dailey

✫✫✫✫✫✫✫✫✫✫✫✫✫✫✫✫✫✫✫✫✫✫✫

ASSESSMENT
OF LIVES

✫✫✫✫✫✫✫✫✫✫✫✫✫✫✫✫✫✫✫✫✫✫✫

Jossey-Bass Inc., Publishers
San Francisco · Washington · London · 1971

ASSESSMENT OF LIVES
Personality Evaluation in a Bureaucratic Society
      by Charles A. Dailey

Copyright © 1971 by Jossey-Bass, Inc., Publishers

Copyright under International, Pan American, and
Universal Copyright Conventions. All rights
reserved. No part of this book may be reproduced
in any form—except for brief quotation (not to
exceed 1,000 words) in a review or professional
work—without permission in writing from the publisher.
Address all inquiries to: Jossey-Bass, Inc., Publishers,
San Francisco, California, USA.

Published in Great Britain by
Jossey-Bass, Inc., Publishers
St. George's House
44 Hatton Garden, London E.C. 1

Library of Congress Catalogue Card Number LC 70-168860

International Standard Book Number ISBN 0-87589-108-X

Manufactured in the United States of America

JACKET DESIGN BY WILLI BAUM, SAN FRANCISCO

FIRST EDITION

Code 7131

The Jossey-Bass
Behavioral Science Series

General Editors

WILLIAM E. HENRY
University of Chicago

NEVITT SANFORD
Wright Institute, Berkeley

To Max L. Hutt

Preface

Assessment of Lives is for professionals and social scientists concerned with human assessment. I have written it especially for those weary of the old models who want a humanistic rather than behavioristic solution to the serious problems of assessment plaguing us—problems of opportunity in our society and problems of validation in our science.

The first premise for a new model is that the problem and therefore the model of assessment transcend the particular institution. For example, the same underlying assumptions and concepts that lead us to put down the patient in the medical model are also putting down the disadvantaged in the industrial model. A second premise for a new model is that these very institutions, in the name of objectivity, use objective procedures in the service of hidden biases. I hardly wish to ridicule objectivity, and I hope that the data presented in this book are objective enough for their purpose. However, it strikes me that the older assessment models—those using objective credentials and test scores—are used for poor purposes. Moreover, even when used for good purposes, the older models are tiresome. I faithfully promise here not to add to the endless literature reporting "a new test of" this or that. The simplistic pursuit of objectivity for its own sake cannot save us from bias (as I suggest in the first chapter), nor can it ensure the fresh discoveries that keep a science young and growing. The old objective models have failed us morally and scientifically.

Thus it seems timely to present a humanistic model of assessment as an alternative to the psychometric and behavioristic models. Advocates of objective methods have been having a field day reporting research that, it is implied, makes the intuitive clinician obsolete in medicine, industry, education, or wherever. Behaviorists freely pronounce psychodynamic theories dead, or else insist they can get along without understanding (or even postulating) the "person." While the intuitive clinician seems neither dead nor ineffectual to me, the research about his skills is too negative to permit us to be complacent. However, the research has been designed not to learn much about how clinicians observe and reason but to ask how valid they are, sometimes using methods that destroy intuition while attempting to measure it. Building a research model consistent with the way clinicians and other intuitive judges of personality function means starting with their kind of data.

As I reflect on my own experience, the life history is the most impressive kind of data, whether one is making decisions or engaging in therapy. My model is therefore built on the life history and on the contention that this form of data is the ultimate criterion of truth about an individual. Such a belief is widely shared by clinicians, but few have formulated it, and still fewer have built their research around it. And yet, as I reread Henry Murray's work, it shows a consistent emphasis on the biography as the long unit of psychological research. It seems also that, in Abraham Maslow's career, the point at which he abandoned the deficiency model came during his collection of lives of creative persons. However, such a widely held belief as the primacy of the life history has not generated much research in assessment. There is probably good reason. Methodologically, the life history is difficult to collect and use. So, we have the life-history paradox: The form of assessment that, by common agreement, is the most fundamental generates the least research.

Why not devote a few decades to learning how to do this kind of research? The process of learning began for me some years ago on a hospital staff, when the medical model began to trouble me. It seemed that patients were being viewed through a filter of assumptions denying much of their potential, dignity, and individuality. The assessment process during therapy seemed distorted by this medical model; the interaction taking place in the therapeutic interview was so heavily distorted by the doctor-patient relation as to obscure one's own individuality as well as the patient's. This model discouraged me so gravely that I left the medical setting for the industrial. Here, in the late 1950s, I encountered and participated in the storm of protest over equality of opportunity. It seemed to me that I was watching the same breakdowns in assessment all over again—blacks, women, and school dropouts could not get a fair hearing. They too were commonly viewed through a filter of assumptions that denied potential, dignity, and individuality. There was no pathological bias, nor necessarily even prejudice, but rather a prevailing negativism about human life chances that was equally oppressive. This negativism suggested failure by assessment judges to respond humanly to human data. Such a response constitutes for me the core of the assessment process.

But neither the medical nor the personnel models seemed as frightening to me as what I came to recognize as the model of man formulated by the bureaucratic system of organization. Applied to assessment, this filter of assumptions does not directly deny humanity but merely affirms policy and the rule of law. In the interests of standardization and objectivity, the bureaucratic system minimizes the personal contact between the assessed person and the decision maker. Under the mistaken notion that bureaucratic organizations are concerned with validity, psychologists have helped large organizations (governmental and corporate) build personnel departments and have contributed objective procedures. Psychological tests and credentials have been drawn into the service of a society moving at a frightening pace toward bureaucratic systems of regulating life chances in increasingly immense organizations, a movement facilitated by the computer. Thus I have completed a professional odyssey from psychiatric hospitals, where one can observe patients put down by the medical model, into industry, where one can see employees and managers put down by the personnel model, and into the study of bureaucratic operations, where one can watch students or employees being processed. I see in all these experiences a common underlying attitude of negativism toward the possibility of understanding individuals.

The view of *Assessment of Lives* is that we do not know how to judge people in humanistic but valid fashion; this ignorance is largely due to the small amount of research done. The idiographic point of view here is closest to Murray's assessment model; but it also incorporates some of the values of humanistic psychology, especially those formulated by Maslow. However, I doubt that humanistic psychology has yet provided sufficiently rigorous and productive models for inquiry. This book is in emphatic opposition to the views of behavioristic psychology on assessment; yet in most sciences there can be creative tension among opposites. I have even presumed to borrow some ideas from reinforcement-learning theory.

Assessment of Lives begins with the social crisis of equal opportunity and the scientific crisis in psychological assessment. It goes on in Chapter Two to find a new conceptual foundation in life history and exemplifies the life-history method in some sample designs in Chapters Three and Four. These explanations are provisional enough for the reader to require some evidence, and I begin to provide this evidence in Chapters Five and Six, in which I present an experimental method for assessment research, with some cross-cultural findings. Implications of the life-history method are traced in Chapters Seven and Eight. Chapter Seven examines problems common to medical and industrial models. In Chapter Eight, I consider the uses of life history in higher education as a tool for learning about personality. In Chapter Nine, I examine the prospects for reform of assessment and the research potential of the methods presented. Part Two of the book—Chapters Ten through Thirteen—presents examples of programed cases.

Gradually, with the help of sympathetic but critical colleagues, I have crystalized the view that underlies *Assessment of Lives* in the form of a particular experimental design. Robert G. Wright's enthusiasm and scholarship were decisive, especially in the critical early stages of design. Gordon Allport arranged for me to give a seminar, from which Raymond Fancher's research eventuated and ultimately also a most useful correspondence with Belgian colleague J. P. De Waele. Glenn Carlson, Samuel Bonette, Wayne Ingle, and I collected data together.

Some ingenious case writing was contributed by colleagues S. P. English, Ollie Backus, Lillian Cleary, Enid Johnson, Edward Lucking, John McCormack, Ann O'Keefe, Philip Marks, Robert Piltz, Karl and Barbara Pottharst, John Price, Sandy Schirmer, Shirley Sperling, Harry G. Woodward, Jr., Robert G. Wright, and

Madeline Wright. Alice Roosevelt Kennedy and Eli Wismer provided key data-gathering opportunities. Editorial and research
criticism—how little one can yet meet!—came from Marcia Berkeley, Victor Cline, Diane Harper, Kenneth Hammond, and Joseph
Matarazzo. Encouragement in applying the model to issues of
employment came from Labor Department colleagues Janet Cow-
ing, Judah Drob, and Joseph Seiler. Planning and executing the
data processing and computerization involved stimulating collaboration with Thomas Baer, Donald Baird, Will Lee, Ann Robinson,
Daniel Sullivan, and Thomas Todd. As the great mass of findings
began to funnel into written form, the talents and unfailing good
humor of Marsha Hollenbeck, Donna Musgrove (wise in the failings of academic writers), Thomas Dailey (who drew case graphs),
friend and editor Carolyn Mullins (who makes things intelligible),
and my wife, Ann (a production genius) were invaluable. They
complete a distinguished roster of advisers and a good company of
friends.

Hanover, New Hampshire　　　　　　　CHARLES A. DAILEY
October 1971

Contents

Assessment of Lives

Personality Evaluation
in a Bureaucratic Society

✯✯✯✯ PART I ✯✯✯✯

ASSESSMENT
OF LIVES

✯✯✯✯✯✯✯✯✯✯✯✯✯✯✯✯✯✯✯✯✯✯✯✯✯

✫✫✫✫✫✫✫✫✫ **1** ✫✫✫✫✫✫✫✫✫

Crises in

Assessment

✫✫✫✫✫✫✫✫✫✫✫✫✫✫✫✫✫✫✫✫✫✫

Every person is both a practitioner and client of assessment. If he has an official position, his judgments can affect others' jobs and lives. And other people—draft boards, bosses, surgeons, professions, and if he is especially unlucky, juries—will make decisions about his job, his life, his freedom.

There are numerous assessment situations. A jury reviews the facts of a case and decides upon guilt or innocence. A psychologist interviews a person, tests him, and recommends for or against therapy (or employment). A psychiatrist takes a medical history and recommends for or against commitment to a mental hospital. A college admissions office reviews a student's high school achievements and test results and decides whether to admit him. All twelve jury members and the three professionals may be ardent liberals and contributors to the American Civil Liberties Union. They nevertheless are participating in the operation of an assessment system that has been accused of creating cul-de-sacs of disadvantage for certain groups of persons who share a characteristic feature (skin color, age, and so on), for whom opportunities are restricted, and who will, in consequence, bequeath some of these restrictions to their children and dependents. Those disadvantaged by the assess-

3

ment system include twenty million blacks, one hundred million
women, several million Mexican-Americans, several hundred thousand American Indians, forty million old people, and perhaps the
young. The restrictions result not so much from obvious and blatant
prejudice as from respected but questionable assessment policies and
procedures. The assessment process is ubiquitous and has always
been challenged, but the questioning today has assumed a particularly strident tone. There is a radical stance. Opposing that stance is
a quite conservative defense of present assessment practices.

The University of Illinois attempted to suspend admissions
standards (substituting a lottery); conservative counterattack forced
a retreat, but the political lesson is clear. Assessment is a public
issue. At Dartmouth, as at other colleges, a small but determined
band of black students insisted upon the admission of black fresh-
men to a proportion of 10 per cent of the class. The admissions
office introduced more flexible selection standards, and the "quota"
was filled. A significant proportion of the general public assumes
that somehow admissions standards at such colleges will eventually
return to "normalcy"; conservative politicians have demanded that
return.

These are dramatic surface manifestations of a deep-lying
problem in the "national assessment policy." The blacks were only
the first of the aggrieved to protest, and quite obviously they detected
the connections between such heretofore isolated assessment systems
as college admission, medical and law school admission, job opportunities, and even credit extension. The protest was joined by
Mexican-Americans and Indians in the late 1960s, and more
recently, they have been followed by the growing "Women's Lib"
movement, which is directing much of its fire toward specific career
obstacles as well as toward the masculine ethos of society.

Many hidden categories of victims cannot or probably will
not protest: a million epileptics, other handicapped persons, older
persons (forty is the magical cutoff age for many good jobs, and age
sixty-five is the line drawn for any job at all), and numerous other
categories. Their common situation is that they are alleged to possess
"weaknesses," defined by national assessment policies as sufficient to
disqualify them for some of life's better chances.

The Civil Rights Act of 1964 was enacted at the federal

level; many fair-employment laws appeared at the state level; and rules forbidding the use of personality testing in federal employment were instated by executive order. Obviously, political concern follows social unrest.

In the Motorola Case, a lower court in Illinois upheld the contention that the use of a certain ability test was unfair. The ruling required administration of a new test that could equate the "inequalities and environmental factors" among "the disadvantaged and culturally deprived groups" (French, 1965). Since such a test has not yet been successfully devised by psychologists, only the overturn of this lower-court ruling by the Illinois Supreme Court spared personnel departments from a frantic revision of practices. Only time was bought, however; the recommendations developed by James Kirkpatrick, Robert Ewen, Richard Barrett, and Raymond Katzell (1968) call quite clearly for reform in the very logic of statistical analysis used in the construction of employment tests.

Legal reforms have provided two remedies. They have forbidden discrimination on the basis of such factors as age (a legal nightmare when one gets to the point of proving discrimination), and they have made it possible to suspend the rules for a period, as in college admissions and industrial selection. These "solutions" buy time for some more basic reform and ease political pressure under the illusion that something is being done, but they are likely to distract us from the fundamental problems: (1) We do not know how to assess human beings, and (2) we have not resolved the inherent contradiction in seeking both equality and excellence (Gardner, 1961). These two problems are interrelated. The contradiction between equality (we want to open up all life chances to as many people as possible) and excellence (we must have excellent surgeons, jet pilots, and so on) *appears* fundamental, but we do not yet know enough about human assessment to say definitely that there is no way to open up opportunities while assuring excellence. Since John Gardner's book was published, no progress has been made toward solving this problem because we have not addressed ourselves to the fundamental problem of assessment.

In the past, psychologists have avoided such emotion-laden issues as justice. I have never seen a psychological book on assessment that discussed justice. Yet the justice of the assessment systems used by American institutions is essentially the issue under attack. Is there a national assessment system—that is, a common body of assumptions, procedures, and decision rules used by most institutions to determine human life chances? Traditionally, we have considered medical decision making to be unrelated to legal decisions, and we have seen neither as related to personnel choices; further, educational decision making has been treated as a fourth, distinct area. But the underlying psychological concepts of validity and utility, as approached by Lee Cronbach and Goldine Gleser (1965), sweep across the lines of all these distinct fields. The experimental methods described by Kenneth Hammond, Carolyn Hursch, and Frederick Todd (1964) and by Lewis Goldberg (1968) can be used with legal, medical, educational, or personnel data. Thus, it becomes possible to search for generalities among the policies of institutions that were previously considered unrelated.

It is the burden of the next section to show the common ideological thread running through the different institutions. As a matter of deliberate policy, decisions about people's life chances are based on *credentials;* and the assumptions underlying this policy are deeply incorporated into thinking patterns of the decision makers—a corps of officials and professionals I shall call the gatekeepers. Only a few hundred thousand officials and professionals make the critical decisions that control the lives of most Americans. These judges of people determine a variety of individual matters, such as admitting to college, granting a loan to buy a home, admitting or releasing a person from a psychiatric hospital, hiring or promoting, declaring a person guilty or innocent of a criminal offense. Such decision makers are called gatekeepers because they control access to opportunities, freedoms, and benefits; they control the gateways into or out of the good life.

Because the gatekeeper serves as mediator between individual and institution, he can hardly conduct assessment without being influenced by institutional values. Consequently, a system has developed, in which the appraisal of credentials has been substituted for the appraisal of persons. Operation of the system is more obvious among some kinds of assessment officials than others. Institutional gatekeepers are officials recognized by society as decision makers who control access to institutional membership or resources. These include admissions officials for college and professional schools, personnel officers, research-grant committees, loan officers, and welfare officials. Less clearly recognized as keepers of gateways are those officials who control freedom *from* institutions and their constraints. These include, for example, juries (particularly in criminal cases), parole boards and officers, and hospital boards that govern discharge from closed wards. Finally, some persons in quasi-official capacities control access to institutional support in a broad sense, and their decisions can be momentous for society as well as the individual. These include voters and members of political committees that choose or encourage candidates at all levels of government.

Professional gatekeepers may not occupy official positions in the usual sense, but their opinions can decisively influence decisions about or access to institutional resources. These include psychologists who assess or diagnose individuals in medical, legal, industrial, or military settings; psychiatrists who make diagnoses or render medical or legal opinions; counselors who advise school, college, and agency administrators about the individuals they counsel; social case workers; and clergy. These professionals differ from the institutional gatekeepers in their educational qualifications, the kinds of clients they serve (individuals rather than institutions), and their memberships in organizations of colleagues. These three factors influence the manner in which they make assessments.

It is possible to improve the assessment done by psychologists, psychiatrists, social workers, counselors, and pastors, albeit slowly. Almost all such persons enter their professions through some form of graduate study, and (in theory at least) the curriculum could be modified to improve their assessment training (see Chapter Eight).

The professional clearly makes an individual assessment. Certainly he cannot appraise a person's chances for job success without knowledge of the job itself, but his major emphasis is on obtaining and interpreting data about an individual. By contrast, the institutional gatekeeper is primarily occupied with the machinery, policy, and data of his institution. A loan officer, for example, notes the size of his budget, the state of the local economy, and his own recent mistakes when deciding how to evaluate a particular application. The professional and the institutional gatekeeper each would be well served by learning something of the other's skills because the interplay between institutional environment and individual life cycle is important for accurate assessment. Recognition of this interplay has been repeatedly stressed by emphasis on the necessity of relating assessment to the environment which the individual is to enter or in which he is to perform.

Gatekeepers have a number of attributes in common. These shared characteristics are probably more obvious to the "under classes" whose fates are regulated by the gatekeepers—or to an anthropologist—than to the gatekeepers themselves. The attributes probably influence the way they do assessment. First, a gatekeeper usually works in an office—in a square box, at a square desk, surrounded by a set of files. This conventional space design expresses a common life style repellent to some in that it is more often designed to accommodate paper and to regulate paper flow than to facilitate human encounter or to encourage communication.

Second, most gatekeepers have had no discernible sign of training that would prepare them to make valid decisions about human life chances. One will vainly search the educational curriculum of the gatekeepers—psychiatrists, psychologists, lawyers, any or all of them—to find specific occasions on which the student physician or other gatekeeper was rigorously trained to review data of the kind seen officially and professionally (given data, rigorous criticisms of his judgment, and so on) and to reach conclusions that are testable for validity, or required to verify at a later date the outcome of these cases. The most advanced gatekeepers are given a graduate-level, technical education in which there is extensive treatment of issues relevant but peripheral to assessment. These most advanced gatekeepers are qualified by boards that primarily verify that the professional remembers what he learned from the technical curriculum. The list of gatekeepers also includes some highly "qualified" persons who possess a liberal or undergraduate education only and who also have not been taught to assess people. And for the most vital kind of assessment function—service on a jury—there is no training at all, peripheral or otherwise.

Third, most pernicious is the fact that the gatekeepers are functioning in an increasingly bureaucratized society. Big organizations that work from explicit policies increasingly dominate this society, and it is at least bad form, perhaps illegal or even dangerous, to deviate from organization policies for a particular case. Such bureaucratic assessment procedures place more value on rationality than on compassion. That is, it would not be defensible for a physician to let the "wrong" patient out of the locked ward because he desperately wanted out; or for a warden to release a prisoner because he is suffering; or for an admissions officer to admit an atypical applicant because he so badly wants to go to medical school. Occasionally, a gatekeeper may make such compassionate decisions, but in a bureaucratic society he would have to resort to increasingly elaborate devices to make the decisions look regular—that is, to make his decisions appear more rational than compassionate. Thus, compassion is forced underground.

Fourth, and last, the gatekeepers who defend their system can do so in a common, logical way. The conservative position on selection decisions is that institutions will collapse unless they are well led; the best persons must be placed in key posts, and the worst must be imprisoned. (The arguments are well summed up by John Gardner [1961].) Similarly, the conservative position on opportunity decisions is that opportunities are scarce and must be distributed to those who most merit them or who can profit most from them.

However, radical criticisms are increasingly directed toward the gatekeepers and such rationales. Critics charge that the gatekeepers' assessments are only superficially rational, that present assessment procedures conceal an iron-fisted determination to restrict opportunities, and that the broad effect of present policies is to preserve the status quo and its system of privilege. The radicals further charge that even in devising a new test for selecting people for jobs, gatekeepers will reveal conscious or unconscious bias. Edgar Friedenberg's (1970, p. 27) assertion about educational measurements is an example of such criticism: "Educational measurement is an inherently conservative function since it depends on the application of established norms to the selection of candidates for positions within the existing social structure on terms and for purposes set by that structure. It cannot usually muster either the imagination or the sponsorship needed to search out and legitimate new conceptions of excellence which might threaten the hegemony of existing elites."

Despite the possible appeal of this radical discontent, most psychologists will not find solutions in it. If one wants solutions, he must seek to reform the training, concepts, policies, or mode of operation of gatekeepers. He may find a conspicuous advantage in serving human needs at the present if he cultivates a radical skepticism toward gatekeeper conservatism, while avoiding radical nihilism. The psychologist who is interested in the reform of our national assessment systems should look for new and equitable procedures for reviewing data in order to make predictions of those kinds of performance that are required for decisions in employment, education, law, and medicine. The search for predictive validity commits him to research, although if the search is not in some fundamentally new directions, I am convinced he will continue merely to reinforce the ways of his conservative clients, as Loren Baritz charged (1960).

Since the invention of projective techniques, psychology has not developed a single radically new form of data in the area of assessment. It continues to generate, every year, hundreds of new paper-and-pencil tests, more and more of the same thing. In order to break out of this box, we shall have to ask new kinds of questions. Part of the walls around his thinking are formed by the psychologist's concepts. In particular, consider the concept of objectivity. In the process of assessment, objectivity conjures up for some images of impartial official boards, testing bureaus, and personnel dossiers. But these images appear objective only to those who are not at the moment undergoing assessment. Consider the employee suing for his pension, the patient waiting to be evaluated by a medical board for his release from the TB sanatorium, or the litigants in a custody suit. These are agonizing situations; bland psychological concepts such as reliability and validity conceal intensely emotional issues such as justice. An entire monograph on testing and fair employment was published recently. In it, the facts were reviewed dispassionately (no doubt a public service) but with no reference to the sense of injustice experienced by the persons tested, no mention of the feeling and impression of discrimination. This monograph at least obscures the human realities of the problem and in this sense renders a public disservice.

CREDENTIALS SYSTEM

The increasingly dominant system of assessment in the United States makes use of credentials as data. There have been attacks on the system in terms of justice and validity. S. M. Miller (1967, pp. 127–128) has charged:

> *We have become a credentials society where one's educational level is more important than what he can do. People cannot obtain jobs that they could well fill because they lack educational qualifications. Negroes who dropped out of the educational steeplechase before a high school diploma cannot get jobs. Employers and the better off do not feel there is discrimination; rather the low educated are "not qualified."*

A credential is a simple fact, readily encoded and usually documented, that is used as a standard of judgment. A positive credential attests to one's competence or fitness; a negative credential certifies one's failures, shortcomings, and weaknesses. Examples of credentials from different institutions are grades, credits, diplomas, and degrees; offenses, convictions, and prison records; symptoms, diagnoses, and lengths of stay in hospitals; work record, earnings, titles, seniority, and companies worked for; I.Q., Graduate Record Examination scores, and aptitude-test scores; honors, awards, papers and books published; merit badges earned in the Boy Scouts; Masonic degrees received. Credentials determine one's access to numerous freedoms and opportunities; they influence, often determine, the decisions that permit access to those opportunities and freedoms. An assessment system in our society, and in all other technical societies, has been built up around the use of credentials. The credentials are the primary data for judgment; their analysis is prescribed by formulas; and the system is actively promoted as just, scientific, objective, and convenient. An entire industry has developed to build credential systems, to install them, and to promote their further use.

The primary scientific argument for the use of a credential is the ease of proof. One can validate a standard by showing through research what kinds of behavior can be predicted from it. The test score is already in a convenient form suited for this statistical proof. The logical appeal is quite simple: if one can specify a hypothesis precisely, he can prove it-or disprove it precisely. Credentials provide such precise categorizations and measurements of performance. The primary administrative arguments for the use of a credential are convenience and economy, which are manifested in processes of obtaining, recording, and computing.

The primary moral argument (which is of questionable validity) stresses the objectivity of credentials. The Boy Scout is impressed when his merit badge is handed out. Physical things, even if they are only paper, seem more objective. The objectivity may indeed offer protection against autocratic whim. However, for blacks and for women, how valid are moral arguments about objectivity if, in spite of college degrees or high school diplomas (objective credentials not to be questioned), their opportunities in life are less?

Secondary arguments for credentials can be elaborated in all these respects. The objectivity of the credential promotes scientific research. Credentials not only are convenient in the obtaining and handling of data, but also make feasible specification and enforcement of policies. Hospital length of stay can be shortened by formulating policies and enforcing them by reference to careful medical records. The percentage of black employees with college degrees can be increased by enforced directive. The moral argument for credentials lies, not only in the inherent protections afforded by objective assessment, which judges all equal who have the same credentials, but also in the hope held out by credentials to the disadvantaged. "Get a college degree," the appeal sounds, "and double your income." Or "Get certified by the American Board of ———, and you will be as good as anybody." These goals also offer something like the primitive rites of passage—they offer milestones of progress and give meaning to human life.

With the support of such arguments, the credentials system seems in a strong position. It receives support from the advocates of institutional values, because these values so often get written into the credentials system itself. That is, when one speaks of a qualified person he tends to build into the qualifications as many of the social values as he can. A clean-shaven executive refuses to hire a person with a long beard even though his own grandfather wore one. In psychiatry, "deviation" becomes part of the diagnosis, or at least part of the etiology. In politics, a qualified candidate must come from an acceptable and trusted occupation, must look right for the job, must say the right things, and so forth. Further, the growing automation of assessment supports the kinds of assessment that provide computerizable data. These social and technical forces combine in a massive thrust toward bigger and better credentials systems. One need not identify particular spokesmen for it. Its size and power are too great to require any advocates.

The failings of the credentials system of assessment will be presented here more vigorously and at more length because this case must be a powerful one even to begin to offset the thrust of such data and decision systems in a technical society. First, consider the scientific argument. Objective tests and other credentials, because of that objectivity and the very form in which they exist, lend themselves to validation. But are they validated? A test publisher presents some validating data, but a test is then used in many circumstances for which it was not validated. When we consider the number of different occupations (40,000?) and changes in them, the many industries and their changing technologies, it is not difficult to predict that the initial validation of a test by its designer is likely the only one it will ever receive. Conscientious industrial psychologists and clinicians do revalidate tests for new populations, but revalidation appears a hopeless task in comparison with the size of the problem. If the problem is immense with the most highly developed form of credential (the psychological test), consider the other credentials. What is the validity of the college grade when used as a criterion for employment? Donald Hoyt (1965) reports a vigorous effort to find an occupation in which performance is correlated with college grades—results were almost entirely negative. What is the evidence for the conclusions usually reached about a person on the basis of his education, age, sex, religion, race, occupation, residence, club memberships, physical appearance, income level, job experience, country of origin, dress, grooming, prison record, accident record, health history, athletic history? It is no doubt true that research can readily establish what kinds of predictions can be made on the basis of what kinds of credentials (and hence what kinds of decisions are warranted). It is doubtful that such research can be done on a sufficient scale to be definitive. Even if so, it is doubtful that it will be done, and I consider it less likely in the future than in the past. Such validation interests only a small number of research psychologists and sociologists. One reason seems to be that the validation of credentials fits neither the life style nor the logic of bureaucratic thinking. The bureaucratic organization (and are not hospitals, schools, colleges, industries, increasingly bureaucratic?) is one that empha-sizes rationality, lawfulness, compliance with policy and procedure, and stability, not critical thinking and not challenging the validity of the laws and customs that hold bureaucratic organizations together. The college is a good example—how many professors are interested in validating the grading system of the college?

Bureaucratic ideals of economy and precision place a high value on administrative convenience, which brings us to the second advantage of credentials. If one has a thousand applicants for a high post, the temptation is strong to collect a small amount of factual data from each, code it objectively, and narrow the field of applicants to a few "well-qualified" finalists. The sheer pressure of the situation gives such economic devices great appeal, regardless of their validity. Thus a professor, who might prefer to read a reasonable number of student essays, may well settle for an objective examination to evaluate two hundred members of a single class. The superior con-venience of credentials drives out more complex data regardless of the relative validity. In industry, the personnel department may prefer to purchase a $5 credit-reference check on an applicant rather than an intensive career review at $500, even if the first has zero validity for selection and the second has considerable validity. By similar reasoning, the credential increasingly is favored for adminis-trative purposes because such data can be more readily computerized than can impressionistic and uncoded data (as from an interview). Our burgeoning computer technology further enhances the creden-tial system. The net effect makes more and more possible the ex-aggeration of the ills as well as the benefits of the credentials system; as has been noted, the computer permits one to calculate either fact or error at lightning speed.

The worst effect of the low cost of credentials is their preemp-tion of the assessment process. Instead of professional assessors (psy-chologists, psychiatrists, attorneys, personnel managers, admissions officers) who are paid for the quality of their judgments, we could increasingly get clerks who are paid for their reliability. A clerk here is defined as a conscientious person who has a high regard for reli-able facts but no inclination or ability to search for their meaning. We may prefer druggists to chemists in a drugstore but one is not yet satisfied that gatekeepers should be clerks. The question of the equal proficiency of clerks will be dealt with in a later section. We will also consider later the kinds of society in which policies, through clerks, control life chances. But it is worth noting here Max Weber's horror at this prospect, when he said (Bendix, 1960, pp. 454–456): "It is horrible to think that the world could one day be filled with nothing but those little cogs, little men clinging to little jobs and striving towards bigger ones . . . men who need 'order' and nothing but order, who become nervous and cowardly if for one moment this order wavers, and helpless if they are torn away from their total incorporation in it."

Credentials can preempt the assessment process at both ends. That is, the data used in assessment eventually become credentials; and, to the extent that there is a desire to validate those data, the natural preference is for precise criterion facts. These too become credentialized. Thus college grades are used to validate high-school grades, and graduate-school grades to validate college grades. There the validation process halts, until the messy criteria from occupational life can be more satisfactorily credentialized.

The moral arguments are the most controversial of all. In a democracy there is constant tension between the struggle to assure excellence in the vital skills and the insistence on equal opportunities for all (Gardner, 1961). The use of objective credentials to determine opportunities (such as admission to medical school and to good jobs) seems at first glance to favor equalization of opportunity. But then one quickly finds that many blacks do not do well on tests. Apparently, while tests do measure competence, that competence is inextricably wrapped up with previous opportunity. Perhaps the argument is less emotional if we consider another situation. A professor is to be appointed. The requirement is set that the candidate have ten years' experience in teaching; this is a rational requirement. However, consider the fact that consequently few women will be considered for the post. The requirement of a specified period of teaching experience assures that primarily men would be qualified for the post since they customarily have uninterrupted career lines and women very often do not. The semantic trick lies in the word *qualification*—instead of predicting who will make a good professor, all aspects of performance considered, the selection committee looks

for the "most qualified applicant," which is not the same requirement at all. The point is that disadvantage is created by the way
qualifications are defined; it is an artifact of the credentials assessment system. Black students recognized this in a number of colleges
when they demanded that the admission requirements be suspended
to get more blacks enrolled.

The moral assets of credentials assessment include the alleged
objectivity of decision making and the presumed virtues of explicit
standards, which permit the disadvantaged to learn in advance the
ground rules for obtaining opportunities. Thus the hospital patient
knows that if he behaves himself and his symptoms disappear he may
be released or receive other privileges. There are several moral difficulties with such practices. One is that they can lead to a system in
which the person is deprived of liberty, property, or opportunity
without an opportunity to confront, cross-examine, or even negotiate
with his accuser. The black person (or anyone) who is rejected by
objective standards has no one to confront. The system thus violates
an elementary consideration of justice—the ancient rule in Anglo-
Saxon law that one has the right to an open court. This ancient
right accounts, I believe, for the instinctive preference for interviewing in employment assessment. The interview, while the least reliable, least valid, and least economic of all selection procedures, is one
most frequently used. I would not maintain that this is the only
reason for its use or that it does in fact assure human rights to the
rejected applicant, bypassed employee, or fired employee; but at
least a crude instinct to provide a hearing is there. Considerations of
justice are therefore obscured by the credentials system. It has, I submit, almost totally distracted reformers who are concerned with
equal opportunities and civil liberties. Instead of questioning the
validity or the justice of requiring a college degree for a job, the
reform movement urges that everyone receive a chance at a college
degree—this merely postpones and evades the real problem.

The moral implications of credentials assessment lead us to
wonder also about the losses of human encounter between physician
and patient if the physician increasingly relies on the computer; on
the losses in the humanity of academic relationships when objective
examinations are used and grades are emphasized; and, of course,
about the kind of society in which computerizable data are the

primary kind of evidence. This is a society in which the computer in one city can advise computers in other cities that an employee has failed to pay his bills (no matter why or that the bills were too high), that a person was alleged to have written his congressman protesting the war, and that a person once had an "epileptic seizure" (no matter which kind or what the conditions were surrounding it).

What kind of society is it in which one looks at a dossier on a person instead of at the person? It is the kind of society, surely, in which the kinds of things that can be and are recorded in dossiers are considered important. Such a society has a plus-or-minus system in which one accumulates merits (or demerits); when the merits are progressively related, or the demerits reinforce one another, we have a society in which advantage or disadvantage can pyramid. Even if one does not concede that the merits are at best caricatures and mockeries of humanistic values, he must concede that the dangers of pyramiding have become all too real now that disadvantage has been known to perpetuate itself through several generations. The demerits of the father are borne by the child.

Some would say that the dossier society is scientific. Technical perhaps, but not scientific. Let us consider whether there is a distinction between such data as credentials, qualifications, standards, diagnostic criteria, and test scores, on the one hand, and scientific measurement on the other hand. It is convention to lump tests and measurements together because they have a similar form; the technical mind does this. However, the usage of the data differs quite fundamentally. There is a world of difference between attempting to learn how intelligence grows in children (a scientific problem requiring some objective measurement) and defining the I.Q. as an instrument for social decision making. That difference lies in the technical man's desire for a decision versus the research man's desire for meaning. It is inconceivable to think of research without some use of objective measurement. But it does not follow that a procedure useful in research will be useful in assessment. The methods useful in dissection of a cadaver are hardly appropriate in surgery.

However, if we wish to do research in assessment, we ought to use some procedures that are consistent with the discipline and nature of that assessment. This is precisely what has not happened in assessment research: Until the last decade, there were few if any attempts to investigate the way clinicians and other professional judges achieve their impressions and make predictions. Just as the growing inequities of credentials assessment have provoked a social crisis, the failures to do relevant assessment research have provoked a scientific crisis.

INTUITIVE CLINICAL ASSESSMENT

There is a rival to the credentials system, and that is the more intuitive system favored by many clinical psychologists. I refer not only to psychologists in clinical settings but also those who were schooled in the clinical tradition but who render services in industrial, educational, and other settings. In this section, I shall examine briefly the claims of this system, its recent troubles, and the prospects for borrowing its more promising features in some new reform system of assessment.

The characteristics of the clinical system are somewhat obscured by the fact that clinicians appear to practice one system while writing about another. That is, when they do assessment, it is on a case-by-case basis; and, in each case, they tend to collect diverse forms of data. However, when they publish assessment research, clinicians tend to descend into particularism, to analyze some specific data-gathering or data-measuring device. If clinical assessment is multiform and case oriented, clinical research is "uni-form" and instrument oriented.

To my knowledge, there has been only one serious effort to validate multiform assessment: the Michigan assessment program (Kelly and Fiske, 1951). The findings were dismal enough to discourage many investigators. However, it is worth noting that the criteria used (performance ratings five years later) were as dubious in meaning as any of the instruments used in the research. Nevertheless, the Michigan assessment group had at least the ambition to do research upon multiform assessment, as Henry Murray urged (1938). A few investigators have heeded this urging. In all such investigations, however, including those of Murray's colleagues, little attention has been focused on the major instrument (the life history) featured in his original propositions; and thus it may not be said that the multiform, Murray-style assessment has ever received definitive research attention commensurate with the emphasis it receives in the practice of assessment. We will, in this book, consider the research and assessment implications of Murray's original set of propositions (1938, pp. 38–49).

A second paradox in clinical assessment is therapists' indifference to it, as documented by Paul Meehl (1960). My own observations, as in a study of clinical utility (Dailey, 1953), suggested to me that one of the prime problems of psychological assessment in clinical settings was not so much that psychologists' predictions were invalid as that their reports were not relevant to decisions about patients. Therapists, who must engage in the management of cases, simply need from diagnosticians very little information that they cannot obtain in the process of therapy itself. Thus clinical assessment, as in formal and projective technique interpretation, seems to be largely an academic exercise. The paradox is that the same psychologist who insists on clinical techniques in diagnosis loses interest in his own findings when he conducts therapy. (See Chapter Three.)

A third paradox arises from the very argument for intuitive method: that it is more human, permits more compassion and openness, than does the credentials system. To test a student, patient, or employee may seem to some a mechanical, cold, and witless process. Instead of such test gathering and credentials collecting, one should engage in a warm, flexible, or empathic inquiry in an interview. However, such an open-end procedure permits other abuses. The same open-end procedure that permits compassion also permits autocracy and even prejudice. Would a disadvantaged applicant for college admission be protected better by suspending objective tests if he is then to be subjected to the decision-making processes of an intuitive autocrat? The paradox is that we cannot humanize assessment without taking risks of abuse.

Although these three paradoxes have an important relation to the proposed solution, which will be developed in following chapters, they are not yet the most serious self-contradiction in the clinical system. This very system, which has been heavily favored by the most experienced professionals and which would seem to be most carefully designed to take advantage of their experience in assessment, is in the most serious scientific difficulties. Before the onslaught of an extremely disappointing series of experimental findings—beginning with the Michigan assessment report (Kelly and Fiske, 1951),

decisively summarized by Meehl (1954), and continuing in still
more recent investigations (Mischel, 1968)—the scientific fortunes
of clinical assessment have been steadily falling. Consider just how
far they have fallen, according to the research findings published.
Psychologists using intuitive methods do no better than clerks making actuarial forecasts from tests (Meehl, 1954; Sarbin, Taft, and
Bailey, 1960). Trained psychologists do no better than graduate
students (Cline, 1955; Grigg, 1958). The clinician who is permitted
to choose his predictions (that is, decides to predict only if he has
enough data) is not helped by this flexibility—because, according to
Lewis Goldberg (1959) and Stuart Oskamp (1965), confidence is
inversely related to accuracy. Nor can we say that the research
should use only "the best clinicians," since this concept of excellence
implies some generality in the skill of making assessments—a generality as yet disputed, although supported in Victor Cline and
James Richards' careful research (1960).

At a quick glance, the situation could hardly appear worse.
Clinical assessment has not been shown effective. How can one consider this system a rival to the far more potent, socially favored, and
institutionally supported credentials system of assessment? Is it no
small wonder that one of its leading recent critics, Walter Mischel
(1968), recommends the abandonment of the "trait and state" (or
dynamic) theories of assessment altogether? Mischel reads the same
evidence we have already cited. He reaches the same appraisal we
have reached: that there is a crisis. He does not, however, recommend a solution in any particular detail. When one reviews the latter
half of Mischel's treatise, he finds much discussion of how behavior
is modified; but, other than occasional references to obtaining the
patient's or client's social-learning history (so that the modification
can be properly planned), no assessment system is proposed. But
wait: perhaps this very "social-learning history" describes an assessment system. I am not sure whether it does or not. In some parts of
his treatise, Mischel sounds as if he is saying some of the things that
will be said in Chapters Three and Four of this work; in other
places, he is merely sketching in an assessment system yet to be devised, described, and validated. Donald Peterson's diagnosis (1968)
is similar to Mischel's. The difficulties of clinical assessment are so
profound that new scoring keys for projective techniques, or for the

Minnesota Multiphasic Personality Inventory (MMPI), are no solution, because "flaws in clinical assessment are not only procedural but conceptual. Not only have we been using faulty methods, we have been trying to get the wrong kinds of data" (p. 4). Peterson then leads us into a behaviorism, as does Mischel. A growing number of clinicians do appear to find this a plausible direction for exploration, and the research literature regarding the modification of behavior is larger (and, I think, richer) than that generated by any other school of thought regarding therapy (Gendlin and Rychlak, 1970).

But we cannot quite write off the psychodynamic wellsprings of clinical assessment so quickly. In the end, perhaps we must and shall. For the moment, so very many of our clinical colleagues continue to follow the modes of thought of psychoanalytic and related dynamic theories that one can hardly hope to divert an entire profession's course of thought in the way proposed by Mischel and Peterson. I do not believe that trait and psychodynamic views of assessment have been clearly disproven by the failure of clinical assessment allegedly based on those views. The reasons are these:

First, clinicians have not reported much research on the ways in which they actually practice assessment. The studies that have been published reflect more the canons of evidence accepted by editors of journals (instrument-oriented) than they reflect the ways clinicians actually look at their patients (case-oriented, multiform assessment).

Second, in particular, the predominant assessment model, multiform assessment, has received major research attention to most of its detailed procedures—except for the one procedure that happened to be central in Murray's thought: the life history.

Third, since traditional assessment data are not especially relevant to the needs of psychodynamic therapists, one might try devising data-gathering procedures that do appear relevant rather than to abandon psychodynamic assessment altogether (this is the burden of Chapter Four). This does appear to be the wise strategy adopted by Mischel: to build assessment around the needs of behavioral-modification therapists.

In brief, the negative findings regarding assessment validity cannot be generalized to the way practicing clinicians do assessment;

but rather they pertain to the kinds of research evidence regarded as publishable. We are not quite out of the woods yet in explaining why clinicians do not do assessment in ways relevant to therapy, even if we were satisfied with their validity. Nor can these defenses satisfy us if we want a science. If practicing clinicians, in spite of reasonable diligence in gathering and interpreting data, do not publish significant findings that reflect the state of their art, then we shall have to find ways to help them do this. If a clinician submits to an experiment in which the validity of his predictions is to be checked against some clerk's, for example, and he fails to do better than the clerk, then he must either accept the evidence or prescribe an experiment in which his claimed skill can be manifest and can be measured. The stark negativism of Meehl's findings remains as hard fact to confront us. What is it that clinicians know about people and how is it to be measured? The assumption here is that they know a great deal but that it has not been appropriately measured. However, it is further assumed that knowledge of persons is not enough to offset the doubts raised by the published research cited above; therefore, the greater interest here lies in the *potential* validity of clinical assessment, which I believe to be immense, rather than its past validity, which may be all too modest.

The hope for psychodynamic assessment rests in the belief that the great thrust of ideas, beginning with Sigmund Freud and Alfred Adler and continuing to find new frontiers with Erik Erikson, have not run their course in science. It rests on one's conviction that the humanity reflected in the writings of such as Rollo May and Abraham Maslow is real, and that the compassion revealed in the writing is shown in the way such clinicians do assessment. If justice must be compassionate, clinical assessment of this kind offers us hope of justice for those oppressed by the credentials machines of our society. But what about validity—is it not also just to be valid in one's judgments? What good does it do to use a clinician to appraise a person's job chances or his potential for doing good research if given a grant, if the clinician is grossly inaccurate?

I am willing to make the assumption that the validity of the clinician's assessment can be improved. But the accuracy of clinical assessment can be increased only if we investigate it through research, learning the conditions under which increments can be obtained. If through the medical and humanistic tradition of the clinician he has compassion for the person assessed, then we can learn further to make that compassionate clinician accurate in his judgments. This is the fundamental assumption.

How can it be done? Something in the way of a consistent model for thinking about the assessment process, the logic of its operation, the optimum strategy for its development, the way in which its humanity is to be preserved while its validity is enhanced —these are the requirements for solving the problem of clinical assessment.

In assessment one collects certain kinds of data as inputs, processes them in certain ways, and produces decisions about life chances as outputs. Among the inputs are the following: (1) Data about abilities from tests, course grades, employment histories, and other sources. (2) Data about values, interests, and motivations from tests and from behavior in social situations (especially situations that evoke conformity, and so forth). (3) Data on social characteristics: age, race, sex, religion, and occupation. (4) Physical and physiological characteristics: data on height, weight, good looks, skin color, pallor, coordination, laboratory findings of a general psychophysiological type (such as skin resistance). (5) Data on status: positions in formal institutions, honors and awards, money, social-class membership, "connections," merit badges, arrests, convictions, and the like. (6) Data regarding the life history or biography of the person.

The rules for transforming these data into decisions operate along lines representing premises about human nature. These premises include a set of propositions about the capacity of people (with certain characteristics) to change and learn, the nature of human abilities, the structure of values and their relationship to human privilege and opportunity, the nature of merit and the duty of an assessment judge to reward it, and the nature of measurement itself. These rules (a postulate system) stand between the data about a person and the decisions reached about him. Theodore Sarbin, Ronald Taft, and Daniel Bailey (1960) have outlined the logic of such postulate systems, indicating how they are used to govern the process of clinical inference.

Postulate systems claim rationality. For example, consider the postulate system involved in our legal doctrines of due process. They *appear* rational. Judge Learned Hand said, "I must say that, as a litigant, I should dread a lawsuit beyond almost anything else short of sickness and of death" (Frank, 1949, p. 40). In spite of this claim to rationality, the institution typically weakens it by imposing several purposes *in addition to* rational decision making. Two of them are (1) the streamlining of assessment processes so that there are minimum unrest, cost to institutions, and trouble for officials, regardless of whether resulting procedures are valid; and (2) the maintenance of social stability by continuing to allocate the most desirable opportunities to persons who support the present structure or belong to its privileged portions.

The design of assessment must cope with these practical and political constraints while making as few concessions to them as possible. In some instances, the credentials system has unwittingly sold out to them.

If assessment is to be multiform rather than singular (and who can disagree with Gordon Allport's view [1961] that there is no "one and only" method for diagnosing personality?), then it must deal with the problem of integrating data from diverse sources. The Michigan assessment program integrated data by calling for unified ratings after each increment of data, and this would be one feasible way. The data can come, in Allport's classification, from several levels (physiological, psychological, and sociocultural) and from diverse techniques (1961, p. 399). Allport's varied list of techniques included personal documents, self-appraisal and other ratings, conduct sampling, tests and scales, projective techniques, depth analyses, and expressive behavior records—which list he appropriately described as an "embarrassment of riches." The device for integrating data was called by Allport the synoptic procedure: one that provides a "general view of the whole or principal parts of a thing . . . a group of methods which have to do with combining or relating information so as to strengthen our assessment of a given personality" (1961, p. 445).

The synoptic procedure has been virtually ignored in assessment research. Thus if there are meanings in the whole of data that are not obvious or visible in the parts, the bulk of research misses some of the meaning of assessment data. Lewis Goldberg (1968) is one of the few to cope with this problem in his model for research. He reports that configural models (those reflecting the meaning of whole sets of data) do not show accuracy levels better than linear models, which deal with the meaning from simpler sets of assessment data. However, the suspicion here is that this problem cannot be solved until we have some theory as to why data should integrate at all. It is quite possible that some kinds of data do not combine in assessment, and efforts to show their configural value will always fail. For example, credentials data or external facts about a person (height, weight, education, income) do not have materially different meanings after combination than can be detected piecemeal. On the other hand, my hypothesis is that more expressive and phenomeno-logically meaningful data will prove to have configural meaning. The main point to make clear now is that the procedure for synopsis, and the general question of integration in assessment, must be dealt with in satisfactory manner before one can claim to understand how humanistic clinicians do or should do assessment. I shall return to this question in Chapters Five and Six. The assessment of actual cases appears to be a synoptic procedure.

Continuing our inventory of the requisites for satisfactory assessment-research design, what about objectivity? How can the values of objectivity be preserved, and what in fact does objectivity mean in clinical assessment? The aim should be not to seek objec-tivity but rather to avoid the dangers of subjectivity without losing its creative and humane values. My proposal (developed in Chapter Three) involves utilization of objective methods as a rough check on the accuracy of intuitive assessment. But the major control over runaway subjectivity should be prediction, not objectivity in data collection and interpretation. The predictive validity of assessment is a central feature in the investigations to be reported in Chapter Six and in the methods of assessment proposed. Whatever achieves ac-curate prediction is accepted as sufficiently objective.

In fact, a limit should be set upon objectivity. One should not seek objectivity at the expense of the human encounter. It would be unfortunately possible to devise an inventory to question a patient or a job applicant about almost any topic at all. A computer can administer and score the answers. There is little objection to this in research, but it must not interfere with the humanity of the assessment encounter. This alleged possible empathy makes it worthwhile to puzzle over ways to save the intricate and problematic clinical assessment system.

By *human encounter* in the present context is meant, first, an assessment procedure that permits the assessment professional or official to judge areas of omission, distortion, or reticence on the part of the informant and to improvise ad hoc inquiries to fill in those areas if the effort seems worthwhile. A human encounter provides also the opportunity for the person assessed to interrogate the judge, even to cross-examine him on his conclusions under certain conditions. It is a situation, ideally, of human equality rather than the traditional doctor-patient, tester-subject, boss-employee, or other such power-imbalanced relation. In practice, any person assessed finds it difficult not to feel at a disadvantage but the style of assessment need not add to this disadvantage by defining him as a guinea pig, an object to be measured, or a problem to be solved. Since Stanley Milgram's experiment (1963), we know how brutalizing the relation of scientist to experimental subject can become under conditions once considered innocuous.

I am not proposing to explain away the negative findings regarding clinical assessment. These findings may not be ignored; they tell us that much is seriously wrong with clinical assessment but without telling us what it is. There must be a radical change, but in ways that are intrinsic to the nature of the clinical enterprise and compatible with the nature of personality, and on this premise I believe most humanistic psychologists would agree to found their investigations. Can the more rigorous investigation of intuitive assessment really hope to solve the problems of justice exposed in our discussion of credentials assessment? The intuitive system has two very serious flaws—the danger of prejudice and the problem of validation. But it has one decisive advantage—the possibility of compassion. In the chapters to follow, I propose that we gamble on this possibility of greater compassion and pursue through research the problem of improving the validity of intuitive assessment.

2

New Foundations
for Reform

It is proposed that vital decisions be based on the most humanistic data we can find and that a formal assessment system be built around the collection and interpretation of such data. It is further suggested that the data that best fit this requirement will prove to be the life history of the person, applicant, patient, client, or student. While the disciplined collection of life history is far from the self-indulgent looseness of a purely intuitive assessment judge, neither can it be done by clerks and computers. Life history must strike a balance between excessive intuition and the tedious meritocracy of the credentials system. This emphasis on the life history is far from new; Adolph Meyer (Lief, 1948) stressed it decades ago. What is new is that the life history should be made the central focus of assessment *research* and that it should constitute the central framework of thought about a person. Thus, properly collected and authenticated, it is the ultimate source of criterion statements about a person as well as the basic source of humanistic understanding of him.

Henry Murray (1938, p. 39) stressed this more explicitly than any other assessment theorist: "The life cycle of a single individual should be taken as a unit, the long unit for psychology. . . .

27

The history of the organism is the organism. This proposition calls for biographical studies."

A man's life is to him the most obvious and overwhelming of all realities. Traces of his past are his constant companions; as for his future, do not most people act as if they will live indefinitely? It is therefore most surprising that there should be any question whether life is a substantial enough form of fact to provide data for an assessment system. Perhaps what has so long delayed the evolution of a life-history assessment system has been the undeniable problem that a person's life is an awesome, intricate, beautifully complex phenomenon, much too complex for the simple descriptive procedures preferred by assessment psychologists in the past. Fortunately, we have some extremely competent guides in the search for ways to build a life-history assessment system. Every major theorist of personality has helped lay the conceptual foundations for the study of life. This chapter discusses those foundations; subsequent chapters describe some sample procedures for collecting and using life-history data in assessment.

Is this task worth doing? There is considerable discouragement regarding personality research today. Favorite techniques have proven weak, and there is more tension and competition than cooperation among those professions which should be coordinating their personality studies. In such a discouraging climate one is likely to begin a radically new quest only if there is some plausible hope of discovery at the other end. Let us pose this skeptical question in the form of analogy. Does a person's life have an organized form, an anatomy? One is not likely to initiate new research methods, go to the trouble of purloining cadavers at midnight for detailed dissection, unless he is willing to assume there is such an anatomy. Is there a researchable problem in life history at all?

The question has two levels. First, there is the molecular level of analysis, the study of particular associations and brief chains of events, as in Alfred Baldwin's study (1942). Molecular analysis has the methodological advantage of simplicity and the immense conceptual advantage of a theoretical foundation—learning theory. Molecular analysis has for us one decisive disadvantage—it loses the person if pushed too far. The second level calls for molar analysis, the study of very long chains and patterns of events, as in the series of inquiries beginning at the Harvard Psychological Clinic in the 1930s and visible in the extensive work of alumni of that clinic (Wessman, 1957). In the study of lives, has any roster of psychologists been more productive than this one? And yet it seems harder to be rigorous in molar problems than in molecular; when one examines the research of this roster of psychologists, a very great preponderance of it is upon questions just as molecular in scope as that of the experimental learning psychologist. Thus the molar level of analysis has a serious disadvantage—its methodological difficulties. The number of psychologists who can prepare "an American Icarus" (Murray, 1955) is perhaps very small; this limits the possibility of replicating Murray's conclusions.

While it will be difficult at times, our search here is for methods of research and assessment that do not replace the life history with abbreviated molecular chains of events. It is our fundamental assumption that there is something in the whole of life that is not visible in each part. Therefore, one aim of research must be to determine the functional interconnections among those parts, just as the vital organs interact in forming the system of the body. It is true, nonetheless, that one may isolate particular cells, organs, or systems of organs for study without studying the action of the whole body. There is surely a gain in precision from isolation; but there is a cost, and this is the loss of understanding of the system as a whole. If we analyze—as on occasion it is necessary to do—we do so with caution. Otherwise, in the name of science, we analyze too far in the molecular direction and undergo a sort of receptive aphasia as to the meaning of events, as Murray (1938) put it, a scientific illness like that in which the behavior is observed but its meaning lost.

How does one demonstrate in the particular case the existence, size, and shape of the anatomy of that person's life? Erikson (1968) and others have spoken of such holistic concepts when they use the terms *ground plans, life plots, course of life,* and *life-history structure*. If there is a ground plan to each individual life, then the data of that life history should become more meaningful when placed within the context of that plan. Thus the ground plan is like a template or pattern that helps the observer think about his own or someone else's life. It brings order to otherwise chaotic or irrational details. It provides a set of architectonic principles showing how the life is built and suggesting why it is so built. If such a ground plan exists then predictability exists, since the claims for a pattern imply an orderly relationship among the elements in that pattern. The pattern would also indicate areas of life in which predictability is impossible because disorder is inherent or inevitable in those areas. For example, predictability would perhaps be less during the period of identity confusion (Erikson, 1968), or during creative expansion in the sense defined by Charlotte Bühler and Marianne Marschak (1968, pp. 92 ff.). This feature of predictability will determine the usefulness of such concepts as ground plan. Prediction is what assessment tools, methods, and judges must demonstrate.

OBJECTIVE VARIETIES OF LIFE HISTORY

No one approach to life history has been sufficiently persuasive to provide a dominant model. Instead, it will be necessary to synthesize concepts and methods from a number of sources. Consider first the objective accounts of life—those that place emphasis on finding solid and reliable facts whether or not the meaning of facts is sacrificed in the process. Objective methods of life history are necessary in the professions and constitute a significant research problem in biology, sociology, and psychology.

Several traditional professions—especially in the fields of medicine, law, and education—compile records of lives and draw inferences from them. Consider hospital dossiers. They are usually heaps of badly organized facts about the patient's previous illnesses, symptoms, remedial measures taken, and notes on his ward behavior. The medical record often seems meaningless and arbitrary to the hospital staff, who thus need reminders to "write up" the patient. Especially is this so under the stresses of heavy case load. In spite of the variable conditions under which medical records are often kept, decades of effort to interpret such dossiers have slowly extracted from them concepts that are serviceable in identifying and describing patterns. One example is the concept of etiology—the deepest understanding of a patient's present condition is obtained when one can reconstruct the chain of events and circumstances that led to his present condition (Gough, 1971).

Legal records resemble medical dossiers in that they exhibit at times a rather stilted and arbitrary character. But the legal model in cases concerned with guilt and intention (which is to say primarily criminal cases) demonstrates a relentless stress on evidence. The ideal legal case (in spite of the depressing deviations from this ideal in practice) calls for careful collection and authentication of testimony in order to reconstruct the behavioral sequences and factual circumstances that indicate the probability and degree of guilt. Courts of law follow rules of evidence for establishing both the credibility of fact and the logical values of those facts (Wigmore, 1931). Due process is only one of many examples of the existence of a methodology for idiographic analysis. This was John Wigmore's intent: to found an empirical science of judicial proof, a *novum organum* to guide the courts in regard to the admissibility and use of evidence regarding the individual case. While his program of inquiry, decades ago, did not ever find sufficient followers to carry out the empirical studies that would be required, the idiographic conception is there.

Educational institutions represent a third stream of professional input. A longitudinal conception of the person is embodied in the records kept of an individual over long periods of time. They chronicle the timetable of his progress through a series of learning stages and courses; they evaluate that progress according to age norms, grading, and achievement tests. The resulting educational record exemplifies the concept of an objective developmental history.

It is true that the objectivity, reliability, and even the validity of medical, legal, and educational records are constantly disputed. But their intent is clear: to document the behavior and life of an individual in the effort to be responsible. Furthermore, the intent is in part scientific. The compilers of such dossiers are usually conscientious enough to try to apply whatever scientific knowledge is accessible to them. Even though this knowledge is piecemeal and the application is inconsistent, the professions have generated such concepts as etiology, due process, and the timetable that we call educational history. Common to some theorists in all three professions—especially in psychiatry—is a stout belief in the existence of individuals. There is no nomothetic-versus-idiographic debate among professionals.

In contrast, consider now the disciplines that do stress the nomothetic view. Biology, psychology, and sociology share with the professions the search for objective ways of depicting historical patterns, but they are not so attuned to uniqueness in such patterns. Consider first the contributions of biology. Stressing the biographic method as we shall, there is little opportunity here to probe the values of physiological and biochemical data in assessment. Rather, we shall content ourselves with mentioning a simple role for biological factors in behavior: one of limit setting. The length of the life cycle is an obvious example. That there is a biological limit seems obvious to everyone, but the nature of that limit is in dispute. Alexander Comfort (1956) delineates three positions:

First, the fundamentalist view that in effect all men are mortal because mortality is a property of living matter. It is in the nature of living things to die. If we say that something lives, we semantically imply that it has a duration.

Second, the wear-and-tear theory of Hans Selye (1956). The "machine" wears out as a result of constant or frequent strains; the body either loses its capacity to resist biological or other attack or the vital organs lose their ability to function and coordinate.

Third, growth theories. In effect, every species has a biological regulator that terminates organismic growth when it reaches a certain optimal size. After that point, the growth mechanism is shut off by the regulator much as a rocket motor is shut off; senescence begins at that point.

Of these theories, Selye's appears the most flexible in that it permits us to include the psychological as well as physical factors influencing the length of life. For example, Selye's theory would accommodate such findings as that death dates show a statistical irregularity; a person is more likely to die soon after his birthday than just before (Phillips, 1971). The data suggest that the person will "hang on" until a crucial time is past. Such stress theory led Richard Rahe, Joseph McKean, and Ransom Arthur (1967) to devise a simple objective procedure for recording significant recent life history events. Their questionnaire lists typical, change-inducing events (for example, marriage) and tabulates an annual life-change unit score for the person being studied. This score is the weighted sum of change-inducing events and has been found to predict the incidence of severe physical illness during the following year. (See Table 1.)

Table 1. Life-Change Units Scale

Events	LCU[a]
1. Loss of wife through death	100
2. Divorce	73
3. A lot more or a lot less than usual association with wife, due to marriage trouble	65
4. Held in a civilian jail or a brig	63
5. Loss of close family member by death	63
6. Marriage	50
7. Courtmartial	47
8. A lot more or a lot less than usual association with wife, due to orders (military)	45
9. Change in health or behavior of a family member	44
10. Major change in dating habits (engagement, etc.)	40
11. Major change in the situation of parents (divorce, etc.)	40
12. Gain of a new family member	39
13. A lot more or a lot less financial problems	38
14. Loss of close friend by death	37
15. Change to a new line of work, or a new type of work than done previously in the rating	36
16. A lot more or a lot less arguments with wife	35
17. Took on mortgage or loan greater than $10,000	31
18. To a Captain's Mast for disciplinary reasons	30
19. Experienced a foreclosure on a mortgage or loan or received a letter of indebtedness	30
20. Major change in responsibilities at work	29
21. A son or daughter married or moved out of the home	29
22. A lot more or a lot less in-law troubles	29
23. Personal successes	28
24. Either begun or ceased attending high school or college	26
25. Wife started or stopped working outside the home	26
26. Substantial change in living conditions	25
27. Substantial change in personal habits	24
28. A lot more or a lot less trouble with superiors	23
29. Eligible for promotion but "cut by quota" (enlisted) or "passed over" (officer)	20
30. Changed high schools or colleges	20
31. Change of residence	20
32. Substantial change in working hours or conditions	20
33. Substantial change in church activity	19
34. Substantial change in usual amount and/or type of recreation	19
35. Substantial change in social activities	18

Table 1. LIFE-CHANGE UNITS SCALE (cont'd)

Events	LCU[a]
36. Took on mortgage or loan less than $10,000	17
37. Marked change in sleeping pattern	16
38. Substantial change in family get-togethers	15
39. Marked change in eating habits	15
40. Taking a leave or a vacation	13
41. Guilty of minor infractions of the civilian law	11

[a] To obtain total life-change score for a time period, add the LCU corresponding to the events occurring in that time period.

NOTE: Reprinted with permission from R. H. Rahe, J. D. Mc-Kean, and R. J. Arthur, "A Longitudinal Study of Life—Change and Illness Patterns," *Journal of Psychosomatic Research,* 1967, *10,* 357. Pergamon Press.

Biological views of the course of life have also been expressed in terms of hypothetical growth phases, psychosexual stages, and theories that assume that different amounts of energy are available at different points in life. However expressed, these stages have a cultural as well as biological meaning. Some sociological landmarks (puberty, for example) are biologically related. Indeed, one of the best known theories of epigenesis is Erikson's (1968), which shows both biological and anthropological influences.

The *course of life* is a sociological term. Leonard Cain (1964) defines this term with reference to age status. At different ages one is expected to behave in different ways and to receive certain treatment from others based on that behavior. In some cultures, acting the role of old age will elicit deference and in other cultures one should act or look young. Chronological age is frequently used as a research variable. However, time may be quite differently structured for different cultures, social classes, and individuals. To be thirty-nine is not the same in New York and in Mexico. Sometimes chronological age is replaced by a grosser concept, stage of life, which has been used ever since Shakespeare's "ages of man." Perhaps the most carefully structured sociological subdivisions of time are those based on the concepts of timetable (Roth, 1963) and careers (Goffman, 1959). There are timetables not only for life as a whole but also for a host of lesser subdivisions within it.

Empirical psychology's greatest contribution to understanding the course of life has been methodology, especially in the specification of age norms. In more recent years, Jean Piaget, Bärbel Inhelder, Eckhard Hess, and others have designed methods that reveal progression or change in not only type but also organization of behavior. In Inhelder's (1953) paper, for example, the structural idea of stages is given operational meaning. This has not been attempted, as far as I know, with more ambitious life-stage systems such as Erikson's. One limitation to the contributions of empirical developmental psychology has been the scope of its inquiry. Studies are frequently reported of childhood or old age but the middle phases of life are largely a void, with a few important exceptions such as the lives published by Bühler (1933) and the work of E. Lowell Kelly (1955), showing what can be predicted over twenty-year spans. These data provide a factual frame of reference within which to view a particular life history. Are they not useful, perhaps even indispensable, templates to lay on the map we are making of the individual's course of life?

The diversity of these sources—from the professions and from several sciences—helps explain why life-history investigation has not progressed more rapidly. Such investigation appears to require interdisciplinary thinking. The difficulties of this kind of thinking are well known; we shall not therefore try in this short space to achieve a serious integration of such concepts as etiology, due process, and developmental history. However, the role of objective life-history facts in assessment should be noted—that of providing an objective background—and the limitations of such facts should be acknowledged. The inherent limitations are in this very objectivity. Such facts speak about life rather than of it, a distinction dating to William James. That is, the professions (in spite of their idiographic intent) and the sciences (because of their nomothetic goals) tend to present facts about a person rather than his experience of those facts. It is assumed here that knowing facts is not the same as knowing the person. To intellectualize about the origin of a person's pain is not the same as empathizing with the pain of one's child. Nevertheless, assessment cannot be wholly empathic; facts have a place in it; that place is to provide objective reality testing for the phenomenological and compassionate side of assessment.

The term *subjective* has been applied in a very broad way to psychology by Heinz and Rowena Ansbacher (1956, pp. 4–5). Among the synonyms for subjective they include *holistic* (rather than *atomistic*), *organismic* (not *mechanistic*), and *understanding* (rather than *explanatory*). The subjective investigation of life seeks to understand soft determinism through the inner nature of life (rather than hard determinism through the analysis of external pressures upon behavior). While this broad frame of reference is acceptable here, our use of the term *subjective* is more restricted than theirs. A subjective life history is one in which the investigator, using methods more holistic than objective, attempts to learn not only what happens but also what it means to the person. However, assessment is both objective and subjective. The fundamental question is how subjective data are to be collected so that objective results are achieved.

Subjective varieties of life history may be loosely divided into humanistic and scientific types. Unlike C. P. Snow's (1959, 1964) two cultures, the two views of life history do not seem especially antagonistic to each other. The difficulty in drawing upon the resources of humanistic scholarship lies not in its antagonism to science but perhaps in its subtlety. The first problem in devising subjective models for life-history assessment is therefore to find a way to draw upon the humanistic achievements in depicting life. Describing emotion is the craft of the novelist and dramatist. What has psychology to learn from them? In recent years, there has been much acknowledgement of the contribution of psychology to the understanding of literature (Garraty, 1957). There has been little appreciation of the use of literary resources by the psychologist. It is not easy to know how this is to be done. There are several generations of prejudice to work through. Consider, for example, the concept of objectivity as the *sine qua non* of science. Literary craftsmen seem less scientific in intent if we think of science as objective data gathering. But there is one critical sense in which authors are more scientific than the diligent data gatherer. They wonder, many of the literary artists, at the marvelous in man, at the intricacy, the unexpected, the contradiction, the absurd. Some of the best biographers stand in awe of the life they are depicting. Are not such qualities of awe more expressive of science than the Puritan diligence of the laboratory worker? Sigmund Freud also had this curiosity; still more, C. G. Jung. Carl Rogers has it; Abraham Maslow conveys it. This attitude of wonder permits the literary man to recognize and portray the irrational; hence, his skill in depicting emotion. Still more, one suspects the attitude gives him courage to recognize and depict the subtler patterns of life. When one asks for the life plot or ground plan of a life history, the novelist or biographer knows what this means. The playwright can tell us his scenario. The fact that writers plot the action of plays does not prove there are plots in life. But the concept of plot may prove useful in examining life records in a search for their patterns. Erving Goffman (1967) has made this sensitivity to brief plots a fine art in his sociological analyses. How are plots to be found in a life history? The methods of the Harvard Psychological Clinic group in interpreting biographic data are probably the most explicit example, as the analysis of episodes into thema and the tabulation of recurring thema provide a large part of the presentation of cases in the work of Henry Murray (1938) and Robert White (1960, 1963).

What can be done about the dangers of subjectivity? Charles Cannell and Robert Kahn (1968) have outlined a theoretical model for analyzing the forces that influence the person to report his life history accurately. Estimating these forces accurately might make it possible to know how far to discount certain reports. Robert Casey, Minoru Masuda, and Thomas Holmes (1967) determined the reliability with which informants described objective events as either occurring or not occurring in a particular year. The reliability coefficients varied greatly by the event reported but in general were in the 60s (correlations .67 or greater over a decade) or higher. The greater the magnitude of the event the more reliable its report in their data. The motivation to report true facts or to reconstruct one's life is perhaps at its greatest at certain points in his career, or at certain levels of anxiety. Such occasions would include personal crises, decision situations, and the onset of psychotherapy. Some of these motivational states foster rumination and reflection, as during mourning and reactive depression. Some such motivational states would not necessarily produce a representative and complete account of the life history. The times at which the person is most highly motivated to review his life may unfortunately be the times at which he is least able to do a good job of it. These considerations prompt us to consider whether psychotherapy itself provides a good model for the collection of subjective life history. Nevertheless, I have assumed so, in designing the sample interrogation procedures discussed in the following chapters. Just as one aim (in many schools of therapy) is to help the patient build insight by telling his story, so the assessment interviewer's aim could be the same. Would not an assessment process modeled on therapeutic interviewing have therapeutic benefits, and might not these benefits provide sufficient motivation to produce an accurate and representative life history? The approach to subjective life history, then, must acknowledge its difficulties but attempt to devise motivational settings in which those difficulties can be overcome.

Consider the implications of the close interfacing among humanistic and psychoanalytic models of biography. Freud and Jung borrowed metaphors and symbolism from imaginative literature and addressed questions provocative to dramatists and novelists. The field of biography after Freud underwent profound change (Edel, 1959). Despite the concern of Jung and Freud with life history, however, neither wrote a great biography; Freud, in fact, published only six complete cases (Sherwood, 1969). It remained for Erikson to emerge into eminence in the field of biography, which some would say he attained with *Young Man Luther* (1958) and, many more would agree, with *Gandhi's Truth* (1969). I suspect that this creative flowering of biographic talent resulted from his ties to both psychoanalysis and cultural anthropology and perhaps from his disinterest in the traditional medical model. Perhaps the models most useful to us, and certainly the most numerous examples of subjective biography, come from anthropologists (see especially the listing by Langness [1965]). However, Lewis Langness is troubled that anthropology in recent years has neglected the development of life history as a method, a concern earlier voiced by Clyde Kluckhohn (1957).

Bühler (1933) has shown a consistent interest in the theoretical problems of life-history interpretation. In recent years she has especially emphasized the role of goals in understanding the course of life (Bühler and Massarik, 1968).

Henry Murray (1938) was the first to call explicitly for the development of a life-history model in assessment. While his model calls for both subjective and objective data, the organismic emphasis and the stress on autobiography lead us to classify it as among the subjective varieties of life history. In the 1930s, there was a flurry of interest among psychologists and social scientists in the use of personal documents, possibly incident to the publication of William Thomas and Florian Znaniecki's *The Polish Peasant* (1927). One result of this interest was G. W. Allport's monograph *The Use of Personal Documents in Psychological Science* (1942). Allport thereafter continued to be interested in personal documents but did not give such data a central role in his assessment schema (1961) in which he appears to regard the life history as only one among many forms of data.

Development of a life-history method of assessment should draw together concept and method from the diverse sources discussed. It should be, in our view, a catholic and not a parochial method, producing data useful in a variety of theoretical frames of reference. The result would be not a theory of personality (are there not enough already?) but a set of interrelated procedures for collecting, interpreting, and validating data and for coping with special problems such as those of motivation and cultural bias. The difficulty of such an enterprise is obvious. Indeed, none of the foregoing theorists who emphasized life history called for its validation by prediction. However, data are presented in Chapter Six suggesting that such validation is feasible.

To this point we have merely identified the major sources from which one may hope to extract insights into the problems and possibilities of subjective life history. Most such sources themselves, however, have laid the groundwork for life-history assessment but without actually formulating it. An important exception is Murray.

MURRAY'S MODEL

Consider now Henry Murray's synthesis of ideas (1938) from Freud, Jung, Adler, William McDougall, and Kurt Lewin; in

subsequent publication (1955, 1959), he reaffirmed the organismic
point of view of that synthesis. In the voluminous publications of
his students and colleagues from the Harvard Psychological Clinic
(Wessman, 1957), a consistent search for empirical solution to the
problems of multiform assessment has been evident, ever since the
original "explorations in personality." Murray's propositions about
the life history (and personality) have been liberally restated below,
but the numbers of these propositions are cited so that one may
refer back to the original version (1938, pp. 38–49).

First, Murray's allegiance to organismic theory leads him
directly to a holistic view in which all significant data possible will
be integrated in the attempt to discern what a whole organism is
trying to do. Murray considers this approach necessary because
organismic reactions to the environmental press must ordinarily be
unitary, that is, show a single, over-all directionality as in survival
situations. He does not contend that all situations have the urgency
of survival but rather implies that they have sufficient urgency to
require this unitary trend. (See his propositions 1, 2, and 7.)

Second, to perceive this unity one must view the organism
over a period of time during the single, creature-environment interaction that Murray called the episode. An episode possesses a duration equal to the duration of a press (the environmental stimuli
relevant to meeting a need) and of the need, which is the hypothetical force accounting for the behavior observed during the episode. One can thus have a single need for achievement shown in two
successive environments; there would then be two episodes. An
organism could react to two successive needs in one environmental
setting; in this case also there would be two episodes. The episode is
the irreducible unit for describing persons, the so-called short unit
of psychology. In each such unit there is a dynamical structure consisting of a press (which sets things going), a need, behavior produced in pursuit of that need, and an end state in which some degree
of realization (success or failure) in meeting that need is apparent.
While the need-reductionist view implied in Murray's concepts
would no longer satisfy all psychologists, his general concept of an
episode and its dynamical structure otherwise continues to appear
quite useful. (See propositions 5, 6, 8, 9, 10, and 11.)

Third, Murray's concept of the time span of assessment itself is long; in fact, it is maximum. If the short unit is the episode,

the long unit is the life history itself. An organism's history is the organism; its history consists of the lifelong series of episodes. These episodes show recurring thema but a particular thema never recurs exactly. This richness of the life history makes biography imperative as the major instrument of understanding. Biography is all the more necessary because of life's time-binding character: in any episode, a person responds to the immediate press but also to very distant events in his past and goals in his future. As Murray put it, most behavior is related "not only to the settled past but also to shadowy preconceptions of what lies ahead" (p. 49). (See propositions 4, 5, 10, 12, and 25.)

Fourth, Murray presents a group of propositions that outline his conception of the ways in which new behavior is shaped and fixated. His learning theory was catholic (some might say vague); and he did not attempt to specify the sources, kinds, and timing of rewards that are necessary to alter behavior. But learning theory is not enough to enable us to understand change and stability, Murray warned; and one should not exaggerate the importance of external stimuli. He stressed the importance of the internal stimuli implied in the rhythms for life; both the diurnal alternations between activity and rest and the longer cycles of living. Murray noted the increasing tendency toward habit with age and the coordinate tendency toward greater interference with new habits. Combined, these tendencies force the adult organism to cope increasingly with internal conflicts and to strive toward synthesis and creative integration in later life. Murray (propositions 3, 11, 13, 14, and 15) dealt more with the products and consequences of learning process than with their inner mechanisms.

The rest of Murray's propositions (dealing with the regnancy of the brain) are not critical for the basic question of how life history is to be collected, analyzed, and used to develop verifiable predictions about individual behavior.

Assessment thus collects episodes in sufficient number and variety to provide a comprehensive, accurate account of a life history. In Murray's system, when assessment data have been shown to provide such an account, the assessment ends. Thus an assessment team at the Harvard Psychological Clinic was presided over by a "biographer," and assessment conferences concluded with description of the psychograph (reconstruction of the subject's personality from birth). Murray's dictum that "to fully understand a trait one must know its genesis and history" suggests that diagnostic classification is itself complete only if it can be shown how the patient's present pathological behavior grew out of and is an expression of his early life. Harrison Gough (1971) also has recently argued for the deepest level of diagnosis as etiological.

These views are accepted, but it would seem equally plausible that the intentionality of present behavior is part of the diagnosis. It was Adler's concept (Ansbacher and Ansbacher, 1956) that the patient's symptoms represent disguised goal statements and are completely understood only when their relation to his style of life or pattern of striving is understood. This future reference of assessment is implicit in Murray's last (or time-binding) postulate, but the logical consequences for assessment method are not so explicit in Murray's system as one might prefer. Chief among these consequences is the requirement of predictability (although neither prediction nor validation is mentioned in *Explorations in Personality*). Future referents are featured somewhat more clearly in Charlotte Bühler and Fred Massarik's work (1968). However, it cannot be said that Murray's model is disinterested in the future of the person. Robert White (1960), for example, regarded his cases as ongoing realities in that he presented follow-up data on them in subsequent publication.

Not only should prediction be explicitly a part of the assessment model, as in more recent programs of research based on multiform assessment (Stern, Stein, and Bloom, 1963), but it should detail the different kinds of prediction that are to be made. Two kinds are differentiated here: passive and active. Passive prediction estimates the probabilities of a person's life if no professional intervention is made. Active prediction estimates what the person will do under various contingencies. Passive prediction appears logically easier, and it is the only kind treated in this book. Active prediction appears to alter the natural directions of a person's life and should logically be less accurate as well as pose ethical problems.

ANATOMY OF THE LIFE HISTORY

It would be premature to offer a model of assessment synthesizing such a rich diversity of conceptual and methodological in-

put from the professions, nomothetic sciences, and subjective biographers. Nevertheless, one can discern common themes that
animate the inquiries of these different disciplines. One of these
themes is the search for a convincing and useful life plot, a grand
division of the life history into major phases. Else Frenkel (1936), in
discussing Bühler's life-history research, delineated five such divisions
or stages; they are derived from the interaction of two broad biological trends, the one referring to the rise and fall of general growth
energies and the other to the onset and later decline of the pro-
creative ability. Erikson (1968) suggests eight stages based on the
sequence in which organisms acquire new capacities and address
themselves to existential conflicts confronting them at those ages.
The conflicts result both from the biological unfolding and from the
expansion of the social setting that is real for the organism. Jung
offers patterns for depicting the afternoon of life as well as the
morning in an exposition too complex for abbreviation here. There
are, in brief, richly promising suggestions from the different theories
as to what these grand divisions of life are, along with a lack of
suggestions as to how one can empirically find them in data.

Time is the substance one is dividing here, but there are
many times to divide. One may speak of chronologic, sociological
(age, career, timetables that accompany certain games and roles),
and emotional timetables unique to the individual (for example,
anniversary depressions). There are psychological orientations to
time: the past, present, and future perspectives, as in Lewin's model
(1936). There are cycles to consider, from diurnal cycles to annual
calendars; some such cycles are clearly biochemical in origin and
some require an appreciation of the ethnic and cultural timetables.
Murray (1938, p. 49) described the uniquely human time-binding
capacity in his final propostion:

Man is a "time-binding" [*Korzybski, 1921*] *organism; which
is a way of saying that, by conserving some of the past and anticipating some of the future, a human being can, to a significant degree, make his behaviour accord with events that have happened as
well as those that are to come. Man is not a mere creature of the
moment, at the beck and call of any stimulus or drive. What he does
is related not only to the settled past but also to shadowy precon-*

*ceptions of what lies ahead. Years in advance he makes preparations
to observe an eclipse of the sun from a distant island in the South
Pacific and, lo, when the moment comes he is there to record the
event. With the same confidence another man prepares to meet his
god. Man lives in an inner world of expected press (pessimistic or
optimistic), and the psychologist must take cognizance of them if he
wishes to understand his conduct or his moods, his buoyances, dis-
appointments, resignations. Time-binding makes for continuity of
purpose.*

Finally, there are the longer swings in mood and the stately
rhythms marked by rites of passage. As Arnold van Gennep (1960,
p. 189) put it: "[Life] . . . is to act and to cease, to wait and rest,
and then to begin acting again, but in a different way. And there
are always new thresholds to cross."

Working down from the molar or grand divisions of life, examining successively smaller loops or segments of time, one finds it
convenient to use terms such as *recurring thema* or *plots;* then
particular thema (or *a particular enviroment-creature interaction*);
learning sequences of particular kinds (such as the sequences of
events that result in learning a new concept); and smallest unit of
all, the so-called short unit in psychology, the *episode.* The episode
could be further unfolded into press-stimulus, need, response, and
outcome, but while plausible in research, this analysis is excessive in
assessment. The episode, as Murray defines it, appears to me the
minimum meaningful unit of analysis.

Life-history assessment therefore must assume some kind of
structure or anatomy, embracing very molar concepts such as
stages of life at the holistic pole and more molecular concepts such
as episode at the opposite pole. What life-history assessment seeks to
do is to collect episodes and from them to reconstruct the whole. If
these are collected without undue bias and under proper motivational
conditions, they should form or reveal larger plots and thema,
ultimately the "style of life" itself as Adler might see it.

The interconnections among these episodes would be revealed to us under whatever behavioral laws from the nomothetic
sciences we could apply; and, still more important, the episodes
would prove meaningfully connected within the behavioral codes

characteristic of the person's culture. A third source of interconnection among episodes is the time-binding character of behavior itself. As an episode preserves some elements of past experience in it, the assessment judge can decipher the past from the episode; as it contains in it some plans and scenarios for the future, the assessment judge can make some estimates of the future. Every episode has to be seen, as Bühler (1968, pp. 24–25) puts it, in a triple orientation. Whatever cannot be seen in this way is accident or isolated reflex without significance to assessment.

.When it is assumed that there are interconnections among episodes in a life, the implication is that the life history is intelligible. That is, if the life history has been reduced in a natural way (without distorting the natural patterns that are there), it should be possible to recover the whole from which those parts were derived and of which they are an expression. This attempt to formulate an image of the whole life seems to be one of the implications of Erikson's (1968) concept of identity. Would it not be possible that the individual's own efforts to formulate an image of his whole life—to integrate—would serve as a useful guide to the assessment judge? Then one strategy for developing life-history assessment is to find out how individuals assess themselves: how they reconstruct their pasts, conceptualize the whole, estimate their own future behavior. Such a strategy can be pursued on a behavioral and not only on a conscious basis; that is, the person's intentions, implicit in his behavior, can be regarded as a better guide to the "as-ifs" or fictional goals he is pursuing (Adler, 1914). Assessment thus asks, "What is this person trying to do?" It asks this question not because one wishes to classify the person's motivations and values, but rather because we want to know what he is about to *do*; and this one wishes to know not because he wants to classify behavior but because action unifies the organism. It is no doubt true that some action can also conceal significant trends, but ultimately assessment must learn to predict overt behavior. Consistent action enables a person to express a consistent identity; and identity revealed in action, consolidated by it, committed by it, is what assessment must predict. One can choose a job or a course or even a marital partner but not an identity; it is grown, out of the slow accretions of behavior, much as a tree grows a branch.

⭐⭐⭐⭐⭐⭐⭐⭐⭐ **3** ⭐⭐⭐⭐⭐⭐⭐⭐⭐

Reconstructing the Natural History

⭐⭐⭐⭐⭐⭐⭐⭐⭐⭐⭐⭐⭐⭐⭐⭐⭐⭐⭐⭐⭐⭐⭐

To translate the foregoing grand theory of life into a valid procedure is a formidable task. We therefore take it in stages. In this chapter, difficulties such as motivation and feasibility are ignored, and life-history assessment is treated in its simplest form— the collection and use of a narrative account. In the next chapter, we take a further step toward operational definition by offering a sample interrogation procedure that extends incentives to the person to participate fully. Later chapters then take up the problems of validating and improving the effectiveness of assessment.

The process of assessment is based on the gatekeeper's role, which is one of mediation between the person and an institution in regard to life chances. He starts with data regarding the person and concludes with predictions of life chances. His role therefore compels him to face value-loaded issues, of which both the person and the institution are aware, and also to cope with the problem of prediction, of which they are not. The person thus expects (and the institution expects) that the values involved (performance of employees, grades, recovery from illness) will dominate the procedure of assessment. Some psychologists have, without much reflection, accepted these values as the determinant of relevance for data collection. One result has been assessment systems that collect data oriented to institutional machinery, to a fragmentary view of the person, and in short to the collection of credentials proving the person a qualified achiever, an able employee, a guilty criminal, or a sick patient.

The life-history assessment system begins instead with a different kind of data because it begins with a view of the person as an organism. He is not a potential student, criminal, mental patient, employee, or any other inmate. What is most real is his life, not the institutional subdivisions of it. Within that life, the organismic view instructs us, the episodes are more real than any conceivable statements one can make about them. Assessment therefore tries to get as close as possible to defining the episodes of life rather than to classifying them or substituting abstract codifications of them. Where the traditional assessor collected data in order to learn about constructs such as the person's ego strength, intelligence, or achievement drives, the life-history assessment interviewer learns about such constructs in order to arrive at data. A construct such as ego strength is like the historian's interrogative hypothesis (Gottschalk, Kluckhohn, and Angell, 1945): It guides him in reconstructing the original episodes composing the biography, after which the thing to do with the interrogative hypothesis is to forget it.

While life-history assessment ignores the institution at the outset (while coming eventually to terms with it), it accepts the person at the outset. True, the person wants to talk about his pains, job hopes, grievances, or other values involved in the reason for assessment. While these values must not be permitted to dominate the assessment process, they are inevitably present in the person's initial self-presentation. The assessment just begins with a disarming request, "Tell me about your life." To the person expecting to talk about a job, the question may arouse initial suspicions; but in general the assessment judge can get across the notion that he has a natural interest in the person and his experience. The traditional view of such broad opening questions is that they are a good way to gain something called rapport and that the data thus obtained are useful background before the assessment proceeds to the more fundamental facts that are relevant. The view of life-history assessment is the reverse of both these propositions: The data that emerge about

his life are the fundamental data of assessment, and the preliminary rapport is the essence of the requisite motivational climate that
ought to prevail throughout.

The initial responses are, however, only a cover story. A
cover story is a series of abstractions and evaluations of himself that
the person has acquired over the years in place of a complete understanding of his own life. In part, the cover story is a convenient and
appropriate cognitive map of himself and in part a set of fictions
that conceal troubling facts and inhibit ambition. It is that part of
his identity that he can readily put into words, or chooses to put into
words in this particular assessment setting, given his hopes and un-
certainties regarding the character of the interviewer. The aim of the
assessment interview is to obtain this cover story and, by judicious
questioning, to transform it into a more concrete, more accurate,
and more useful account of the episodes in life. The practical problem is how to transform this cover story within the permissible time
frame and in view of the institutional forces operating. The general
human readiness to talk about one's life and to recount specific
episodes is such that, from most informants, an acceptable narrative
account can be obtained within an hour, and a remarkably searching account within a half day. These time costs are within the conventional bounds of most assessment with which I am familiar.

DATA OF LIFE-HISTORY ASSESSMENT

Life-history assessment refers to the collection and interpretation of episodes from natural-life settings (Willems and Raush,
1969) for the purpose of making predictions in connection with
decisions about allocating life chances to a person. Naturalistic study
has been defined as that in which "an investigator records, or commits to analyzable form, descriptions of phenomena he does not
bring about" (Willems and Raush, 1969, p. 273). So defined, life-
history assessment does not directly qualify as naturalistic because
the data are not original but are estimated by various observers including the person himself. However, the *referent* is the natural life.
This is the domain of events that have already occurred without the
influence of investigator and those possible events in the future that
will occur without his intervention.

In this sense, objectivity refers to those natural data outside the scientist's control; objective research provides the scientist with an opportunity to learn something he did not know before beginning the research; and assessment offers the person the chance to be appraised without bias. Naturalistic investigation is thus a way to discover something new and is not at all a means to prove what was already suspected before the data. Roger Barker (1964, pp. 5–6) put it strongly: "A science which does not include among its data phenomena as they exist unarranged by the investigator and without input from the methods used to reveal them, describe and enumerate them, is only half a science."

The naturally existing history is an ideal. It is what we try to reconstruct and predict and is the criterion for the truth of everything that we collect and say about a person. The written life history represents that natural history. The data that are collected, then, should reflect the original history as closely as possible. If one assumes that data, *in vivo,* are formed in episodes, that episodes are found in historically dated, natural chronicles (that is, in real time), that episodes appear to recur in patterns one calls thema; then episode, chronicle, and thema represent reality. This is assuredly not the same reality meant by the experimentalist who contends that only what he can produce under controlled conditions in a laboratory is real; it is not the same reality meant by the trait theorists who assume that behavioral phenomena are but surface phenomena.

Assessment data are behavioral. But this is not to say that they are only behavioral. The episode, as Murray defined it, includes a stimulus situation *and* other features. An episode contains a press (that part of the environment that is relevant to the person's needs at the moment), a need, action in response to that need, and outcome of this action. Careful examination of this definition shows that one usually cannot determine what the press is without knowing both the environment and the organism's need. How does one know the organism's need? Something the individual does or says permits us to infer a need. Thus an episode contains need-revealing data. Such data can be behavioral, introspective, or both. The action or instrumental part of the episode then follows the activation of the need and the influence of the press; action (the actone) is not interpretable in the episode unless one first knows the press and need. Finally, the reward or result of the action cannot be determined unless one knows what the need and press were. Clearly the critical parts of the episode, as Murray defined it, are need and press.

Certain other features of episode are apparent in this discussion. The episode is the short unit of the biography. The biography or life history is composed of the total series of such episodes. Thus each episode has a particular location in historical or real time. It occurred on October 11 in 1912, and therefore at no other time. Because the press is a selection of stimuli from actual physical environment, it too possesses a particular location. These features may be summed up by saying that every episode has a unique time-and-place index. If one wishes to assume that the organism can engage in only a limited number of need-oriented pieces of action at one time, then the total number of events in a lifetime is finite though huge (Barker and Wright, 1951).

The reconstruction of an episode from the past can be attempted from memory, physical records, and testimony of observers. There are available in historiography two kinds of authentication: internal, the determination of internal consistency among separate pieces of information; and external, the determination of the data's logical consistency with outside factors (Gottschalk, Kluckhohn, and Angell, 1945). While the preference would generally be for external authentication of assessment data, there is no logical reason why data that have only internal support may not produce better predictions than externally authenticated data. When we measure the validity of predictions, however, externally authenticated criterion facts appear logically essential. The dilemma then becomes this: Shall we test the validity of data that are more real by predicting facts that may be more credible (because externally authenticated) but less real? This distinction between what is real and what is credible is necessary in organismic theory. A fact can be very reliable and precise but tell us little about the organism. And some vital data about the organism may be vague.

If the natural life history is assumed to consist of a large but finite number of episodes, the question is how these are to be sampled. Is there such a thing as a representative sample? One cannot easily visualize a random sample, for example, but it is not beyond imagination. Somewhat more within the bounds of feasibility

would be a sample representative as to the times, phases, and places
of life. I suggest, as a very crude first approximation, that a representative life history should sample every year of life; every significant environment; and relationships with every significant person.
The significant environments are assumed to be those in which
people spend the most time: work, home, school, and leisure. This
inventory of settings can be expanded by applying a value system
such as Gordon Allport, P. E. Vernon, and Gardner Lindzey's
(1960), in which case there are economic, political, religious,
aesthetic, social, and theoretical settings. Thus, the major institutions of society contribute the inventory of environments or settings
to be sampled. A life history is representative only if it includes episodes from each of those institutions relevant to the particular year
of life.

Such institutions also provide authenticating credentials. Credentials show the child enrolled in school, and the adult registered
voter. The worker is named on the payroll and is listed as a member
of a bowling league team. The hospital keeps records of illnesses and
symptoms. The military maintains a personnel record. Such facts
provide external validation of what the person privately reports. An
objective history may be written describing the passage of the individual through the records of each institution. This history records
his passage from one status to another. The term for this documented
movement is *career history*. Since there is also a future time perspective, however, there is also a prospect before the individual of future
movement through the institution or social structure. This anticipated movement is variously called career line, job prospects, or even
romantic expectations. It will be termed *scenario* here. A scenario is
the future anticipated for a person by himself, by the institution, or
by the assessment judge. Many of the questions put to the gatekeeper
are about the probabilities of this scenario.

The subjective side of this career line is the person's own
account of his movement through the social structure or through the
settings that have been chosen for analysis. The basic units describing this movement are those particular episodes that contain conventional successes or failures as their end points. It must not be
thought that the whole of life is bound up in the movement from

status to status within social structures. The subjective life history is not an account only of institutionalized behavior, but the external authenticating data are usually obtained from institutions.

Where the individual's own account of life is grossly at variance with the account of institutions, the external authentication fails; not necessarily, however, the internal. The assessment interviewer may well find the subjective account of life of the individual more credible than the institutional records available for authentication. This is particularly the case in regions where the bureaucratization of institutions has not proceeded far, and among under classes who are poorly served by institutions. Even if the credentials are mistrusted in the particular case, the assessment judge can still be alert to objective public events mentioned by the informant such as sporting events, elections, riots, disasters, freeway construction dates, places, and names. In general, the episodes of life history are rarely devoid of all historical reference. These external orienting facts appear in casual accounts of life and can support their authenticity.

The internal authentication of data begins when a judge tries to determine the intelligibility of data. Intelligibility is the richness of connections among episodes. If intelligibility is based on the data's conformity to known behavioral laws, their credibility is greater, especially if the subject person is unlikely to have heard of those behavioral laws.

This decisive role of behavioral laws in the authentication of data is offset by what I suspect will prove their inferior role in assessment prediction. Thus one would not be surprised to learn that knowledge of the principles of psychology or other behavioral sciences is not helpful in making life-history predictions. For example, the research studies cited in Chapter One indicated that graduate-level education does not help psychologists to predict behavior in individual cases. Since the principal orientation of graduate education is nomothetic, one would suppose that the research studies would lead to questioning its relevance to assessment. Instead, the inference has been drawn without warrant that it is clinical psychology whose predictive relevance has been disproved in the research. For these reasons, assessment judges participating in this life-history research (see Chapter Six) are primarily nonpsychologists, therefore ruling out the explicit use of nomothetic knowledge as accounting for the findings. (What is needed, of course, is a population of clinical judges whose education has been primarily idiographic, but this population does not yet exist.)

When a person tells his history to a lawyer, physician, psychologist, social worker, or other professional, he produces a long string of material in which actual events, confusing circumstances, evaluative judgments, and objective facts are intermingled. There is a confusion among levels of abstraction (Korzybski, 1941). Clinically, one hears mingled facts and interpretations organized around symptoms and fears about health and adequacy. The person has already begun a process of self-diagnosis or he would not have come willingly to the clinic in the first place. A social worker listens to a string of information organized around the informant's cover story about the state of his marriage, his economic situation, or his job. A divorce lawyer hears a cover story organized around a set of grievances. Whatever the setting, a judge needs an interrogation outline or written document to help order the string of information so that the data begin to flow in a more coherent manner. In industry, one such outline or document is the application blank. It orders behavior and facts into institutional settings such as education, health, military, and job history.

The careful interviewer then proceeds to sort and round out the picture in his own way. At this point, some interviewers lose the informant's humanity by a premature, categorical, and excessively logical decision. A more careful interviewer lays the groundwork for progressing further. He should proceed to teach the informant how to be assessed by recalling the critical episodes of his life history. Chapter Four describes a sample procedure to guide a judge in sorting the informant's initial story into episodes, objective facts, and evaluative statements regarding these episodes and facts. Facts function simply to authenticate the episodes, and put them into an interpretable framework. For example, the informant's eyesight may in fact be exceptionally poor and the assessment judge may then interpret some episodes under a hypothesis that the person is overcompensating. Evaluative statements have many functions. They help identify biases in reporting episodes and facts. They help clarify the values that a person will use in constructing his scenarios for the future.

What kinds of facts are essential? In general, the demographic facts that are usually relevant are age, sex, educational level, occupation, socioeconomic status, and residence. If the I.Q., physical appearance, and physical condition are unusual, these would be relevant facts. If a person's self-evaluations imply that he has an exceptional I.Q., appearance, or condition, then facts on these matters would be relevant. Such facts are credentials. (Not all credentials are irrelevant to assessment.) Their role in assessment is to modify, qualify, and help verify the basic life history; they cannot substitute for it.

MODEL OF THE PERSON

While episodes and external facts make up the raw material of life history, they do not alone make it understandable. Some arrangements of the data are necessary. The simplest of such arrangements is the chronicle—a narrative listing of episodes and facts. This preliminary grouping of episodes by time sequence makes it convenient to group them further by whatever grand scheme for subdivision is preferred. Erik Erikson's eight stages (1968) might be used here. Within each stage, it might be well to group episodes by environment. An alternative arrangement might be to group the episodes within a stage according to the significant person depicted in each. These groupings are more mechanical than revealing. They are the prelude to the search for relationships among them. The relationships to be found are if-then relationships: "If episode X occurs, would one expect Y to occur?" Thus the primary tool for ordering events is expectancy relationships. If these occur within short time spans, they tend to be conceptualized as social codes (for example, roles) and if over longer spans, as traits or thema, as psychological codes.

Ignoring for the moment where these expectancies come from, let us consider how they appear. They have the logical form of prediction itself, as found in diverse applications: If the stock price is 85 today, what are the odds that it will be 85 or higher tomorrow? If it is third down and three, will the quarterback pass? The search for relationships among episodes takes this form: Given an episode, what is the subjective probability of its relationship to each of the other episodes? Across the judges used in an assessment research experiment, consistently stated relationships between an episode A and an episode B indicate a subjectively probable relation between A and B. The experimental method developed in Chapter Five is based on this assumption. A life history with many such relationships is intelligible; if there are few such connections it will be perceived as barren.

Every pair of episodes potentially has such a relationship; thus an exhaustive study of these relationships requires a paired comparison of every possible combination—somewhat impractical in an extensive biography although it can be done with shorter ones (Dailey, 1959b). More simply, one looks intuitively for themes— groups of episodes that fall into a type (such as a thema) or form a sequence (such as course of development of an illness). Leopold Bellak (1963) illustrates this intuitive search in his thematic analysis of Somerset Maugham's stories.

At this point, psychology's traditional approach has been to define the particular variables that should be encoded or determined from the analysis. If we are looking for thema, what are they? If thema contain needs, what needs exist and how are they to be defined and perhaps encoded? If thema also contain presses, what kinds of presses exist and how are they to be defined and encoded? There then might ensue a long discussion of which human abilities, traits, and personality types should be defined and extracted from the analysis. Such discussion of theoretical variables is deliberately avoided here for several reasons.

First, there is no basis for specifying any one set of concepts as more useful in life-history analysis than all others. Second, our view that episodes and thema naturally exist within the life history requires us to find such phenomena in it rather than to implant them artificially. If the assessment judge wishes to use concepts more elaborate than these very simple ones, let him formulate them in his own way. I do not think them necessary. The intent of life-history assessment is to describe a metatheory or language for talking about almost anyone's life history. This metatheory is broad enough to accommodate any personality theory that is concerned with human development over the life span.

The model of the person that emerges from analysis is a series of concrete statements summarizing what he has done in the past and hinting in terms of recurring themes at what he has been trying to do. Examples of such summaries are found in Henry Murray's "Icarus" (1955), Erik Erikson's Shaw (1968, pp. 142–150), Althea Horner's Darrow (Bühler, 1968, pp. 64 ff.), Robert White's Hartley Hale (1960, pp. 55–64 and 80–91), and Nevitt Sanford's cases on acting out of impulses (1963, pp. 19–24, 35–36). The summary statements, which "model" the person, constitute a biography. A good biographic model should be clearly derived from the data in the history, should have useful implications, and should lead to testable propositions about the person.

Utility refers to the importance of the decisions suggested by data (Cronbach and Gleser, 1965). To evaluate a person in life-history assessment means to place some value on the implications of his life, behavior, and performance. Since assessment decisions generally refer to a person's future more often than to his past behavior (there are exceptions to this, as in jurisprudence), utility is intimately related to prediction. However, consider the two conceptual processes separately before combining them.

There are, in general, two sets of utility in assessment. The person assessed has his own hopes and aspirations for the future. The institution has expectations for that person if he should become a member, student, patient, or employee. Consider first the institution's views. Its scenario calls for the person to reach certain goals or subgoals, which are expected to be reached at a certain rate. This statement is limited to positive scenarios, those in which the goals are desired. But by a slight transformation of terms, one may also discuss negative scenarios, in which a person (such as a patient) deteriorates until he reaches a certain hazardous or devalued state, passing through various way stations en route. These status sequences represent career lines, whether they are promotion sequences in industry or degenerative sequences as in the "moral career of a bum" (Spradley, 1970). In medicine, positive scenarios hopefully predict positive results from particular treatments within set time limits; negative scenarios dolefully anticipate deterioration over a time period. In industry, positive scenarios predict promotions and earnings; negative scenarios are not often discussed. In education, positive scenarios describe sequences of learning from course to course or from year to year; negative scenarios are ignored. Criminology postulates both positive and negative scenarios.

A person has scenarios in each institutional setting. The adolescent may have precise expectations as to the year when it is normal or expected for him to begin to date, become affianced, and marry. Later, the timetable may be extended to include children and a home in the suburbs. The college scenario from the student's standpoint calls for courses but also adventure, sexual experience, and increments in autonomy. Among patients, timetables are often concerned with status progressions toward recovery and a normal life.

Julius Roth (1963) gives us a provocative description of the timetables tuberculosis patients have regarding the rate and bench marks of their recovery. For example, the patient expects to be promoted to the next exercise class within a few weeks or else told why not. He expects the medical staff to know exactly how he is doing and if they do not appear to know, he feels that "the doctors don't give a damn." By contrast, the staff physician is less precise about times, first because, as he well knows, his knowledge is not precise enough to make analyses in the detail the patient expects and, second, because the

physician does not have the same desperate concern about the time of treatment as the patient has. Whereas the patients think in terms of the weeks and days—and sometimes even of the hours— when something will happen to them, the physician is more likely to round off treatment events in terms of months and, in the case of the "old chronic" patients, even of years. . . . He is, after all, spending the patient's time and not his own [p. 22].

One result is persistent tension, occasional conflict, and periodic bargaining over such matters as surgery and discharge dates. Roth develops his concept of contrasting timetables for a variety of institutional settings—psychiatric patients, polio convalescents, military men, students, children, and airline pilots.

To evaluate a person's life chances implies comparing his own characteristics with these bench marks and timetables. Will he likely behave in such a way as to progress (or deteriorate) along the institution's or his own career expectations? This evaluation is absent from unvalidated credentials-assessment systems. Instead, the person's characteristics are compared not with the scenarios but with a set of criteria or standards. In a credential-oriented company, a job applicant is not appraised against the performance improvements and career progressions expected but rather against standards such as age, experience, seniority, and education.

The evaluation of scenarios in the life-history assessment process introduces some complexities not found in older systems of assessment. First, the gatekeeper has to be concerned with both the person's scenario and the institution's, no matter who is paying his fee. This interest in the person's scenario is required because an interviewer who lacks interest cannot engage in a very human encounter and therefore cannot obtain a searching history. The gatekeeper has to be interested in the institution because the person's scenarios lie in that environment. Second, life-history assessment is very often concerned with several kinds of personal scenario rather than just one artificially segregated scenario. Consider, for example, the choice of an astronaut. The ultimate question is whether he can walk on the moon. To make such forecasts one must evaluate the scenario, getting through training, getting into the sky, handling space emergencies, and other technical subgoals prior to the walk on the moon. But one must also estimate the life chances in some more personal scenarios. The astronaut's family life is not irrelevant, because this scenario is inextricably interwoven with technical scenarios. An astronaut with an alcoholic wife has a different probability of completing training than other astronauts. In brief, evaluation in life-history assessment is based on complex sets of data and is directed toward several kinds of interrelated scenarios.

Just as the past history of a person has a structure (the episodes falling into networks of meaning called thema) so also does the entire life history. Now, if the entire life has a structure, this includes the future; hence it is logical to postulate that it has a prospective structure. The person's future then consists of a very large set of if-then relationships or contingencies just as does his past. One difference: One is more likely to regard the future as having less probability than the past. To mark this distinction, one refers to desired episodes in the future as goals while past data are events. Future undesirable episodes are hazards. Each goal or hazard in a scenario therefore has probability as well as desirability. The term commonly used by decision theory for these attributes taken together is *utility*.

Richard Jeffrey (1965) and Ward Edwards and Amos Tversky (1967) show ways to analyze judges' inferences with reference to their value system as well as their validity. For example, utility is defined by Jeffrey as the sum of the products of the probabilities and desirabilities of particular events. Thus the total future of an individual in a particular scenario can be appraised for utility, and separate scenarios can be added together for an over-all estimate of all his life chances.

What are the bases for such estimates of the future? We must return to the if-then logical form used to analyze life-history data in order to put together a model of the person. Every if-then relation has a probability of being correct. Consider the total model of the person, arrived at through analysis of thema of his life, as a complex "if." The "then" consists of the alternate scenarios that are being considered. What is the total validity, in the particular life history, of this if-then relation? And how is it to be determined? And why is it that predictions can be made at all? In the experimental analyses of assessment to be reported (Chapter Five), judges were asked to predict specific episodes by choosing among alternatives, on the basis of known data. When a judge was asked to do this repeatedly and his accuracy was determined by comparing his predictions with known occurrences, the average validity of his predictions could be determined. By varying the data known to different judges (and particularly by varying the amount of data), it could be determined just which aspects of a model, and just which episodes contributing to that model, produced the validity.

Why should intuitive prediction be possible? It is assumed that a life history has some organization. Occurrences at time 1 have consequences at time 2. Episodes are part of a web of meaning. It was suggested earlier that behavioral codes or implicit theories (Bronfenbrenner, Harding, and Gallwey, 1958; Fancher, 1966) are involved in this web of meaning. It is, in fact, difficult to imagine a social order in which there were no such predictability; people do honor contracts and do fulfill roles. Life-history analysis implies that

there is predictability whether or not actuarial tables exist. There
was a social order before there was an insurance industry, and the
prudent conduct of life was known before the concept of probability
was formulated.

My concern is for prediction, no matter how attained. There
is no special virtue in using actuarial tables unless it be shown that
they matter significantly. In very limited instances this is no doubt
the case. It is assumed, however, that the complexity of life chances,
multiple scenarios, and assessment in a changing society is much too
great to warrant dependence on known tables of relationships between particular kinds of facts and particular scenarios. There is a
certain archaic curiosity or even value in comparing actuarial
formulas with intuitive judges, of course, but the role of actuarial
thinking is far more important than such "cookbook" experiments.
This important role concerns the relationship between subjective and
objective probability (de Finetti, 1964), which has received scarcely
any exploration in the context of assessment. The laws governing
the ways in which intuitive assessment judges receive, combine,
process, and use life-history data in order to formulate accurate
images of the future will be statistical laws. It is suggested here that
these statistical laws will prove to have a great deal to do with our
exploration of social structure and the role systems of society. What
determines the realism of one's views of a person's future is the
judge's comprehension of that social structure (the probabilities of
movement along its career lines) as well as his comprehension of the
person. As Roger Brown (1965, p. 637) put it, "A knowledge of
social structure alone will take one smoothly through a large part of
the day's routine."

There is no conflict, then, between idiographic and nomothetic views of prediction. The assessment judge studies the unique
life of the person in order to make forecasts. If he is accurate, there
must have been lawfulness or order within the life. While there is no
conflict, there *is* a difference in strategy. The idiographic strategy
herein followed is to derive laws and regularities from the way
judges intuitively respond to data and especially from the way they
respond when accurate. The nomothetic strategy attempts to prescribe (or limit) the way judges respond to data on the basis of
known laws. It is difficult to say that one strategy is more scientific

than the other. The real issue is: Which one is more productive? One cannot draw conclusions about the productivity of the idiographic strategy until an attempt has been made to use it in research, and very little research has been done using life-history episodes to estimate the probabilities of life chances.

Should idiographic assessment be done if research proves it grossly inaccurate? Assessment receives its moral justification only → from the ability of a judge to predict events. If a gatekeeper makes a decision that implies no future benefit to anyone, there is little reason to make it at all. If his anticipation of future benefits is consistently wrong, the decision making is a charade. Hospitalization is expected to benefit the patient or his family. Such a decision is later deemed wise if the benefits obtained outweighed the costs and ill effects. Over time, a physician whose prescriptions are consistently followed by ill effects and heavy costs without compensating benefits will be deemed very poor and possibly will be sued for malpractice. In industry, hiring and promotion decisions are made in the expectation of good performance. The decision is later deemed wise if the person has performed well. Performance can fail for many extraneous reasons; but, on the average, the industrial gatekeeper whose choices consistently fail is considered inadequate. Medical and industrial prognostication are not exact sciences, but the inexactness does not indicate that they deal in random guesses. If this is shown to be the case, the costs of diagnosis and personnel appraisal should be saved and coin flipping should be substituted. Or, what is for me almost as dismal a prospect, we should return to credentials—and then be swept forward into the computerized society.

Motivation for
Assessment

A variety of assessment procedures can be generated from the fore-going model. Some procedures would be short and would take their chances with superficiality; some would be long and would assume the burdens of cost. Some would be two-person situations between professional and client or patient; some would be small-group situations, as in assessing the common life of a family. Even larger groups can be instructed in the preparation of life history, and while the limits for this seemingly outrageous procedure must be carefully set, in certain contexts it is appropriate; we will consider its applications in later chapters. Here we will deal with the particular situation in which it is desirable to develop the life history of one person, and it is assumed that a four-hour period is feasible for this purpose. We begin with this procedure because it suggests a way to solve the problem of providing sufficient incentives to the person assessed: the very great problem of motivation for assessment. The assumption is made that intensive assessment provides incentives to the informant because it can be insight building and in that sense therapeutic. While such insights and therapeutic benefits have the best chance to emerge from one-to-one assessment situations, in my view all assessment should compensate the person by building insights. One can assess persons or real estate; one difference between the two, how-ever, is that real estate does not care. Few undergo a searching assessment without wondering, worrying, or thinking deeply about it. Assessment should leave the subject person with a more helpful image of his life, a more valid impression of what he is and what he can do. Classical assessment paid little or no attention to this side effect. For life-history assessment it is a main effect.

Meehl (1954) recommended that assessment be left, for the most part, to actuarial instruments; the psychologist should con-centrate on therapy or other matters that he does well since he can-not best the objective tests on validity. Meehl's analysis stops short of an important insight, however. The psychologist should engage in therapy *in order to learn* how to do assessment. In this way, he can discover the potentialities of assessment. Assessment is continuous with therapy, both emotionally and cognitively. It is emotionally continuous with therapy because, properly handled, assessment provides a relationship that is rather emotion laden and places the kind of human demands on the judge that are placed on therapists. To stress this therapeutic obligation, this chapter substitutes the word *clinician* for the more general term *assessment judge*. It is implied that anyone who wishes to engage in life-history assessment must have some appreciation of the clinical point of view. Further, a minimum bond of trust is required for the kind of authentic self-declaration that permits valid assessment data to emerge. Assess-ment is *cognitively* continuous with therapy in that the basic data of assessment—the life history—are also basic to therapy. Therapy works by altering the assessed person's image of his life, and it is proven valid only when the course of his life changes.

Psychologists often lose interest in traditional assessment after they have had some experience with therapy. I believe that this disinterest develops not because they find psychotherapy power-ful but because traditional assessment registers only dimly the life processes that come into dramatic view during therapeutic inter-action. This process becomes visible not because the psychologist is seeing a real patient (that fact is true also during diagnosis) but be-cause in therapy the two are communicating about something deeply meaningful—a life history. (Of course, none of these arguments pertain to therapies that are limited to here-and-now encounters.)

The by-products of the life-history process, when properly done, are (for the clinical assessor) a valid impression of the person assessed and (for the person) a beneficial clarity about his life. Both can gain from successful assessment conceived as a joint task. For assessment to be done otherwise is to make the clinician either an authoritarian diagnostician who intends to acquire some magical insights denied to the person himself, or a "real estate appraiser" assessing an inanimate object.

In general, the intensive method outlined here, like others of the large family of possible methods, is an operational statement of our premises about life-history assessment. In brief, the method assumes that a person's life is a set of episodes and that only the person knows what those are (although he will probably need help in telling them). It also assumes that these events are interrelated in a semantic network of meaning that makes sense to the person and hopefully will prove intelligible to the clinician. If the person's network of meaning is not known to the clinician or does not make sense to him, then that person's behavior will appear irrational and unpredictable. It is further assumed that the clinician will then be unable to make valid estimates of life chances.

The procedure for doing life-history assessment is to teach a person how to tell the events of his life, identify the more significant occurrences, and interrelate them in the person's own pattern of meaning. The clinician needs to teach the person what an event is and point to whatever has not yet been completely described. It is especially difficult at times to get people to fill in the feelings that are an indispensable part of a complete event. A more serious difficulty is that sometimes an emotionally overwhelmed person can narrate feelings but cannot allocate them to time and place in the form of events to which those feelings refer. Such a person is not yet ready for assessment.

Consider now a clinically simple case: a person in a state of realistic anxiety, the judge (clinician) being the only professional in the case at the moment, and the person presenting clinical symptoms not severely disabling to either the conduct of life or his ability to give a coherent account of himself. Further, assume that he has some motivation or incentive to offer a fairly complete account of his life. A twenty-year-old appeared in my office ostensibly for help with a draft counseling problem. Normally such a person would have gone to a legal specialist (to whom I actually did refer him at a later point). He poured out his story. No one had to tell him that assessment requires dealing with life history! Speaking under considerable pressure of ideas, he spoke of an urgent need to "pull my thoughts together" so that he could decide whether to study music or return to a major in history. This led him back very quickly to an account of his recent role in campus dissent, his relationships to the Establishment in general, and his deepening romantic involvement. From this he moved to consider whether he should fight with his Selective Service board, apply for conscientious-objector status, or just disappear into Canada. Every element in this complex puzzle of life was invested with emotion; every element touched on his relationships with his parents and his girl. Each episode from the past suggested a train of possibilities for the future.

We had several interviews. I did not "treat" him. Instead, it would be more accurate to say that he engaged, with my help, in trial reconstruction of his life. He sorted out what had happened; revised his story. He invented certain themes among these events and then decided that these themes did not, in fact, represent true relationships. He viewed the past as in part established fact and in part creative new scripts. The future, to him, was of much the same character. The episode of "the day I will confront my draft board" was almost as real as "the day I occupied the administration building." (See Figure 1.)

He talked of his family, of the possibilities in Canada, of alternative courses of action for the future, and of their troubling implications for the style of life he hoped to share with his girl. There was no single decision to be made; all was ramified, like a set of simultaneous equations. It could not be thought an intellectual problem, however; it was all invested with too much emotion— mingled apprehension, hopes, and even joy at times. But somehow decisions came to be made. They grew out of his life (not mine); but, still more, they grew from one of the numerous scenarios he had tried on for size. One of these seemed best to fit his identity, his lifeline; and, when he found it, he chose it.

In this case, I functioned as institutional gatekeeper from college to the outer world. The decision to be made was whether the

Figure 1

Diagram of a Therapeutically Simple Case

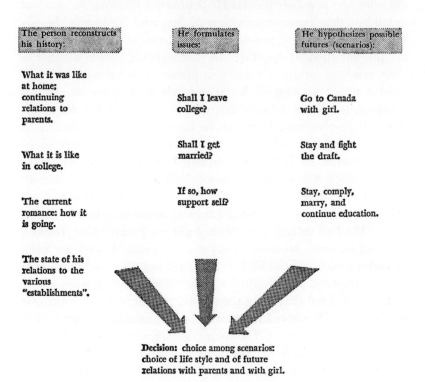

The person reconstructs his history:	He formulates issues:	He hypothesizes possible futures (scenarios):
What it was like at home; continuing relations to parents.	Shall I leave college?	Go to Canada with girl.
What it is like in college.	Shall I get married?	Stay and fight the draft.
The current romance: how it is going.	If so, how support self?	Stay, comply, marry, and continue education.
The state of his relations to the various "establishments".		

Decision: choice among scenarios:
choice of life style and of future
relations with parents and with girl.

student should leave or not and which of the several alternative scenarios he should pursue. I was engaged in helping him face the outer institutions he would subsequently face, such as the draft board. However, completing the job of such mediation required a counselor, to whom I next referred him, to steer this student through the complex technicalities of draft boards and other institutions. Thus my role was closer to the student than to the institutions involved. It was to help him find the life line, the natural scenario that integrated the previous significant trends of his life, the style of life. He was in an identity crisis; and, in finding his way through it, he had to identify the trends of his own life. To do this, he had to know something about it and to sort out these events and facts. This is what the clinician attempts to do in the following series of questions. The end result of such questions is a case history that has been built out of the collaboration of clinician and person. The series begins with a global view of things and then works back to questions intended to render the history more precise, more balanced, and more insight inducing.

Life-history assessment ultimately requires a clinician and his client to build a case. A series of questions to stimulate such case development would begin by probing the person's present view of his situation and work back to a more complete picture of his life history.

Tell me about your life. A literal-minded or apprehensive person might want a more specific request than this. The request can be elaborated in several ways: (*a*) *Tell me about your life. Where are you heading? What do you want to do?* (*b*) *Fill me in on what has happened to you. How did you come to be in this (college, hospital, job or whatever)?* (*c*) *What made you come in to see me?*

How do you hope things will turn out? This question is phrased in an academic, vocational, social, or medical context, whatever is appropriate. Once the person has voiced a goal, question him specifically on two points: (*a*) *How badly do you really want to do this?* (*b*) *What are your chances? Would you estimate them?*

What makes you think so? This question is designed to provoke a series of self-evaluation statements. Usually there will be both positive and negative statements, several of each. The question is phrased as a mild challenge to justify this estimate of the chances. If the person does not answer the question in that light, ask him to give a list of the strengths and weaknesses he believes he has as a person. These lead directly to the next question.

You speak of being —————. What has happened that leads you to make this evaluation? This question takes the first element of the person's self-evaluation and provokes an example. It marks the beginning of the clinician's attempt to teach the person to describe specific events and thus to produce approximations to the original episodes of that life. Thus the clinician responds to each reply from the person with a request for more details: (*a*) *What happened?* (*b*) *What was the situation?* (*c*) *When and where was it?* (*d*) *Who was there?* (*e*) *What was the outcome?* (*f*) *How did you feel about it?*

These are the attributes of an event as defined throughout this book. After the clinician has conducted such a didactic interrogation for several events, the person begins to recognize the kind of discourse intended.

The next question is the initial try at *developing a life history*. It produces a biased and limited history but contains specific and verifiable occurrences. These should be recorded rather fully. Evaluation of these events leads to the next series of steps in assessment. A review of the several episodes obtained in answer to the previous question show they are drawn from limited periods of life and are not sufficiently comprehensive to portray the entire person. Their purpose is simply to begin moving the assessment process along lines about which the person has feelings. In order to go beyond this cover story, the next questions attempt to obtain one or two very positively toned events from each year of life in effect asking for self-actualizing events as defined by Maslow (1962).

This year, has anything happened that "turned you on," deeply and fully expressed the kind of person you think you are, or in some way constituted a peak of experience—an emotional high? One of these questions is used rather than all. The language has to be phrased differently for different age, ethnic, social, and educational groups. But the concept that every life history has some high points (as well as valleys) is not difficult for most people to grasp. When the person begins to answer this question, he is again encouraged to produce sufficient detail to constitute an event.

What about last year? And the previous year? And . . . ? In this fashion, the clinician continues back throughout the person's life until one or two events for each year have been recorded verbatim. This procedure may be initially difficult for persons determined to maintain a facade of inadequacy, and it is inappropriate for very depressed persons. For those who can respond, it can be an enlivening experience, opening up new lines of inquiry into themselves.

The person is now ready to consider gaps in time spans, relationships to significant persons, and areas of life.

We have been writing your life history in effect. Naturally no one can tell everything that ever happened. However, let's take a look at what has been left out. There are, first of all, certain periods of life we know little about. The person may be able to think now of important events that he forgot to name in his childhood, school years, and the like.

Let's consider now some of the other people in your life. We haven't talked much about your ———— (whoever has been conspicuously or consistently omitted). The person may not be able to think of any events characterizing his relationship with that person but he can at least describe the person and why he thinks he has heretofore omitted him.

Most people are active in several areas of living: they work, study, play, love. We haven't talked much about ———— (whatever area of life has been conspicuously or consistently omitted). Data about each of these areas should be filled in so the clinician begins to probe where the person has lived, as well as how; where he has received satisfactions and where life has been too barren to report. If the person cannot remember some of these areas, he can be asked to name all the cities in which he has lived or to visualize all the houses in which he has lived and tell something about each.

The account of life can be supplemented by different facts from different assessment settings. In a hospital, the hospital provides clinical and psychological tests, a medical history, and a social history. The college generates grades, nonacademic achievements, and a health record. The assessment doctrines on such supplementary data have been too well developed to require summary here. What does need emphasis, however, is that these data are intended to modify, amplify, authenticate, and supplement—but *never* replace—the life history. They are distinctly secondary evidence for personality assessment. This does not mean that they are unimportant; indeed, they may seem very important to the person being assessed. But they are not viewed here as the mainstream of the life history, and they have no meaning outside that history.

The events of life should ideally be prepared verbatim and placed in chronological order. In this account, by itself, the person may well see new aspects of himself that are fresh and valid. And in any event, the clinician will probably not be able to make coherent sense of the data until they are in temporal sequence.

In length, such a history will, in fact, quickly outrun the clinician's powers for comprehension and recall. I would recommend

grouping and numbering the events as an aid to organization.
Notes on authentication and credibility should be added to these as
footnotes. Even in a simple case, between fifty and a hundred events
will be thus assembled. With each step, more parts of the life
naturally unfold, and the person is progressively better able to reconstruct events that are related to what he has said. A life history
comprising fifty to a hundred such events will total 5,000 to 20,000
words, or from twenty-five to a hundred typed pages.

This length makes it almost mandatory to deal with token
events. Once the person has learned how to report detailed events
and once he appreciates their importance, he may be able to substitute token phrases referring to original events. The person can
then amplify upon demand. A list of such token events can be outlined on only one or two pages. These constitute a skeleton of life
and can be fleshed out when needed. For example, the person's
token list might include entries in his own shorthand such as, "The
time my dog died; my first fishing trip; death of Uncle Charlie; the
first dance; first sex; day I left for college; broke leg first time
out on skis; tried pot and didn't like it; roommate's bad trip; boot
camp. . . ."

Last of all, one needs to know the person's view of his future.
What next steps might he be considering? What are his short-range
and longer-range goals? Essentially, the question is:

In light of all this, how does the future look? A person may
respond to this in various ways: emotionally, practically, wishfully,
fearfully. The clinician may wish to know how the person interprets
the question. Eventually, however, the clinician will need to learn
both the cognitive structure of the future and the evaluation the
person makes of it. To get the person to clarify his view of the
future, one may compare it to a map of country he is exploring and
ask him to imagine the features he expects or hopes to encounter.

Finally, one should ask the person to name specific goals so
that several questions may be raised about each, for example: *What
would you like to be doing this time next year?* or *Where would
you like to be living five years from now?* Then ask about these focal
goals: (a) *What are the chances that (this goal) will actually come
about?* Most people, with various shades of reluctance, can answer
in terms of the probabilities 0 to 100, and it is important to translate

verbal thinking about life chances into these numbers. (*b*) *How good will it be if you actually reach this goal?* A desirability scale is needed for this question. We have been experimenting with various scales that might express how people feel and I would have to leave the final choice of such a scale open. But in general, desirability for life goals varies from indifference to "If this happened, my entire existence would be justified."

What will have to transpire in order to bring about this goal? This question is asked not so much to test the person's practical plans as to provoke an evaluation of his life's means as well as its ends (true also with question 10). Thus one asks the person to evaluate the means toward his goal as well as the goal itself.

When you think about the future, does it express more the kind of person you have been, or the kind you want to be? This question is designed to determine whether or not the person sees his identity in the future. It confronts his hope for the future with the fact of his past. The clinician should therefore confront the person with the past, if necessary—not the bitter parts of the past but the peak experiences in it. The phrasing of this line of questioning is the most delicate in the series, and it should be done uniquely for every person. A clumsy wording or tone in it can further embitter a person whose entire history is defined by him as sad and deprived. With an old person, obviously, the question should be phrased in plausible form.

Having completed this process, how shall we determine whether an assessment has been well done? This question must be answered from the standpoint of both the clinician and the person. It should be answered in a measurable way if we hope to do research that will reveal the best assessment methods. There are primary (indispensable) goals; and occasional goals (appropriate only under certain conditions). In the assessment evaluation system to be described it is assumed that a tangible end product, a written document, has resulted from the assessment. The seriousness of the issues and the complexity of the material are too great for the clinician to do analysis "off the top of his head."

The life history has been well constructed and the assessment process well done if the following primary goals have been achieved: (1) The clinician can accurately predict events that are not in the history. He can test himself by predicting past facts about the life history that were not reported by the person as well as by predicting future events, whose ultimate validity can be determined only by follow-up study. (2) The clinician can accurately predict clinically significant events not contained in the history. These are such an important subcategory of criterion 1 that I have listed them separately. The dangers of suicide, the probabilities of addiction, the success or failure of the person's impending marriage, all illustrate situations for which many clinicians want to be able to make valid estimates.

Moving to the person's primary goals, what kind of therapeutic benefit can he expect to receive from such a searching analysis of his own life? The life history has been well constructed if (3) he can accurately anticipate the outcome of his hopes and goals; and (4) he knows how to devise substitute goals and plans when the first ones fail or have to be abandoned. The person should profit from going through the emotionally demanding process of reviewing and constructing his life. Criterion 3 indicates that he knows his life and his potentialities. He knows what he himself can do and is likely to do. This is a kind of insight. Criterion 4 shows that the person has learned enough about the life-history construction process that he, too, can use it on a later occasion; he has acquired some planning skill. This feature of therapeutic assessment will lead some to wonder whether it is not as well called counseling. In the sense that what is said here is intended equally for normal as for "sick" people (and, indeed, intensive assessment is better done with a person after extreme anxieties or other disabling symptoms have subsided), perhaps *counseling* is not an inappropriate term. However, the first two goals listed (criteria 1 and 2) are imperative requirements for assessment, and they derive from the clinical tradition. In particular, the model of life history developed by Henry Murray is a clinical organismic model.

There are numerous secondary goals that should be considered therapeutic aims. While they are intended to benefit the person, the clinician will recognize their benefits more fully than most patients or clients. For this reason, they are more the clinician's goals than the person's. The life history has been well constructed if (5) the person now recognizes the most significant events of his life and can link them both conceptually and emotionally with the rest of his life; and (6) the clinician can identify not only events that the person admits are key events but also can identify those that the person treats *as if* significant.

These goals are all measurable in the following ways. To determine those events that are recognized as most significant ask the person: *You have given me the following account of your life. Would you indicate the single most important thing that has ever happened to you?* Or ask: *What one event would be the best example of your life if someone asked what it had been like?* Then the clinician may go on to ask for the next most significant event, and so on for at least ten such events or until the person finds he can no longer offer a meaningful answer. My observation is that intelligent people can usually produce at least twenty.

With this subjective nucleus of the life in hand, the person is now asked to account for it. The clinician asks about the first event in time, "What led up to this?" The usual reply will be a chain of external circumstances and events already in the life history. It is of the greatest importance to note new events that had not previously been reported and those that are manifestly significant (in the clinician's view) but that the person does not designate as such. These inquiries move toward achievement of criteria 5 and 6 above. Answering this question for each significant event should produce a sequence of events that will link the significant events with the rest of the life (criterion 5). And in this discussion, the person may report some events as if they were significant (criterion 6) even though they were not in his original list. One may wonder whether this process of evaluation is not part of the original assessment—after all, it is producing new information. Its intent is evaluative but if it is good evaluation it should indeed provide additional clarification. Among the special problems of this line of questioning is the danger of uncovering repressed material and events that unduly arouse anxiety. The clinician who notes carefully the manner in which events are connected will perceive that this connection is not only cognitive (as defined earlier in this book, for example, the paired comparison) but affective. The affective connection between two events is indicated in the feeling expressed as the person discusses the connection in retrospect. These tell the clinician whether to probe a connection further. However, the assessment questioning

should be limited, not so much because of the infrequent dangers
but because the searching explorations characteristic of deep therapy are simply not needed.

There is one final secondary goal of assessment. The life history has been well constructed if (7) the clinician knows the current self-impression of the person. This impression is the verbal
image that the person offers of himself. The simplest way to express
this image, for quantitative purposes, is the Q-sort form (Block,
1961). The Q-sort requires the person to describe himself in a particular standardized way. He rates each of a series of statements for
its accuracy in describing him. The accuracy is judged relative to
the other statements in the list. For example, a person may decide
that he is more intelligent than emotional. The clinician asks the
person to do a Q-sort, and he also does one on the person. A high
correlation between these can mean that either (1) they are describing the same false image or (2) the clinician has empathy for
the person. To rule out the false image, one simply compares the
impression yielded by the Q-sort with the impression yielded by the
most significant recent events of the life history. A Q-sort impression
that resembles the impression left by these events is probably not
faked. One may compare his impression with those of close friends
and family members. Cline and Richards (1960) checked their
trait descriptions against the views of families. My own view is that
relatives often describe a person as he was more than as he is.

In some assessment settings and professional situations, the
clinician may have some or all of the following occasional goals. A
life history has been well constructed if from it (8) the clinician
can communicate to another professional a valid impression of the
person, (9) the clinician can communicate to another professional a
valid impression of the person's clinical situation, and (10) reports
can be written that enable others to validate the clinician's credentials as a professional. These goals are measurable in the same
manner that the earlier goals were. For example, consider requirements that predictions can be made by the clinician (criteria 1 and
2). If the clinician who took the history writes a report from which
another judge can make valid predictions, then criteria 8 and 9
will be satisfied. Criterion 10 can be interpreted to mean that any
or all of the previous goals (criteria 1 through 9) are manifestly met

in a series of reports written by the clinician. There are legal accrediting or licensing agencies in most states, and their means for evaluating such documents are beyond the scope of this book.

The effects of a searching examination of one's life by a judge can be therapeutic. The criteria of effectiveness for assessment should enable the clinician to determine whether a therapeutic result has been achieved as well as other goals of assessment. I have attempted to describe criteria that can be objectively determined and that all grow out of the logic of life-history assessment. The goals or criteria are not so ambitious as those sought by psychotherapists. However, they appear attainable; and, still more important to the empirically minded, it should be possible to determine whether they have in fact been attained.

I have deliberately intermingled the gatekeeper's rational goals and the person's goals in the criteria for assessment. We are in need of assessment systems that view the person and not only the institution as beneficiary. The credentials system deferred almost entirely to institutional needs. Pure counseling and psychotherapy defer almost entirely to the welfare of the person. The intensive assessment system depicted here is a compromise. Such a compromise is justifiable not only in the interests of justice and compassion but also the very practical problem of incentive. The person should gain enough from the process to make his investments of time and emotion worth while.

✰✰✰✰✰✰✰✰✰ **5** ✰✰✰✰✰✰✰✰✰

Experimentation with Programed Cases

✰✰✰✰✰✰✰✰✰✰✰✰✰✰✰✰✰✰✰✰✰✰✰✰

The chief difficulty with clinical assessment is that it has been subject to so little research until recent years. Not even a minor fraction of the staggering amount of research in actuarial and psychometric assessment has been devoted to learning how intuitive judges do assessment (Oscar Buros' yearbook [1965] lists hundreds of new tests in each edition!). Thus when the findings are negative as to how accurately clinicians or other professionals predict, this can be interpreted as the inevitable consequence of research neglect.

The life-history assessment method (of which the procedure in Chapter Four was a sample) defines accuracy in intuitive prediction as its primary criterion. It is time to say how this can be measured and how experiments can be performed that establish the conditions for valid predictions. Since not everything can be investigated at once, we have to justify the decision to investigate prediction, instead of beginning at the other end of the assessment process, with data collection. There are already in process numerous investigations of interviewing and data collection (Matarazzo, 1965). But it is crucial to what we have said here that we demonstrate predictability. If this cannot be shown, there is little point to proceed to the study of data collection.

Consider the question of why prediction is possible. Earlier we suggested that prediction results from the judge's recognition of intelligible interconnections among the episodes of a life. Based on this conception of prediction, a specific kind of experiment has been designed for the study of life-history assessment. It presents behavioral events to the judge and measures his ability to predict other behavioral events in the same history. The design is called the programed case, a hybrid of the terms *programed instruction* and *case study*. The programed case is a life history structured in such a way that the judge learns to make increasingly valid predictions in the case and the experimenter obtains measures of the validity of the judge's predictions. The basic unit of information given the judge is the event, an approximation to the earlier concept of episode. The judge receives the case in increments of one event. After each increment, he predicts the next event. The prediction is made by discriminating among alternative events. Usually a trio is presented in each discrimination, the one correct event and two distractors. After recording his prediction, the judge receives immediate feedback, informing him which event is correct. At this point, he now knows what he knew before, plus the increment. In a typical programed case, the judge makes fifteen discriminations and reinforcements, and thus receives fifteen increments of data. In general, the process resembles the collection of life-history data in that an interviewer also obtains increments of data in response to his questions.

Thus the programed case presents a judge with a learning problem: getting to know a person. The immediate feedback serves as an incentive. At the end of the case, the learning process is shown in the form of a learning curve in which accuracy is shown as a function of increments in life-history data (Figure 2). The design of the programed case was suggested by B. F. Skinner's analysis (1954) of the teaching process. It fits Lewis Goldberg's analysis (1968, pp. 493–494) of the conditions that must hold if skill in making "complex clinical inferences" is to be acquired:

Some form of feedback is a necessary, though not necessarily a sufficient, condition for learning to occur. Second, . . . it may be necessary to disturb the natural sequence of cue presentations—to rearrange the order of cases—so that one's hypotheses can be im-

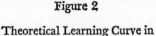

Figure 2

Theoretical Learning Curve in
Life-History Assessment
(Increments in Data Known)

Number of events known to judge at time of prediction.

mediately verified or discounted. [Third] . . . it may often be necessary to tally *the accuracy of one's hypotheses.*

The presentation of such a case to the assessment-research judge follows this sample sequence: (1) Instruction; an initial fact (usually a demographic fact such as occupation) about the person. (2) The judge is asked to record which one of three events is most likely true: (*a*) the correct event, (*b*) an alternative fictitious event, and (*c*) an alternative fictitious event. (3) The judge then turns the page and receives the correct event (*a*), restated as confirmation or disproof of his prediction. He is then asked to record which one of the next set of three events is most likely true: (*a*) an alternative fictitious event, (*b*) the correct event, and (*c*) an alternative fictitious event. (4) The judge then turns the page and receives the correct event (*b*), restated as confirmation or disproof, and so on.

This cycle of prediction and reinforcement is repeated throughout the case. An example of such a programed case is given in Chapter Ten. Other formats are shown in Chapters Eleven and

Twelve. The uses of these other formats are explained in later chapters. However, all programed cases have the elements in common of authentic events, prediction, feedback, and incremental design.

To construct a programed case, the investigator requires a narrative life history, as well authenticated externally as possible; a set of facts that serve as acceptable criteria for understanding this history (the prediction of events from the history); the facts presented in the form of discriminations; and a means for providing the judge immediate feedback regarding the validity of each discrimination. The technical details regarding construction have been presented elsewhere (Dailey, 1966a; Fancher, 1966; De Waele, 1971).

Construction generally follows the organismic premises about life history presented in previous chapters. The unit of information in the case, called event, is an approximation to the episode, although we do not ask case writers to look specifically for Murray's criteria. Instead, a simpler definition of event is normally used; the case writer is instructed to divide the narrative life-history material into events that meet the following definition: *a behavioral episode occurring at a particular time and place, in response to a particular situation; the account of behavior is to include overt behavior, words, and gestures which indicate the feelings and probable motives of the person.* The length of each event in the case is normally no more than 100 words. Examples of events follow:

1. During World War II, although his job did not require it, he went on at least twenty-five bombing missions. His superiors protested his taking such risks as a civilian. One colleague said, "At first I thought he was afraid of being a coward—but it was more complicated than that."

2. In spite of long hours, he still found time to study his law books. In the law he seemed to find something otherwise missing from his life. One friend recalls, "His only mother was the law." With special permission, he took the oral state bar exam at only seventeen, made a high grade, and became the youngest lawyer in the state.

3. When his favorite son died, he turned to alcohol. Asking the advice of a friend when things got bad, he was told, "Lay off that bottle." He said, "I'm going to show you that I am the master of my own soul." He went into the bathroom; and, when he emerged, there were two shattered bottles of bourbon on the floor.

The case writer then prepares distractors for each event: two plausible but fictitious events from a similar situation and time of life. The distractors are then placed with the true event in the discrimination triad. While guessing would lead to correct choices one-third of the time, some events might be chosen more or less often than this, on the basis of appearing psychologically plausible or implausible in themselves without any reference to the rest of the life history. Therefore it is necessary to determine the a priori probability of choice of every event to assure the triad is not unduly hard or easy. The average level of difficulty in the ideal case should neither increase nor decrease from start to finish.

The instruction to the judge is usually "Get to know this news commentator" (or other occupation). The judge then proceeds to make his first discrimination of a childhood event, receives his first feedback, and so on, proceeding through the life history in chronological order. He records his inferences, scores them himself, and adds up his total score at the end of each case. In recent programed cases, we have also asked the judge to record the code number of the preceding event(s) that he used as his basis for the current discrimination. In this way it is possible to study the behavioral cues used by the judge.

In a typical experiment, up to a dozen programed cases (each requiring about an hour of analysis by the judge) are presented to each judge. Each case may be regarded as an experiment in which the independent variable is amount of information (number of events known at the point of discrimination) and the dependent variable is prediction accuracy. The series of cases may be regarded as an experiment also, in which the number of preceding cases completed is the independent variable. Prediction accuracy is is the dependent variable in this instance also.

If cases are equated for difficulty, improvement in predictive accuracy represents generalization or transfer of learning from case to case. Other analyses can determine the kinds of inferences that are most easily made, the cues that are used by judges most often when they make valid predictions, and biases (such as certain kinds of events overused or underused as cues). (See Table 2.) Intracase

Table 2. HYPOTHETICAL DATA-BASE MATRIX: PROBABILITY
OF EVENT *y* GIVEN EVENT *x*

Events *x*, reported as data bases for events *y*	Events *y*							
	2	3	4	5	6	7	8	*Mean*
1	.25	.25	.25	.70	.00	.50	.50	.35
2		.60	.50	.40	.25	.00	.00	.29
3			.70	.00	.70	.25	.50	.43
4				.00	.00	.25	.00	.06
5					.50	.60	.60	.57
6						.80	.40	.60
7							.00	.00
Mean	.25	.42	.48	.28	.29	.40	.29	.33
Zero Level	.25	.25	.30	.20	.20	.30	.20	.24

NOTE: This hypothetical case has no idiographic or learning structure.

improvement in accuracy (as a function of amount of information) would support the assumption of idiographic meaningfulness. That is, the events of such a case evidently possess meanings that become increasingly clear as more of the case is made known to the judge. A total score across cases can be computed for each judge. If this score proves reliable, the finding would support the hypothesis of a talent for life-history assessment.

The case viewed as a network of events may be analyzed in the following way. Let each cue-prediction probability (as in Table 2) be transformed into a 0 or 1 entry; for example, all the probabilities .50 or better are 1 and all others are 0. Place these 0 and 1 entries in a cue-inference table (Table 3). From it, certain con-

Table 3. Matrix of Valid Data Bases (Events 1 to 8)

Data bases	Inferences								Out-degrees
	1	2	3	4	5	6	7	8	
1		0	0	0	1	0	1	1	3
2			1	1	0	0	0	0	2
3				1	0	1	0	1	3
4					0	0	0	0	0
5						1	1	1	3
6							1	0	1
7								0	0
8									
In-degrees	0	1	2	1	2	3	3		12

cepts of graph theory (Harary, Norman, and Cartwright, 1965) can be derived. For example, the in-degree of an event refers to the number of cues that predicted it. The out-degree of an event refers to the number of subsequent events for which it was a cue. In-degrees and out-degrees are useful tools for analyzing the way in which effective assessment judges differ from ineffective. For other graph-theory concepts possibly useful in assessment, see my paper on graph theory (Dailey, 1959b). In Figure 3 the case graph represents the case as an information network. In theory, the network reveals the properties of the case as well as the manner in which judges reasoned about it. Some cases are more understandable; to the extent that this understandability depends on the intelligibility of the network of relations among events, the case graph should be a useful visualization. To the extent that the events in the case are a representative sample of the life history as a whole, the case graph is also an approximation of the structure and hence intelligibility of the life history itself.

The most obvious use of such cases is testing hypotheses about life-history assessment. It can be determined whether

Figure 3

Hypothetical Case-Graph Based
on Matrix of Table 3

Instructions for Case-Graphs:
"Draw a line A to B if Row A, Column B = 1, otherwise do not."

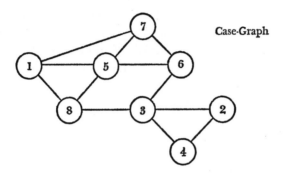

Case-Graph

most persons can make accurate predictions in most cases and whether clinical (or other) training improves this accuracy. The rates at which predictive accuracy improves (if it does) within cases should show something of the economic feasibility of life-history assessment. That is, if the learning rates are too slow, the use of life-history data might be too costly even if it achieves ulti-mately high levels of validity. Turning to variations in type of case programed, it might be determined what kinds of person can be assessed in this way. Perhaps psychotic persons cannot. Perhaps persons from cultures other than the judge's cannot. The limitations of life-history assessment can be empirically determined. The type of judge who can make accurate inferences of behavior would be a possible line of questioning. Do women make better judges? Are warmly empathic judges better at prediction? Do some institutions have better judges than others—for example, are psychiatrists better than industrial personnel managers?

Certain social issues lend themselves to analysis in this man-ner. Elsewhere, I suggested that prejudice in employment decision making can theoretically be detected and its ill effects reduced by methods such as the programed case (Dailey, 1966b). The assump-tion was made that prejudice—or, literally, pre-judging—causes an arrest in data intake. It would be shown in the learning curve in programed cases (see Figure 2) as a plateau or premature cessation of learning. One research question would be: Under what conditions do we get such arrest in learning? The hypothesis that prejudice can be reduced by such a method implies that the programed case can be an instrument of learning for those assessment judges whose decision making is based on unwitting (not deliberate) prejudice. This suggestion is made theoretically, under the assumption that the programed-case experimental design will eventually permit us to determine the optimum conditions for assessment. As we systematically vary the conditions for learning (the independent variables including not only the amount of data but also attitude toward the task, assumptions about life history, and the like) in a variety of populations of judges and cases, we should eventually be able to summarize the conditions for the greatest possible level of predictive accuracy. Chapter Six summarizes what has been learned to date.

COLLECTING DATA

In the experiments to be reported, we used programed cases for which the data had been collected in a variety of ways. Data collection can be designed at any point on the objective-subjective continuum. Objective method would refer at an extreme to the encoding of behavior by an eyewitness (Barker and Wright, 1951). It is almost impossible to conceive of very many feasible studies of life history collected in this manner. Somewhat less objective but still in that direction would be the method used by Richard Rahe, Joseph McKean, and Ransom Arthur (1967), Thomas Holmes and Minoru Masuda (1967), Holmes and Rahe (1967), Masuda and Holmes (1967), Robert Casey, Masuda, and Holmes (1967), Allen Wyler, Masuda, and Holmes (1968), to record the occurrence or nonoccurrence at a certain time of standardized events, each of which was subject to verification because relatively public. Examples of such events are marriage, serious automobile accident, college graduation, and a job change. (One should note with caution that many procedures labeled as biographic inventories do not describe particular events but are in essence inventories of personality traits without reference to any particular situation, time, and place; such inventories are not biographic in our sense of the term, neither subjectively nor objectively.)

Moving toward the subjective pole of life-history data-collection methods, one can permit more freedom to the informant in both stimulus and response. Instead of presenting a list of possible events (and asking the informant to check which ones have happened to him this year, for example), one can limit the response category and open up the stimulus. For example, "What were the happiest times of your life?" would limit the kinds of events with which he can respond but would delimit their definition and location in time and space. Or one can limit the stimulus and open up the response category. For example, "Tell me about a time when you had a blind date this year." Or one can open up both the stimulus and the response in the interview by suggesting to the informant, "Tell me about your life." Then the person selects the stimuli in memory to which he wishes to respond, and selects the kinds of response he is going to make. These variations on data-collection method will be called Standardized-Stimulus, Standardized-Response, and Unstandardized, respectively. A fourth variation used in collecting data is a combination method in which a Standardized-Stimulus method is used to obtain event descriptions from the person; then he is asked to choose the events from among these that best satisfy certain criteria (verifiability, representativeness, significance, and the like). In this combination method, the events described can then be verified by interrogating observers, family members, or other witnesses and significant persons (Baer, 1970).

Other methodological issues involve questions of whether a retrospective or concurrent account is to be obtained and whether the history will be obtained from published or from original sources. No concurrent histories were involved in the research reported in Chapter Six, but programed cases were written from both published and original (interview) sources. Twenty-eight programed cases were used in the experiments reported in the research. Three series were prepared, in the following ways.

Data for the first series of cases were collected from the published life histories of eminent leaders, all essentially normal. From each biography were taken fifteen brief (fifty to a hundred words) incidents that met the criteria that define an event (see above, pp.

79–80). These incidents spanned the life of the subject and described his behavior in diverse situations. Little selectivity was exercised because the typical biography provided such a small number of usable incidents and, in order to obtain fifteen such events, one had to use about all available. The cases were written and programed by twenty different case writers under my instructions. There was no theoretical orientation common to these case writers. This early series of twelve cases was criticized by reviewers as too heavily male, upper class, and North American. However, it produced quantitative findings that met statistical requirements of reliability, and the cases were used in the research reported in Chapter Six. One of these cases is presented in Chapter Ten.

To meet the criticisms, the second series was of considerably greater diversity. These eight cases included women, Latin-Americans, several persons of lower-middle-class status, and three disadvantaged persons. None was hospitalized, although two had consulted psychiatrists. Data for four of these cases were collected in open-end interviewing (that is, unstandardized in regard to both stimulus questions and response categories). The interviewer, a psychologist, essentially began with the simple request "Tell me about your life; start at the beginning." When the informant appeared to have a particular incident in mind but was glossing over details, the interviewer would ask him, "Could you tell me more about that?" Data in the other four of these cases were collected in open-end interviewing by a sociologist, who began by administering a broad inventory of values and then asking the person to comment on his experiences in respect to the more extreme of his responses to the value questions. Then the interviewer proceeded in these four cases to obtain data in a relatively open-end way. Thus, he used the inventory to stimulate the person initially. In two of his cases, the sociologist-interviewer verified the statements made by the informant about his job history, arrest record, educational and social history, and medical record. These eight interviews were tape-recorded, transcribed, and then divided into events. The events were presented in the written case in chronological order. No events were omitted but those parts of the interview that were not part of events were deleted. In this series, the programing shifted from the initial triad-discrimination design to a variety of other kinds. The basic design of prediction with immediate reinforcement was always followed, but the case material was presented in long narrative passages rather than in increments of one brief event (as in the eminent-leader series). The predictions made were of several kinds, true/false, multiple-choice, and other. This created problems in summing the scores that we had not met in the first series of cases. Judges reading the second series of cases found them more meaningful but for research purposes these narrative cases gave us more problems than did the first series. Two of the eight narrative cases are given as Chapters Eleven and Twelve.

The events predicted in the first two series of cases were both objective and subjective. They were objective in the sense that every event occurs objectively (at a particular time and place) and has objective behavioral content. They were subjective in the sense that, in many cases in the first two series (though not all), the events were obtained from the person. The research was criticized as being too subjective by some. Perhaps a judge could match the events reported by a person because of their subjective aspects but would not be able to predict more objective facts. A third series of cases was constructed in which the informant was not the sole source of data. Ten employees of a manufacturing corporation were interviewed by an experienced personnel manager. He used a standard stimulus procedure (administering an application blank) on which he encouraged the informant to write freely and fully. The personnel manager independently interviewed the informant's boss, obtaining a performance rating and other descriptions of performance. The performance ratings, while based on the subjective opinion of the boss, were at least independent of the informant's reports. In later assessment experiments, the ratings were used as the criterion to be predicted by judges after they had reviewed the data in the application form on each informant. In this design, only one prediction and immediate reinforcement per case were used; the entire ten cases were presented as a single series to each judge. The personnel-selection series of cases has face validity in measuring selection ability. It does not, however, present data in intracase increments with many trials in prediction as in the earlier series. Therefore, it is not, strictly speaking, an idiographic procedure. Chapter Thirteen is a sample such case.

These three series provided the programed cases used in the experimental findings to be reported. Some of the cases were translated into Korean or French for use in intercultural experiments. In addition to these twenty-eight cases, Raymond Fancher programed three eighty-event cases of Harvard students (1966, 1967) and J. P. De Waele programed three fifty-event cases of Belgian juvenile delinquents (1971).

There are not many possible programing designs; but, as indicated above, there seem to be endless ways to collect the original cases. In spite of the criteria suggested by John Dollard (1935), Gordon Allport (1942), Lewis Langness (1965) and others, no commonly accepted discipline exists among those who prepare cases, biographies, and life histories. This profusion results in part from the inherent intricacy of life history and in part from the many uses to which cases are put. Some investigators use cases simply to illustrate concepts, presenting their more substantial evidence in the form of quantitative data. Others regard properly prepared cases as original observations to be treated with appropriate discipline as much as any other scientific data. The latter view is our own. Another source of variation in case collection results from confusion about the term *case*. A statistical case is simply a datum like any other datum and it can prove nothing because it is a one-shot single instance that could well be an accident. In assessment, however, a case is a complex set of data regarding an individual. It is the total of what one records of him. This latter is the sense in which the word *case* is used here.

Another issue is the personal character of the case. The intricate and perhaps unique organization of the original life history, most clinicians assume, make it undesirable to standardize the data collection too far. However, if one remains at the extreme intuitive end of the continuum of standardized versus formless case collection, it will prove impossible to solve such problems as life-history sampling. For this reason, I lean toward multiple approaches in future research, especially toward collecting both objective or standardized biographic inventories (see Table 1) and more subjective and free-form autobiographic accounts on the same persons. The total life history, composed then of both objective and subjective parts, should meet the following criteria: The series of incidents or facts must all be located in real time (occurring at particular times and places), must span a considerable portion of the person's life, and must present such demographic and objective facts as help in the interpretation of the subjective part. In its subjective part, the history should describe both behavior and the person's feelings about that behavior; the incidents should describe behavior in a variety of settings and not in only one setting; these settings must be part of the person's habitat (his customary life space) and not a contrived part of the clinician's or experimenter's environment.

An assessment judge is expected to predict events. These are normally events of a certain class, for example, clinical events. In assessment research, however, we have taken the position that it is life as a whole that should be understood. Thus we make no effort to segregate events into classes. A judge receives the same credit for predicting a clinical event as for predicting a legal crime, for anticipating a job change as for anticipating a marriage. This generalized ability is our initial research interest; subvarieties of it can be studied at a later point. The methodology of the programed case is as well suited, logically, for the analysis of the conditions for general prediction as it is for specialized prediction.

✿✿✿✿✿✿✿✿✿ **6** ✿✿✿✿✿✿✿✿✿

Talent for Assessment: Findings

✿✿✿✿✿✿✿✿✿✿✿✿✿✿✿✿✿✿✿✿✿✿

The most serious problems of intuitive assessment have been the repeated demonstration of inaccuracy, causing a scientific and professional crisis in assessment. However, almost none of these negative findings utilized the life history as data. It has been repeatedly suggested here that life-history assessment is potentially valid.

PREDICTION IN PROGRAMED CASES

Twenty-eight programed cases were prepared and used in experiments with more that 1,400 judges in two cultures; see Table 4. In addition to these experiments, Fancher (1966) and De Waele (1971) developed their own programed cases (six additional cases). De Waele's judges were Belgian graduate psychology students. Fancher's were graduate students at Harvard. In brief, then, judges from three cultures (United States, Korean, and Belgian) have interpreted standardized life histories (programed cases). Were they able to predict accurately?

Accuracy. Recall that some programed cases begin by presenting a judge with a discrimination among three possible events: one true and two false. After making his forecast, he is immediately told what the prediction *should* have been. This feedback adds one

Table 4. POPULATIONS OF JUDGES INVOLVED IN PROGRAMED
CASE RESEARCH

Population		N	Institutions
Employment counselors and supervisors		492	U.S. Employment Service
College students		380	
Korean	85		Yonsei and Ewha Universities, Seoul
American	295		The American University
			Dartmouth College
High school students		225	Korea
Soldiers (U.S.)		92	U.S. Army, Korea
Peace Corpsmen (in training)		65	University of Missouri
Industrial executives		59	Control Data, IBM, Interstate Bakeries Corp.
Federal interns		28	U.S. Civil Service Comm.
VISTA Workers (in training)		28	Office of Economic Opportunity
Federal and state officials		28	Bureau of Employment Security
YWCA administrators		14	Kansas City (Mo.) YWCA
Denominational executives		14	United Presbyterian Church in USA
Total		1,425	

event to his store of information (his data base) whether or not his prediction was correct. When he faces the next discrimination (and the next, and so on), he possesses the same information as every other judge.

Table 5 shows the results of two ways of determining whether judges were merely guessing at future events. In the one method predictive accuracy is compared with statistical chance (33 per cent in most of the cases used). In all cases for which

Table 5. Mean Accuracy of Predictions for Selected Populations

Population	N	Case(s)	Predictive accuracy	Chance level[a]	Zero level
				Per Cent	
Korean high school					
Group I	30	b	51	33	32
Group II	55	b	61	33	32
Group III	30	b	50	33	32
Group IV	57	b	52	33	32
Group V	68	b	57	33	32
U.S. high school	62	b	54	33	32
Korean college					
Group I	30	b	55	33	32
Group II	26	b	51	33	32
Group III	30	b	53	33	32
U.S. Military	30	b	49	33	32
Peace Corps					
Men	24	Kaiser[e]	49	33	28
		McClelland[e]	43	33	30
		Anderson[e]	54	33	37

	N				
Women	36	Kaiser[e]	50	33	28
		McClelland[e]	48	33	30
		Anderson[e]	55	33	37
U.S. College Group I	54	McClelland[e]	49	33	30
		Murrow[e]	62	33	33
Group II	159	Richard[d]	65	50	Not available
	159	Richard (negative)[d]	75	50	Not available
	176	Sam Grant[e]	44	28	Not available

[a] Differences between the empirical predictive accuracy column and the chance level can be tested in significance by use of the formula, $SD_M = pq/N$, where pq is the product of the right and wrong proportions in the triads ($\frac{1}{3} \times \frac{2}{3}$ in these cases). N is shown to the left. The largest such SD_M is .09, and no critical ratios are less than 1.8 for particular groups. The population as a whole can also be tested in this way, but the results are obvious. The zero-level null hypothesis is tested by a more complex method to be presented at a later point.

[b] A set of five cases, in the form shown in Chapter Ten, each consisting of fifteen events with each of the fifteen predictions consisting of a discrimination among three alternatives, one of which was correct. Feedback was given after each prediction.

[c] These cases are of the form shown in Chapter Ten (see note b above). To provide a more direct basis of comparison between Peace Corps males and females, and also with Group I of the U. S. college students, mean predictive accuracy scores are shown for each individual in those populations.

[d] The Richard case is in Chapter Eleven. The total score is based on the number of inferences of antisocial behavior correctly predicted by the case analyst. The "negative" score is a subset consisting of the antisocial behaviors which Richard was known to have committed.

[e] The Sam Grant case is in Chapter Thirteen.

statistical chance could be determined—as in the examples shown
in Table 5—predictive accuracy exceeded statistical chance by a
significant amount. This table shows that even Korean high school
students judging American cases (based on the lives of Edward R.
Murrow, Henry Ford, Henry Kaiser, Robert Anderson—Secretary
of the Treasury under Eisenhower—and John McClelland) were
able to predict at an average accuracy of 54 per cent. The cases
were in the programed format of Murrow (Chapter Ten). For
those cases, a more rigorous method of determining chance was also
used; the predictive accuracy of each triad (or discrimination) was
determined by judges who knew nothing else about the case. The
mean accuracy of these predictions-in-isolation are shown in the
zero-level column in Table 5. This method requires a score called
the zero level of accuracy (zero level referring to the fact that the
judge knows nothing about the rest of the case). Some investigators
would call this method psychological chance because, by psychological reasoning alone, some judges could predict which of three
alternatives is more likely. The zero level of predictive accuracy was
determined for seven of the programed cases. Comparing zero level
with predictive accuracy, we found in every case that predictive
accuracy was greater than psychological chance, an indication that
judges benefit from information in a case; the finding supports our
assumption that predictive accuracy measures ability to interpret a
case and not merely ability to pick out right answers.

Does predictive ability necessarily imply *understanding* of a
case? Judges sometimes expressed a sense of unease about their task,
indicating they felt they lacked sufficient data for the events they
were asked to predict. And yet measured by either the statistical or
the zero-level method, they clearly were not guessing. How do we
interpret this lack of confidence? Perhaps in a technical culture
most people do not consider behavior scientifically predictable.
Everyone "knows" physical phenomena are predictable but human
behavior is not! Another interpretation is that the programed case
is what it was designed to be: an intuitive procedure, tapping unconscious judgmental processes. It poses severe confidence problems
among judges who mistrust such processes.

The reader might consider a 54 per cent accuracy in prediction rather imprecise. But these levels were found among *naive*

judges. It is not presently known how accurate the predictive level would be for trained judges, that is, judges subjected to a very long series of programed cases. Not shown in Table 5 were results from ten personnel cases programed in the manner illustrated in Chapter Thirteen: application blank and other data presented to the judge, after which he attempts to forecast a performance rating. Thirty-three graduate students in personnel, completing a series of seven of these cases, made 229 predictions of a four-point performance rating. The chi-square was 98 (with 9 degrees of freedom, significant at the .005 level). Results from one of these cases are shown in the last line of Table 5, used with a larger N of United States undergraduates. In this instance, the case score is based on accuracy in predicting both the supervisory rating (two triads in this particular case) and supervisor's qualitative description of Sam Grant's performance.

General Talent. Is intuitive prediction an ephemeral process, solid enough to produce statistical findings but not tangible enough for replication? Is the method reliable for the individual judge? Are there, in other words, individual differences; are some judges systematically better at prediction than others? There are two ways to answer this question. The first method simply computes an "odd-even" reliability coefficient: sum the number of accurate predictions made for odd-numbered events across all cases, and independently sum the number made for even-numbered events across all cases. Do the two proportions correlate? The finding, for every population in which the correlation was computed, was a significant reliability coefficient (usually about .77). The second method intercorrelates case scores. If a judge earns a predictability score of 45 per cent on his first case, will he earn that same score on the second case? The intercorrelation of case scores produces a matrix of Pearsonian correlation coefficients for the total group of judges.

A case with only fifteen predictions would naturally produce a less reliable measure than the odd-even coefficient determined on the basis of seventy-five predictions—as in the above coefficient of reliability (.77). The median correlation between such single case scores was about .40 for most groups, but it differed systematically from group to group. Figure 4 shows the different populations of

Figure 4

Intercorrelations Between Case
Scores for Various Occupations

The correlation between the mean accuracy of eight occupational groups
and their median intercorrelation among case scores was .75. The number
of subjects in these eight groups was 207. Korean high school subjects
omitted. Number of cases intercorrelated varied from five to twelve.
Decimals omitted from correlations.

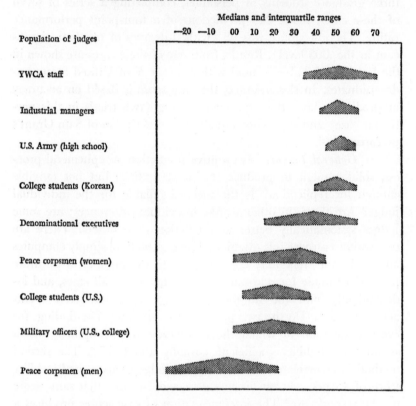

judges arrayed in order of median correlation. If the median correlation measures consistency of the talent for prediction, then the
data suggest that older judges were generally more consistent than
American college students. (The exception was an American military group, which was erratic.) The median consistency for a group
was closely related to the mean accuracy of its predictions. Thus,
prediction ability behaves as a variable like most known talents,
which tend to become more stable or controllable as they develop.

However these tables are interpreted, it is quite clear that they do not contain random phenomena. There is a systematically high or low ability to predict events in these cases. Even without training in psychology or case analysis, some judges show a consistent ability to predict life-history outcomes not known to them.

Cross-Cultural Prediction. It was reported above that Korean high school and college students could predict the behavior of Americans in programed cases. Is there other evidence of such cross-cultural generality? Two studies have examined this question. In one, fifty Peace Corpsmen were asked to make predictions in thirteen programed cases, including three based on the lives of Colombians. In the other, graduate students in psychology at the University of Brussels made predictions in two American programed cases and three Belgian (De Waele, 1971). To test for cross-cultural generality in the Peace Corps study, the accuracy of the corpsmen's predictions on the Colombians was summed (a total score for the three cases). This Latin-American score was then correlated with a similar score, the sum of corpsmen's predictions on the American cases (the North American score). Latin-American and North American scores proved to be correlated (.44 for all fifty corpsmen, .61 for twenty-eight women corpsmen); the result supports the hypothesis of cross-cultural generality, at least for women judges. The twenty-nine Belgians analyzed three very extensive programed cases of Belgian juvenile delinquents and two American programed cases (De Waele, 1971). The correlations between the Belgian and American case scores were .46, .31, .31 for the first American case versus the three Belgian cases; and .48, .74, and .59 for the second American case. Belgian judges' ability to predict Belgian case events was correlated with their ability to predict American case events.

Idiographic Understanding. Summing the number of correct predictions in a series of cases and dividing this figure by the number of attempts obscures the possibility of learning whether judges improve their predictive ability as a case progresses. Is there such a thing as idiographic learning—the ability to develop a progressively more accurate impression of a particular person?

The research explored this question in three ways: (1) The accuracy of a judge early in a case (analogous to the get-acquainted stage) was compared with his later accuracy; if accuracy increased, this fact was interpreted to mean that the judge had learned by the amount of the increase. (2) The accuracy of a judge late in a case was compared with his zero level (guessing level) for those same events. If accuracy achieved in full knowledge of the case was greater than the zero level, this fact was interpreted to mean that the judge had learned by that amount. (3) The accuracy of a judge was correlated with the amount of information he possessed up to the point a given prediction was made. The size of this correlation coefficient was interpreted as a learning rate.

These methods utilize some overlapping assumptions and should therefore produce similar results. Method 1 uses the judge as his own standard, asking whether he knows the person better than before. It assumes equal difficulty in items in the different parts of the cases. Method 2 uses a nomothetic opinion (judges' opinions as to what most people would likely do) as the control, asking whether the judge knows this person better than he would likely know most persons. Method 3 assumes that predictive accuracy should vary directly with number of events known, asking whether the judge is making profitable use of his increments in information. It assumes equal information value in events in different parts of the cases. All three methods were used to analyze findings from the 402 judges who participated in the Korean experiments (see Tables 6, 7, and 8). For methods 1 and 3, American judges showed more idiographic learning than Koreans; not so for method 2. For method 2, women judges showed more idiographic learning than men. College-educated Koreans learned idiographically better than high school Koreans by all three methods.

Recalling the lack of differences in average prediction scores between Korean and American judges, consider the significance of this idiographic learning finding. Possibly the knowledge of culture (American judges had this advantage on the American cases) affects idiographic learning but not the simple average accuracy of prediction. This interpretation of *culture* reverses the view that knowledge of culture implies knowledge of general behavior (that is, customary behavior removed from the context of an individual's life).

When does idiographic learning occur? Tables 7 and 8 suggest that nine cases programed similarly (so that comparisons

Table 6. Idiographic Learning Curves of Koreans and Americans: Differences in Accuracy Between First and Last Third Predictions in Each Case[a]

	N	Case 1		Case 2		Case 3		Case 4		Case 5	
		Mean	SD_M	Mean	SD_M	Mean	SD_M	Mean	SD_M	Mean	SD_M
Americans[b]	92	.14	.15	−.25	.14	.92	.13	.87	.13	1.11	.17
Koreans	326	−.43	.08	−.17	.08	.73	.08	.40	.07	.48	.08
t-tests		3.3		ns		ns		3.2		3.4	

[a] The first and last third of a case each contained five predictions. The number correct on the last third minus the number correct on the first third constituted the difference in accuracy. The mean difference in accuracy, for example on the first case, was .14 (indicating little improvement within the case) for Americans, and −.43 (indicating a decrement) for Koreans.

[b] The ninety-two Americans were soldiers on duty in Korea. This group included sixty-two high school and thirty college graduates.

Table 7. Zero Level of Information in Seven Programed Cases: Accuracy of Guesses in Successive Fifths

Case	Q1	Q2	Q3	Q4	Q5	Total (%)
A	34	46	24	48	32	37
E	18	39	45	42	42	37[a]
G	44	20	38	40	22	33
I	26	34	36	18	36	30
J	27	27	27	24	36	28
K	40	24	20	26	28	28
M	44	36	24	46	14	33
1. Average	33	32	31	35	30	32
2. Average[b]	36	31	28	34	25	31

[a] This case seemed to produce an artificial learning curve due to the decreasing difficulty of its items, and was not used in most subsequent research analyses.

[b] The sums and averages for successive fifths of the other six programed cases (omitting case E), which were used in research, are shown in the second average.

of their learning properties could be made) show idiographic learning patterns. Analysis of the remaining three suggests that their sequencing separated quite widely the predictions to be made from the behavioral cues necessary for the predictions. Superior judges could apparently compare events from widely separated time periods in life. Most judges, however, apparently confined their analysis to comparing events that were grouped closely in the text of the case and thus became confused or otherwise unable to interpret the subtler programed case. To state this finding in another way, perhaps any programed case will yield an idiographic learning curve if the cues are properly placed so that anyone can detect them. However, would such a case teach a judge anything? And how typical would such a programed case be of the way in which lives are actually patterned? Our conclusion is that presenting

Table 8. IDIOGRAPHIC LEARNING CURVES IN TWELVE PRO-
GRAMED CASES: ACCURACY OF PREDICTION IN SUCCESSIVE
FIFTHS[a,b]

Case	Q1	Q2	Q3	Q4	Q5	Mean
A	45	40	65	82	70	60
B	61	52	57	62	80	62
C	29	60	67	76	55	57
D	45	67	50	88	50	60
E[c]	49	72	72	74	78	69
F	62	56	67	66	75	65
G	67	58	58	76	62	64
H	55	71	73	74	59	66
I	52	58	63	76	76	73
J	64	74	76	72	84	74
K	63	68	65	63	83	68
L	69	77	69	72	79	71
Mean	54	62	65	73	71	

[a] Case scores are percentages, uncorrected for variations in difficulty level in different parts of cases.

[b] $N = 59$ YWCA administrators and industrial managers.

[c] Case E is the case described in Table 7 as having a sharp zero-level learning curve.

events in their natural sequence produced idiographic learning in most cases, and we suspect that this will prove generally true. However, idiographic learning can be prevented by deliberately separating cue from inference. Figure 5 shows the idiographic (method 2) learning curve of fifty-nine industrial managers, formed by combining their scores on six cases done in common.

CONCEPTUAL TRAINING FOR ASSESSMENT

Most studies that compare professional assessment judges with less-trained judges indicate that professionals have no advantage (Sarbin, Taft, and Bailey, 1960, p. 262). Such studies

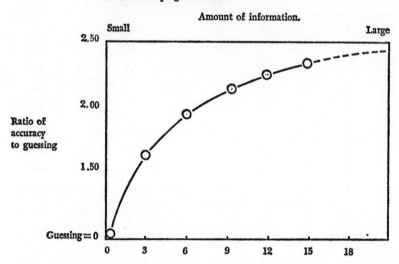

Figure 5

Idiographic Learning Rates

Based on fifty-nine judges making fifteen predictions
in each of six programed cases.

were not made with life histories but used more traditional criteria
such as the prediction of ratings or personality-inventory responses
(rejected here as criteria because they are not events). It is significant, therefore, that using programed cases, De Waele (1971)
found contradictory evidence: He reports that training in psychology may facilitate accurate prediction. One might ask what kind
of psychological training could logically be expected to improve
assessment.

When psychologists and psychiatrists study diagnostic and
other assessment processes, they spend considerable time learning
concepts (for example, concepts of personality theory). The assumption, clearly, is that these concepts are useful tools for assessment. However, if assessment is a learning process, we must ask
what kind of learning is occurring. Learning processes fall into a
hierarchy (Gagne, 1965) ranging from the simplest levels of conditioning to very abstract forms such as the learning of principles.
The programed case, by utilizing the reinforcement form of learn-

ing, assumes that assessment is a fairly primitive learning process. The implication of this assumption is that previous assessment theory has been too abstract in its notion of the level on which assessment can be learned. It is as if surgical residents attempted to acquire their art by reading and talking about surgery to the exclusion of actually doing it.

This judgment on the assessment process makes us want to know how, if at all, a judge's concepts affect his assessment process. One way to determine the role of concepts is to obtain data regarding a judge's conceptual behavior and determine what degree of predictive skill accompanies the use of what kinds of concepts. The experiments reported here used a simple design in which judges made predictions and then did a Q-sort of their impression. If concepts did not matter (it was our suspicion that they did not), then it should be possible for a judge to describe a person in almost any manner and still make valid predictions.

The problem of research design was how to get judges to express their concepts of a person in such a form that the research question ("Do concepts facilitate prediction?") can be answered. The decision was to ask judges to characterize each case in terms of a standardized list of adjectives or phrases. The one devised by Leary (1957) was chosen because it is comprehensive. In constructing his original list of 128 traits, Timothy Leary drew on almost every school of personality theory. The forty-eight items drawn from this checklist represented the eight major categories that he postulated but are limited to the milder, nonpathological form of each item (Appendix A). The checklist yielded the eight trait scores used by Leary: autocratic, competitive, blunt, resistive, submissive, docile, cooperative, and concerned. Each judge was asked to describe the person in a case using this checklist, rating each of the forty-eight traits according to how well it described the person. Each item was encoded 1 (least descriptive), 2, 3, 4, 5, 6, 7, or 8 (most descriptive). In the Q-sort method, each judge may be instructed to use each code a limited number of times. For example, only three 1's (out of the forty-eight) could be assigned, three 2's, six 3's, and so on. This preset distribution made it possible to make correlations very quickly since the distribution is standardized; these advantages have been outlined by Jack Block (1961). The usual procedure was for a judge to do the programed case in the normal manner, making his predictions as he proceeded. At the end of the case, he Q-sorted his impression.

If conceptualization affects prediction, then the judge's estimates of trait scores for a given case should correlate significantly with his predictive accuracy in that case. A negative finding in such an experiment might, however, merely mean that the traits were not visible in that case. To guard against this possibility, analyses of the programed cases were first made to determine whether each contained distinctly recognizable traits. Three judges Q-sorted eleven programed cases (using the checklist in Appendix A). Their Q-sorts were correlated with one another, and the results were divided into two groups: Q-sorts in which two judges were describing the same case, and Q-sorts in which the impression of one judge on a case was correlated with the impression of another judge on another case. The same-case correlations varied from .48 to .81, indicating a moderate reliability of trait estimates for particular cases. The different-case correlations varied from −.25 to .43, indicating that the same-case correlations could not be attributed to stereotyped similarities among all the cases.

One hundred thirty Dartmouth students were given five of these programed cases including (A) disadvantaged person (Chapter Eleven), (B) industrial personnel case (Chapter Thirteen), (C) football coach, (D) Murrow (Chapter Ten), and (E) Robert Anderson. Letter designations are the same as in Table 9. Before the experiment, each student made a Q-sort description of himself and his ideal; some also Q-sorted significant persons—mother, father, and fiancée if student had one. The student also asked his roommate to do a Q-sort of him (the student). The Q-sorts, the inference-making accuracy scores, and a total accuracy sum for the five cases were intercorrelated (see Table 9). The findings were as follows: (1) In general (and to my surprise) the null hypothesis can be rejected. A total of 480 correlations between trait and accuracy scores were computed. Random association would find five of these significant at the .01 level; thirty-three such correlations were in fact obtained. Only four of these, however, were between trait scores attributed to a case and accuracy scores in that same case. (2) In four of the five cases, a particular trait was identified that related significantly to the accuracy of predictions in that case. These were four *different* traits; each appeared subjectively to fit the content of one of the cases, except that no such trait was found for case D. (3) A much larger total of correlations was found between Q-sort descriptions of significant persons and accuracy scores on various cases. In spite of the smaller *N* of students doing Q-sorts of significant persons, there were fifteen such significant correlations. Characterizations of father, mother, and fiancée were especially related to the cases of the commentator and federal administrator (cases D and E). (4) Student's self-description and roommate's description of student were correlated on all eight traits (median correlation .48). In spite of this evident validation of the self-impression, however, the roommate's impression of the judge did not correlate, for the most part, with accuracy in case prediction. The only correlation was between the roommate's characterization of the student judge as managerial and the student's accuracy on case D ($r = .23$, $N = 73$). (5) There were five significant correlations between traits attributed to self and accuracy scores in cases. Four traits characterized the accurate judge: managerial, competitive, not resistive, and not docile.

The most significant finding was the least expected one. Why are there significant correlations between what a judge says about his parents and fiancée and his ability to do cases? Note the particular traits: for the father, validity-producing traits are managerial, competitive, frank, not submissive and not docile. Is this the image of a dominant, adequate, and perhaps stereotyped male father figure? These traits especially helped (that is, were correlated with accuracy scores) students to understand the case of the administrator (case E). The paternal trait competitive may also have been relevant to assessment of the industrial personnel case (case B). Note in Table 9 the "validity-producing" traits attributed to the mother: docile, withdrawing, cooperative, not managerial and not competitive traits; these are mirror images of traits that, in the father, were validity producing. These traits in the mother were especially relevant to the assessment of the administrator (case E), but also to the assessment of the commentator (case D) and of the disadvantaged person (case A). Traits attributed to the fiancée, which appear also to fit a stereotyped feminine image, were validity

Table 9. TRAITS ATTRIBUTED TO CASES COMPARED WITH
ACCURACY OF PREDICTIONS: CORRELATIONS BETWEEN AC-
CURACY SCORE ON CASE AND TRAIT ATTRIBUTION SCORES[a]

| | Attribution to | | | | |
Traits	Case A	Case B	Case C	Case D	Case E
Judge by Self					
Managerial	—	—	—	.27	.19
Competitive	—	—	.19	—	—
Submissive	—	—	—	−.23	—
Judge by Roommate					
Managerial	—	—	—	.23	—
Case A by Judge					
Managerial	—	—	—	−.21	—
Submissive	.22	—	—	—	—
Case B by Judge					
Frank	—	—	—	.34	—
Resistive	—	−.21	—	—	—
Docile	.23	—	—	—	—
Case C by Judge					
Frank	—	—	−.20	—	—
Case D by Judge					
Docile	—	.34	—	—	—
Compassionate	—	—	.29	—	—
Case E by Judge					
Compassionate	—	—	—	—	.32
Father by Judge					
Managerial	—	—	—	—	.44
Competitive	—	.38	—	—	.57
Frank	—	—	—	—	.41
Submissive	—	—	—	—	−.52
Docile	—	—	—	—	−.53

producing in relation to the case D. Finally, the following traits
attributed to the self were validity producing: managerial (helpful
in assessing cases D and E); competitive (helpful in assessing case
C, the coach); submissive (harmful in assessing case D).

We can speculate about the meaning of the data. The Dart-

Table 9. TRAITS ATTRIBUTED TO CASES COMPARED WITH
ACCURACY OF PREDICTIONS: CORRELATIONS BETWEEN AC-
CURACY SCORE ON CASE AND TRAIT ATTRIBUTION SCORES[a]
(cont'd)

Traits	Case A	Case B	Case C	Case D	Case E
Mother by Judge					
Managerial	—	—	—	—	−.56
Competitive	—	−.52	—	—	−.56
Submissive	—	—	—	—	.49
Docile	—	—	—	.56	—
Cooperative	—	—	—	—	.59
Fiancee by Judge					
Resistive	—	—	—	−.65	—
Compliant	—	—	—	.48	—
Cooperative	—	—	—	.55	—

[a] All correlations significant at .01 level or better. However, *N*
varies from 18 (Q-sorts of Mother) to 124 (Q-sorts of case C).
All blanks indicate correlation not significant. Table does not
include trait-attribution correlations with sum of accuracy scores
of all five cases.

mouth students' responses to cases may reflect their general search
for a social identity (Erikson, 1968). If a student is helped in that
search by an identification with paternal figures who play conventional roles on the social stage, he can accurately perceive certain
cases that would otherwise present him with value problems. For
example, case E is a kindly, firm, and responsible father image. If
a student already possesses such an archetype in his perceptual
repertoire, the case will be easier for him. He can recognize case E
because of resemblance to his father. This suggests that the student
with a conventional father will understand conventional cases regarding adult males. The original intent of the experiment was almost
forgotten in the wake of these findings. Traits are not irrelevant,
according to the data. But perhaps the data show too much! How
can trait theory explain the fact that accuracy on a programed case
is related to traits attributed to someone other than the person in

the case? One way to resolve this issue is to take Walter Mischel's (1968) position that the attribution of traits is a general conceptual process, more a characteristic of the *judges* than of the persons judged. In other words, traits are useful analytical tools, but not because they tell what is in the person judged. One might compare the trait, as a tool, to a pickaxe. It is useful in digging out gold ore, but it is not gold. Nevertheless, some types of pickaxe are more useful, durable, and effective than others. That is what research must learn about traits: Which ones help, and when?

Thus trait attribution is related to accuracy of prediction. Too many small but statistically significant correlations were found to warrant discarding trait analysis as irrelevant to assessment. For each case, it is possible that no more than one key trait may exist, but its correct identification facilitates valid assessment. These traits are not the same for every case. Thus it is futile to rate all traits for every person; not all of them matter. The cases themselves varied as to whether trait attributions made a difference to accuracy. The first three cases generated only three significant correlations each; the last two generated nine and eleven respectively. Some cases may be far richer in relevance to trait analysis than others. These findings lead us to wonder about the past strategy of personality-trait research in psychology. That strategy (see Cattell, 1957, or Eysenck, 1952) has been to devise systematic measuring instruments and employ them in assessment. Unfortunately, the presence of reliable traits and the development of valid measurements of them do not tell us what kinds of traits would be useful in the idiographic assessment of what kinds of cases. The present experiment suggests that trait analysis is relevant but not vital to assessment. It matters, but perhaps not very much.

TRAINING THROUGH PROGRAMED CASES

The foregoing experimental analysis implies doubts about trait theory. If trait analysis does not prove to facilitate prediction, what will? Heretofore, graduate and professional study have been heavily conceptual. Whatever the merit of this for other purposes, one questions it as adequate preparation for assessment. I submit that assessment skill is far lower in the hierarchy of skills and would benefit more from reinforcement training than from conceptual instruction. Training might, for instance, consist of a long series of programed cases—in which valid inferences are repeatedly reinforced. Such feedback is a prime factor in skill learning. Theoretically, then, one should be able to demonstrate transfer of training from case to case. Transfer of training assumes that the essential skill is use of information. A judge is taught to use idiographic information. Yet the information itself is not transferred, only the skill of building an increasingly valid image of a person, as information about that person is increased. The transfer differs from learning a particular case. Statistically, the two learning curves would crudely resemble one another, but psychologically they differ: information is generalized *within* a case; a skill is transferred *between* cases. This transfer should not be surprising if demonstrated. Certainly, professionals contend that they learn from cases in their practice. Why should there not be learning from cases that have been programed specifically to teach?

Two methods were used to determine transfer of training from case to case. In one method (see Table 10), half the judges received a series of twelve programed cases in one sequence; the

Table 10. TRANSFER OF TRAINING WITH CASE CONTENT CONTROLLED BY REVERSED ORDER METHOD: MEAN ACCURACY SCORES IN SERIES OF TWELVE CASES

	Case Number											
	1	*2*	*3*	*4*	*5*	*6*	*7*	*8*	*9*	*10*	*11*	*12*
Order I	A	B	C	D	E	F	G	H	I	J	K	L
	70	64	70	75	73	75	68	83	76	60	69	78
Order II	L	K	J	I	H	G	F	E	D	C	B	A
	65	64	71	63	64	72	70	69	70	86	74	73
Mean %	67	64	71	69	69	73+	69	76	73	73	71	75
Rank	2	1	6	4.5	3	9	4.5	12	9	9	7	11

Rank order rho = .74, $N = 12$ cases.

other half received the same series in reverse order. The content
was thus controlled so that any change in accuracy could not be
attributed to doing easier cases last. In this experiment, the finding
indicated that transfer of training did occur. The mean score for a
case in each position was correlated .74 with the position order
number (1 to 12). This correlation represented a gain in accuracy
of about 8 per cent between the sum of the scores on the first three
cases and the sum of scores on the last three cases. This is a modest
but definite gain for the twelve hours of case analysis required for
the experiment (it should be noted that clinical students sometimes
spend this much time working up one or two cases with no feedback
at all checking their predictions). Another approach (see Table 11)
utilized data from fifty-nine judges (managers and administrators)
on the same twelve cases. Because the same cases had been used at
different points in the learning sequence, it was possible to compute
a separate mean score for each case, for each of the several positions

Table 11. TRANSFER OF TRAINING WITH CASE CONTENT
CONTROLLED

Mean accuracy of inference[a] (%)	Case administered early[b]	Case administered late
75	0	3
70	2	2
65	1	3
60	4	5
55	2	3
50	10	4
45	1	1
	$t = 2.57$[c]	

[a] Means are those of groups of judges.

[b] There were twenty separate instances in which a case was administered to one group in the first half of a case series (usually
a series of twelve) and to another group in the second half of its
case series. Twelve cases are involved in these comparisons.

[c] t based on a formula correcting for correlation between means
of particular cases.

Figure 6

Changes in Accuracy of Inference
in Different Portions of Cases

Legend:
X = mean accuracy of 325 Korean judges. O = mean accuracy of
92 American judges. Dotted line shows zero level of accuracy.

(a) inferences based on 0 - 4 units of data.
(b) inferences based on 10 - 14 units of data.

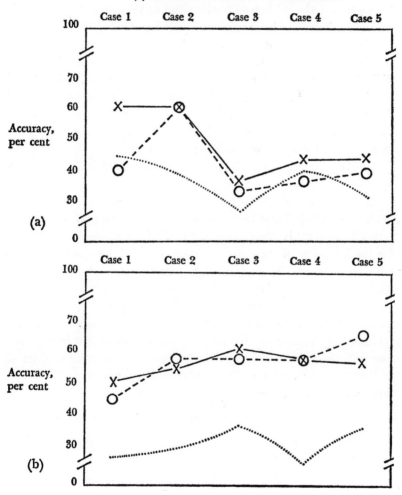

(1 to 12) in which it was administered during the experiment. For example, a case might be administered second (position 2) to one group and last position (position 12) to another. The mean scores were compared and found to differ significantly, indicating transfer of training with case content controlled. A third experiment measured the amount of transfer among Peace Corpsmen doing Latin-American cases. Three cases were presented in varying order to sixty judges. If transfer of training was occurring, the mean scores for each case should increase according to the position in which it was administered. The results were consistent with the transfer-of-training hypothesis but were not statistically significant. Perhaps the failure was due to imprecise programing (fewer predictions were elicited than in the earlier cases); or perhaps there is no transfer of prediction skills among cases depicting persons of different social classes (the three Latin-Americans were lower, middle, and upper class). A fourth study explored what was being transferred from case to case if transfer was in fact occurring.

For this study (see Figure 6), the idiographic learning rates for a series of five cases were measured by the gain method; a judge's accuracy for the last third of a case was compared with his accuracy in the first third. For Korean judges, the gain method indicated a probable transfer in idiographic learning ability; accuracy increased for the last parts of the cases but there was no case-to-case increase to transfer on the initial parts. This experimental outcome argues against the judges' skill as merely learning what the game is or learning to predict what the case authors defined as correct responses. Such trivial learning would not explain why the judges progressively learned to predict the events occurring last in the cases and not the early events. In the experiments measuring transfer of training, the rates of improvement were slow—not more than 1 per cent in accuracy per hour spent in case analysis.

HOW JUDGES REASON PSYCHOLOGICALLY

Most of the 1,400 judges in our experiments were not trained in the behavioral sciences. Why is it, then, that lacking formal instruction, they were able to begin to make accurate predictions anyway? The suggestion offered earlier was that an intelligible case is a network of meaning. The events in it are interrelated. Case writers did not set out to prepare such cases. In our theory, this is the way most cases will appear, if they represent the original life history. Judges make accurate predictions when they grasp the network of meaningful connections among events. Why? It is proposed here that just as a person's language makes his words intelligible, his culture makes his behavior intelligible to his peers. They share his behavioral vocabulary, syntax, semantic. In brief, each judge possesses a calculus of behavior that enables him to make predictions when he applies it to a case appropriately. How can such a notion be tested empirically? First, it implies that judges make similar interpretations of the events they read or view. Second, it implies that these interpretations help them understand cases and therefore predict other events. Third, it implies that the behavioral calculus is derived from the judge's membership in or experience in a social system. The first two of these implications are tested in the following experiments.

The experiments involved 180 Dartmouth students in an undergraduate introductory course in personality and abnormal psychology. In the course's laboratory, the student's assignment was to complete a series of programed cases and to input his findings into the computer. Three programed cases were used: football coach (ten-event case), news commentator (Chapter Ten), and the federal administrator. The last two were fifteen-event cases. After making each prediction, the judge was asked to identify the one preceding event that was his evidence or data base for the prediction. On completing each case, the judge input his inferences and data bases at a computer teletype. The computer immediately printed out an analysis of his performance, identifying the biases he showed in using cues and their effects on his predictions. The computer also added the judge's inferences and their data bases to its master file on all judges. The computer printed out several matrices for the investigator. One of them (see Table 3 in Chapter 5) shows data base (rows) versus inferences (accurate or not) made from those data bases by most judges. A second matrix shows the data bases (rows) versus the accurate inferences (column) made from those data bases. Other matrices accumulate data bases and inferences for judges who consistently scored high on the case. The findings showed for these three cases that judges who made a particular prediction correctly reported the same data bases as those who made it incorrectly ($r = .80$). Thus the judges tend to see the same event network. But the finding does not yet show that the detection of an event network leads to accurate predictions. Two pieces of evidence point to this, however. One is that the in-degree of an event (the number of data bases judges say they use in predicting it) is correlated with the predictability of an event. One way to establish this finding is to correlate (across fifteen inferences within a case) the in-degree of the event (as determined by another group of judges making a paired-comparison analysis of the case) with the predictability of that event. When such a correlation was computed for each of seven cases, the median correlations varied from .26 to .42. (Populations of judges other than Dartmouth students were used in this particular analysis.) Another way to determine the role of the event network in prediction is to compare *consistently* high-scoring judges with consistently low-scoring judges. The finding was that the high-scoring judges agreed upon a larger number of relationships than the low-scoring judges, especially when the data base was physically separated from the event it predicted. Put another way, low-scoring judges were as well able as high-scoring to agree upon whether a pair of events were or were not related if adjacent in the case. It was distant events (distant in time, in situation) that the superior judges could better agree were related or unrelated. The result is a richer (more interconnected) graph of the case as a network of meaning for the high-scoring judges, as shown in Figure 7.

We know that some cases facilitate idiographic learning and general prediction better than others. Perhaps differences in richness of the event network account for this. One way to study richness is to measure the salience of events (that is, their tendency to be cited more often as data bases) and to determine what kinds of events have greater salience. The finding is that earlier (or childhood) events have greater salience, both when viewed in the context of the case and when studied in isolated form (judges merely matching event pairs rather than obtaining cumulative information within the particular case). A more general way to study richness is to measure the total number of other events related to one event, either as data bases for it or inferences from it. This would be the sum of the in-

Figure 7

Graphs of High-Scoring and Low-Scoring Judges

(a) Graph constructed from data bases agreed on by consistently high-scoring judges (a ten-event programed case).
(b) Graph constructed from data bases agreed on by consistently low-scoring judges (same case).

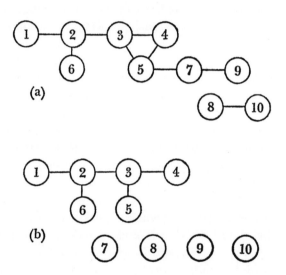

degree and the out-degree for each event. This variable (total degree) is at its peak for Dartmouth students in the middle of each of the three programed cases they analyzed. However, when total degree is computed from the paired-comparison analyses of other judges, we can see in contrast where the richness is distributed in the case when events are viewed in isolation from the total case. Total degree for seven cases is highly concentrated in the first third of each. Thus the Dartmouth students did not "catch on" to the meanings potentially available in their three cases until midway. The paired-comparison analysis of isolated pairs of events enables us to see that there are meanings present that were overlooked in the confusion of case analysis.

The preparation of such case graphs may prove useful for elucidating the information network properties of longer cases as well. I analyzed Freud's case (1947) of Leonardo da Vinci. Numbering each fact in order as he presented them, I made a comparison of each pair of the sixty-eight such facts making up the bulk of the body of his case. The question, for each pair, was "Do these two facts appear to be related?" The responses could be entered in matrix form in which each row and column corresponds to a fact. The matrix is symmetrical, since the term relationship is symmetrical. Each cell (or intersection of a row and a column) would show a 1 if the pair was judged related, or 0 if not. The matrix can be manipulated algebraically to show such properties as the number of facts that are related at a distance of two steps, three steps, and so on. The matrix is too large for presentation here, but its graph is shown (Figure 8). The graph shows two separate domains of meaningful interconnection. The smaller one, labeled G, consists of nine interrelated events describing his early life in relation to parents. The larger domain or subgraph shows several themes, or clusters, of which the largest (F) is composed of events depicting da Vinci's curious habits of work. Others included discussion of the smile of Mona Lisa (A), sexuality (B), love of beauty (C), fantasy life (D), and naturalistic interests (E). Only fifty of the sixty-eight events are shown on this graph; the remaining episodes are omitted, because they are unrelated to any shown or else are duplicates of them.

Frank Harary, Robert Norman, and Dorwin Cartwright (1965) provide a mathematical language for talking about such networks and inferring important properties that are implicit in them but not obvious. In an earlier paper (Dailey, 1959b), I have discussed the potential values of their model for the analysis of life-history structure. Without attempting a formal coordination here, I will simply point to certain relationships in this figure to illustrate the nature of their concepts. One is that of centrality. In the subgraph G in Figure 8, the central events are 39 and 47. These would be events that, if known, would generate the others. They are psychologically closer to the other events. For example, in subgraph G, event 37 is five steps from event 44; event 39 is no more than three steps from every other event in its subgraph, hence central. There are also bridging points in these subgraphs. Events 13 and 47 are bridges (if known, they theoretically permit the judge to reason psychologically to data that are otherwise not predictable).

Figure 8

Graph of the Case of Leonardo Da Vinci

Legend:
Numbers refer to order in which Freud stated the particular fact. Letters refer to themes; shading arbitrary, to help identify locus of theme.

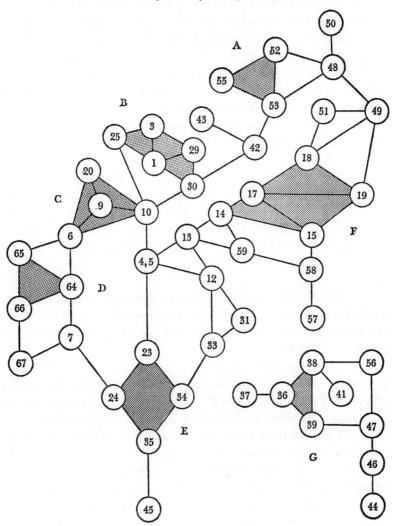

Event 13, for example, unites clusters E and F. Similar analysis shows the interrelationships of the clusters or themes of the case. For example, bridging points or lines connect clusters $A–B–C–D–E–F$ (in that order) and also $C–E,$ but not G.

These associations suggest that the major mystery in the case is not Leonardo's sexual behavior, but his early life or parents. Another question is whether one might detect still broader themes in the case than those mentioned. The chain of themes $A–B–C–D$ suggest the fantasy side, the private life of Leonardo. The other chain $D–E–F$ suggests the visible production and reality-oriented side. Were we able to ask for anything more about Leonardo da Vinci's life, the implication is that we need events or inferences connecting these two broad domains, such as between events 14 and 30, 17 and 42, 23 and 64. Perhaps the network is there and I have overlooked it.

Now, it is obvious that this analysis, like that of the other cases as interpreted by the Dartmouth students, is searching for meaning in subjective judgments. The analysis of Leonardo is conjectural. But in the earlier cases, these subjective judgments of event-networks were reliable and involved in valid chains of reasoning.

CONCLUSIONS

When hearing new proposals in personality assessment, psychologists have learned to be cautious about claims. Let us be precise about what has been shown, and yet let us also consider the potential of the method.

The programed case is not a precise simulation of the way people are assessed in legal, medical, or other situations. We cannot generalize from these findings to assessment practices. What has been done is to collect life histories of a variety of types, reduce them to events, present those events in chronological sequence, and determine how well predictions are made when based on increments in events known. It seems established that judges in a variety of populations were able to predict events. Judges predicted the behavior of persons in their own culture and from another culture. Was it prediction? From the standpoint of the experimenter, the judges were discriminating known behavior. But from the standpoint of the judge, he was being asked to estimate unknown events in the future of the person in the case.

Based on correlations between scores of cases programed in various ways, we find evidence of a general talent for prediction. Judges who predict the events in the lives of eminent men (our first series, as in Chapter Ten) can predict the events in the lives of more ordinary persons (as in the second series—note case in Chapter Twelve).

Prediction ability measured throughout a case (gross prediction) is not the same as idiographic ability (the ability to profit from cumulative amounts of information). Idiographic ability, the skill of learning to recognize the events in a particular life, was found to be greater among Americans learning American cases than Koreans learning American cases. In other words, we speculate that knowledge of culture facilitates idiographic prediction more than it facilitates ability to predict behavior. College-educated Koreans showed more idiographic learning than high-school-level Koreans, but these two groups did not differ in gross prediction.

A way to validate trait perception is suggested in the experiments correlating student Q-sorts of cases with student ability to predict. The unexpected findings in this experiment were more interesting than the intended analyses, however. The traits attributed by a student to his parents were more closely correlated with prediction scores on certain cases than were the traits he attributed to the cases. While trait analysis may not be discarded as a relevant skill, we expect that reinforcement of valid inferences will prove a more effective model for training judges than will the traditional conceptual training favored by departments of psychology and psychiatry. We obtained enough evidence of transfer in gross prediction skill to encourage us, but not enough to be very certain. However, if present rates of transfer of training were sustained (about 0.5 per cent per hour, or per case), a series of approximately 200 programed cases would double the accuracy of assessment judges. More conservatively, because of learning decay and due to the diversity of cases in different assessment situations, it is estimated that several hundred programed cases would either establish a high level of general assessment skill or would indicate that a given judge would not likely ever attain it.

The same data that document the assessment skills of judges can logically document the predictability of the particular case. What kinds of cases generate accurate predictions? We have pursued the implications of our assumption that judges have a calculus of behavior (an implicit theory or set of if-then relations permitting them to see the connections between events) by analyzing the relationships between cues and predictions in several programed cases. It appears that judges do perceive the same networks and that this has some connection to their prediction skills.

A graph is a network of points and lines, where every line has two ends and no more than one line joins a pair of points. A digraph (or directed graph) is a special case in which some lines may go in only one direction (the clinician infers illness from fever but may find illness without fever)—hence, "directed." Graphs make it possible to visualize large structures which hopelessly confuse us when put in words, and the mathematics of graph theory make it possible to compute the properties of such large structures of life. It is our hope that the mathematical model of digraphs will prove useful in depicting clinical analysis of the structures of large and complex cases such as Leonardo da Vinci. Experiments can then selectively prove or disprove these clinical analyses by the use of simpler versions interpreted by large numbers of judges. I have attempted to show an example of this kind of partnership in the case of Leonardo da Vinci. The use of matrix algebra and of graph theory are of promise in this regard.

I will not generalize from these findings of associations among idiographically rich events to more molecular forms of case analysis. The event is the irreducible unit; it is quite possible that our findings can be replicated only with cases composed of events, but not with those composed of increments of information such as stimulus-response (S–R) units or traits. This restriction hardly connotes a hostility to behaviorism—after all, consider our use of the reinforcement method in the programed case—but rather it asserts that the life history is validly treated only as a humanistic document. The logic of personality assessment demands that the data not be cut too fine—like a portrait, this phenomenon we call a person is not visible in small pieces. Some might think the programed case has already cut the data too fine.

What is it that the assessment judge must learn to do? I have, as has Mischel (1968), expressed skepticism that he should learn to find traits in data. But if not traits (or S-R connections), then what? The conception offered earlier was that the judge must find the natural structures in the phenomena. Events exist in life in clusters and sequences called thema; the judge learns to recognize these structures and use them to predict other events. A life, then, is an information network. In that sense, the events of the programed case are expressive and the skill of the judge is to interpret that expression. The data support the measurability of this skill and its generality, and they encourage us to think that it can be improved through training.

☆☆☆☆☆☆☆☆☆ **7** ☆☆☆☆☆☆☆☆☆

Credentials as Inherently Prejudicial

☆☆☆☆☆☆☆☆☆☆☆☆☆☆☆☆☆☆☆☆☆☆☆

In light of the prospects that life-history assessment is potentially a valid system, we take a look again at the social system in which assessment is done. In particular, consider why we persistently have groups of people whose privileges and liberties are sharply limited, as side effects of the traditional assessment systems. These groups are the emotionally ill and the socially or legally disadvantaged.

NEGATIVE-ASSESSMENT SYSTEMS

Society regulates the movement of people from one institution, social class, and place to another by imposing certain standards to govern this movement. A child begins to learn this fact when he is told he must pass certain courses in order to be promoted; by the time he is an adult, he is well accustomed to the notion that he must pass certain milestones before arriving at a desirable destination. The regulation of this social movement is generally by credentials. The road passes through a series of gates, manned by officials who halt the traveler to examine his passport. The gatekeepers discussed in Chapter One are backed by custom and sometimes by law. The system is under constant scrutiny and change. Children now are often promoted automatically, indicating that the social costs of the old credentials system are considered excessive. But, in general, society defends its credentials vigorously. It constantly reiterates that it is better to have more education than less; better to be well-to-do (possess economic credentials) than poor; better to have a good job record than an erratic one. Consistency among the various status signs is regarded as normal and is promoted actively by the use of credentials. While each standard is under erosion, the fundamental idea of a system of standards is not. What do such standards do to assessment? They halt the process too soon. A credentials judge fails in three ways: (1) He does not collect enough humanistic data to arrive at an understanding of the person; (2) he does not collect enough data to learn that the standards do not work very well; a person lacking certain prescribed qualifications may have some personal qualities that would more than compensate, but the judge never learns about them; and (3) the judge acquires a negative point of view that strengthens the credentials system's effects in many ways.

In personnel selection, the concept of a "knockout factor" is the simplest illustration. This is an objective fact that makes it theoretically impossible for a person to do a job or unwise to permit him to try it. When an interviewer detects a knockout factor (for example, an applicant has served time in the penitentiary), he spends no more time considering the person's potential. This single negative factor outweighs all possible compensating factors. Among the knockout factors used in industry (although varying from one company to another) are age limits, sex, physical handicaps, conditions such as epilepsy, lack of a high school or college diploma, race (until recently), apprenticeship for construction jobs. The general attitude toward any applicant is a negative one, according to B. M. Springbett (in Webster, 1964, p. 22); and Edward Webster went so far as to suggest that the real decision in military and employment selection interviews studied might as well be made in an interview not exceeding five to ten minutes (p. 102).

A second type of credential is more subtle in its operation. For each job, there is a general system of preferences for certain kinds of people over others. Where the knockout factor is a matter of deliberate policy (in some instances explicitly required by bonding or by insurance regulations), the preference system is a matter of custom, sometimes unspoken, intuitive, *sub rosa*. The word *qualifications* is used as a general umbrella over all these preferences. A person with more years of experience is considered to be more qualified. Men are preferred to women for certain jobs. Political conservatives might be rated higher for certain financial jobs and liberals for jobs in the news media. Of two applicants for a research grant, if one has published extensively and the other has not, the former will be judged better than the latter. We do not here discuss whether a company, government agency, or union has the right to such preferences; we are concerned primarily with their effect on assessment and on the person's right to a fair hearing. It can probably be demonstrated that society conditions everyone to accept these preferences, even those who lack the preferred characteristics. They are systematically put down until they believe in the system themselves. Companies that decide they do want to hire blacks (and universities that want more black applicants) have trouble getting blacks to apply: in words of the title of a recent novel: "been down so long I don't know which way is up."

A third type of credential is organizational membership. A person is assumed to have the properties (good or bad) of that organization. One is a Phi Delt, a Princeton graduate, and an IBM employee. He is a naval officer, a General Electric manager, or a member of the Bucks County Birdwatchers. The contents of a *Who's Who* entry will be largely a list of such organizations. So also will be the contents of an FBI dossier, a credit-reference dossier, and the political poopsheet written up by a candidate's supporters (or the opposite version written by his opponents). Some memberships are positive credentials for some judges and negative for others. Interpretation of membership in the Black Panthers, Republican Party, or Nader's Raiders depends on the judge. Regardless of the judge, though, does organizational membership constitute valid data in any sense? Consider the Black Panther. Even the most virulent critic of Black Panthers should inquire about the sense in which a person was a member. How identified was he with which purpose? What actions did he, in fact, take? The worst evils of the McCarthy era (Joseph, not Eugene) resulted from naive judgment based on formal membership in allegedly subversive organizations. No one bothered to inquire into the meaning of membership in the individual case. McCarthy's probes have been denounced by many as witch-hunts.

However, the substitution of credentials for human assessment is practiced nowhere more often than among physical and behavioral scientists. Consider the following actual case (Greenberg, 1964), which created some controversy when *Science* printed it. A man we shall call William Fox applied unsuccessfully to several federal research-fund sources, from 1953 to 1958, for grants to conduct chemical research projects. (These were to be carried out on equipment that was installed in his basement, in spare time from his regular work, which was with the New York City Police Department. He was a Lieutenant, Central Park Precinct. He had joined the force in the midst of the depression, thus financing his college studies. He received a B.S., New York City College, in 1935, and, in 1944, a Ph.D. in chemistry from Columbia University.)

In 1959, William Fox attempted a new tack. He noted that most grants went to people affiliated with organizations. Fox formed a nonprofit organization known as Oakland Research Associates (ORA), which had one employee (William Fox) and whose address was on Oakland Street (at his home); he asked the Office of Naval Research (ONR) to decide whether ORA was eligible for research support. Fox offered the following facts to support his research request: his Ph.D. from Columbia University; several papers published in *The Journal of Physical Chemistry* and in other chemical journals; and several papers presented before the American Chemical Society. Yet the ONR reply rejected his research proposals, stating that, "The statutory authority (of ONR) permits the making of grants only to educational institutions and certain other nonprofit organizations and only for the purpose of basic research." In 1961, William Fox proposed to the National Aeronautics and Space Administration (NASA) to investigate the physics of fluids in space vehicles; he received a rejection, which stated, "We have carefully evaluated your proposal . . . but do not feel that the work is closely enough related to our space-sciences mission to warrant support. Please feel free to submit any future proposals you may have to this office." His Columbia University professors made these statements about Fox (Greenberg, 1964): Columbia Chemistry Professor Haynes: "One of the most determined and highly motivated students encountered in 40 years of teaching and research. . . . My attention was originally called to him because he was the only student who came to lab with a pistol." Another professor: "He would never skim over anything. He had to understand everything thoroughly, and if he didn't get something, he would insist that you go over it again and again. He was never embarrassed to say he didn't understand." Professor Kusch: "Obviously competent and enthusiastic. He has made an investment in science at his own expense. He didn't dream up projects to get support, as some people do. He followed his own curiosity, he had a vision of what life could be and that's what led him on." Would it be relevant to consider his Police Department performance? He received the rare meritorious duty award given him for acquiring evidence in a murder case. It was said of him at the department: "He's a lot more than a hothouse cop" (police jargon for a policeman who has led a sheltered career). When last heard from, Fox had been accepted (at the Fourth International Congress on Surface Active Substances [Brussels, 1964]) to give a paper. He applied to the National Science Foundation (NSF) for travel funds. The NSF was apparently a bit short; having funds for six of the twelve persons applying, it funded six, *not* including Fox.

Most people who hear the facts of this case are instantly agreed that the research agencies will not fund Fox's work, and many agree that they *should* not do so. In particular, a small seminar of research and development administrators taking a graduate course from me in 1966 reviewed the case and gravely assured me— without qualification—that Fox was a "poor" prospect for research funding. Since I felt otherwise, I cross-examined my audience on their opinions. A typical exchange went like this: *Dailey:* Why would you not grant Fox the funds? *Response:* He is not qualified. *D:* What do you mean? *R:* While he has a Ph.D. in chemistry, he is not seriously pursuing chemistry as a career. *D:* He is doing it in his basement and buying his own equipment. *R:* Yes, but don't you see, it's an avocation. He is not serious. Really, he is a *policeman*. *D:* Do you think any of his thoroughness as a policeman indicates he can do scientific things well? *R:* You can't be serious. Performance of police duties is not relevant evidence. *D:* Well, what do you think about his scientific performance? Are you aware that most Ph.D.s never publish anything at all after their dissertations but that Fox has done so? *R:* As an individual, Fox is impressive. But when you get right down to it, he is not a part of an organization which does research, and the days of creative individuals are past. You've got to be part of something big, have big resources. *D:* Let us summarize your position. Fox has produced chemical research of evident merit, and as a person is considered by his professors to be likely to do so in the future. But you believe his career line is not purely scientific because he moonlights and he is basically a policeman because that is what he does for his salary. *R:* No, basically Fox is just not qualified for a grant. His request just does not add up the way successful grant applications add up.

The case of William Fox instructs us in the subtleties of assessment. Many of the persons who sympathized with my attacks on the credentials system nonetheless disagreed with me on William Fox. I would argue that the critical decision in grant making should turn on the probabilities of an individual's life. From that perspective Fox looks good. All the rest is pseudo-reasoning.

Fox was washed out by grant policies negative in character. By that I mean the policies not only accepted objective facts that were negative in character but were a void in the sense of psychological reasoning about a human life. Fox's application was scored by bureaucrats against rules, not used to document his career and to estimate his possibilities. This lack of any sense of possibility arising in novel ways is what I mean by a negative frame of reference. In this chapter, I will try to show how this frame of reference cannot be avoided but should be made to interact with other frames of reference in assessment.

We might expect this kind of negative response from a grants committee, but what about professional assessment situations? Let us start with clinicians.

When clinicians began to do assessment work, society took a giant step in progressing from a demonological model to a mental-illness model to account for symptoms and deviant behavior. The concepts of symptom, illness, and pathology have dominated clinical assessment and have affected employment and educational assessment. Chief among the critics of the myth of mental illness is Thomas Szasz (1964). Whether it is a myth or not, the label "mental illness" leads to a number of disasters for a person. Depending on attendant circumstances, he may be denied insurance, deprived of his freedom, given electric shocks through the brain, given an indefinite sentence in prison and thereafter regarded with dismay and reserve by an unfeeling family or ignorant community. Worse still, he may believe the label himself; play the role—begin to live it—of the crazy or emotionally damaged neurotic person. It is quite a career, this being a "mental patient," and Szasz says much of it is unnecessary.

From the standpoint of assessment, however, what is bad about the medical model is its systematic search for incompetence, weakness, and childishness in the patient. William Soskin (1954) calls this the pathologic bias. The assessment professional working from this bias ignores, screens out, signs of ability, potential creativity, hope; he cannot write a well-balanced life history. He looks for signs of organicity, schizophrenia, oedipal difficulties, and the like; and assessment ceases when he finds them in clearcut form.

Evidence for the clinical and legal effects of a negative frame of reference is available in Thomas Scheff's study (1964). His data throw light on the interdependence of that frame of reference with social process. Scheff showed that in ambiguous cases of involuntary commitment, the court (judge and examining physicians) assumed illness. In doubt, it was judged better to commit the patient (this was called being conservative). How were doubts resolved? In one courtroom, the judge supposed to question the patient averaged only two minutes of such questioning per patient. The length of psychiatric interviews in court-ordered examinations varied from five to seventeen minutes (average, ten minutes). The observers of these examinations report that the examiners did not credit the patient with correct or sane responses but continued to search until the patient gave an incorrect or confused answer. One physician, after an eight-minute interview, explained to the observer: "On the schizophrenics, I don't bother asking them more questions when I can see they're schizophrenic because I know what they're going to say. You could talk to them another half hour and not learn any more." Another said of cases initiated by the patient's family (petitions): "The petition cases are pretty automatic. If the patient's own family wants to get rid of him you know there is something wrong." Scheff suggested that these commitments and the uncritical examining procedures are based on a policy of presuming illness. Presumption of illness is a good example of negative frame of reference.

Erving Goffman's term here is useful: discrediting. At Saint Elizabeths Hospital, the medical records revealed to him a widespread discrediting process. The typical chart did not seek to "record occasions when the patient showed capacity to cope honorably and effectively with difficult life situations. . . . [Rather, it extracts] from his whole life course a list of those incidents that have or might have 'symptomatic' significance" (Goffman, 1961, pp. 155, 159). Luis Kutner (1962) described the policies of the Cook County mental health clinic:

> *Certificates are signed as a matter of course by staff physicians after little or no examination. . . . The so-called examinations are made on an assembly line basis, often being completed in two or three minutes, and never taking more than ten minutes. . . . The doctors recommend confinement in 77% of the cases. It appears in practice that the alleged mentally-ill is presumed to be insane and bears the burden of proving his sanity in the few minutes allotted to him.*

In recent years, psychologists have blamed such excesses on the medical model. One might think the remedy is more clinical psychologists. However, it is specifically clinical psychological assessment that is in difficulty, according to studies cited earlier in this book. The suggestion has been made that actuarial clerks can replace the more expensive clinical psychologist. But neither more clerks nor more psychologists can get us out of the inherently negative effects of credentials systems. Jerome Fisher (1959, p. 405) summarizes these effects about as simply as anyone: It is simply easier to predict what a person cannot do than to predict what he can and will do; in brief, "Whatever validity a measure may possess for predicting adaptive behavior, it is likely to be more accurate in predicting nonadaptive behavior." Thus pathology-preoccupied assessment will always be more effective than health-seeking assessment, especially if one ignores the costs of false positives, as Scheff's study indicates is done in law courts (1964). Prediction of failures,

pathology, and inadequacy is naturally more accurate than prediction of achievement, creativity, and competence. If one attempts to
predict a complex achievement, one depends on the combination of
many interdependent factors or abilities; the absence of any one will
be decisive. Thus negative assessment needs to find only one decisive
link or reason why a person will not be able to do a thing to break
the chain of causation. In this sense, negative assessment is always
cheaper than positive assessment. It can and does halt after the discovery of a critically important but negative fact, as in the examining psychiatrist's interview.

Negative assessment is cheap not only in the amount of time
required of the judge but also in the sense that it induces a superficial attitude toward the persons assessed. It takes no great sensitivity to offer the banal observation that a cripple cannot run the
four-minute mile. An excripple once did, indeed, nearly do a four-
minute mile, but the odds are heavy against such a feat. In fact,
the odds generally favor inferences made on the basis of cheap assessment. In Figure 9, I have shown how the cost of assessment—
to the extent that information is a cost—favors the credentials and
negative-assessment systems up to a point. In theory, beyond this
point, the validity should favor the judge looking at a more human-

Figure 9

Hypothetical Cost Analysis of
Two Assessment Systems

It is assumed that the cost of assessment is proportional to the amount of
information required to achieve a given level of prediction. In shaded
zone A, credentials assessment has a lower cost. In zone B, a more
humanistic system would have a lower cost.

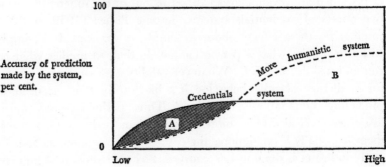

istic form of data, for example, life-history data. There are no experiments demonstrating this, although in a later section we will report some data measuring the effects of the superficial frame of reference allegedly resulting from emphasis on credentials.

I believe it is true, as the psychiatrists in Scheff's study (1964) assumed and as the personnel officers in Webster's study (1964) appeared to believe, that a person can tell a great deal about his general outlook and situation in about ten minutes. This cover story should, however, be cross-examined and replaced with a more representative set of episodes; this replacement of the initial cover story requires an hour for the average person. To go through the still more demanding steps described in Chapter Four requires from two to four hours. At what point the validity of predictions made from these histories begins to exceed the validity of predictions made from credentials and psychological tests is an empirical question not yet investigated. There have been a few investigations of life-history validity using other than programed cases. In one, the investigators showed that clinicians could match autobiographies against other data better than they could match projective protocols and objective test scores. Fifty-five per cent of the correct matches of the twenty clinical psychologists involved biographic data, against 45 per cent for the objective tests. Perhaps of even more significance was the observation that "without having been so instructed judges used the biography as the criterion" (Holsopple and Phelan, 1954). In Albert Kostlan's study (1954), two projectives, the MMPI, and a one-half-page to two-page social case history, were used to predict the data in progress reports written by the patient's therapist. As control, predictive accuracy on the basis of minimal or identifying data was used. Since our view is that therapy deals with the life history, this study could be said to involve comparisons of projectives, tests, and history with *history*. Kostlan found that minimal data were as predictive as projectives; in general, the accuracy of the total battery dropped to about the level of the control or minimal data when the social case history was omitted, showing that it provided the most critical data. (The next most critical was the MMPI.) The investigator concluded, "There seems to be a superiority of the Social Case History both as a source of cues and as the background against which the tests were interpreted."

The question might now arise as to whether the social
worker's role in assessment should not be increased, rather than
changing the data used by the other kinds of assessment judges.
This is a possibility. Another is that the social worker should continue to gather such data, but perhaps do it more systematically and
with objective verification. The other professions should contribute
also to the case report; but perhaps the contribution of psychiatry,
psychology, and other professions is in the development of verifiable
models of the person from the case history and in the collection of
subsequent data that verify or disprove the hypotheses derived from
these models.

APPLICABILITY OF LIFE-HISTORY ASSESSMENT

In discussing general assessment, we have proceeded on the
premise that there are some general erroneous assumptions being
made about the nature of assessment. Therefore, reforms can be
similar in the many different institutions that assess life chances.
While the concept of negativism in the view of life is held here to
pertain to many different institutions, we must first admit the many
specific conditions for assessment peculiar to each institution. For
example, it seems that life-history assessment is feasible only in situations in which the person can tell his story without undue inter-
ruption, without the risk of disclosure to unsympathetic listeners,
and in which the interviewer can record. Over-the-counter interviews (as in many welfare offices) and booth interviews (as in most
employment counseling offices (Dailey, Carlson, and McChesney,
1968) obviously preclude life histories. A person who is too anxious
to report his life or who is grossly inarticulate (a minimum I.Q.
might well be 70) would not be able to provide a life history. A
paranoid patient would not be able, perhaps, to muster the trust
necessary to give his story. In spite of these exclusions and reservations, the conditions necessary to obtain a life history seem to be
more frequently present than the conditions necessary to take a test,
while less universally feasible than a short objective medical or employment history. An apparent exception would be group testing,
as among military recruits. Would this not be more feasible than the
collection of life-history data which, as we have described it in
Chapters Four and Five, was confined to two-person across-the-

desk interviews? This would be a logical implication of our method. But recently, I have been experimenting with groups as large as 160 college students, instructing them in the preparation of life histories.

Moving from data-gathering feasibility to utility problems, what decisions can be made from life histories? Lee Cronbach and Goldine Gleser (1965) use the term *broad-band*, and that seems to be a correct designation for life histories. When one does not know what decision he will have to make, or assist another person to make, broad-band data are what he requires; life histories are a logical contender for broad-band data par excellence. In the area of employment, decisions about complex executive and middle-management positions would appear to warrant life-history data more than would blue-collar, skilled, and semiskilled positions. This is true in the sense of the willingness of companies to pay for more extensive studies in such positions; it may also be true in validity. V. Jon Bentz (1968) reported some astonishingly high validities in predicting managerial performance from objective biographic data. Perhaps this can be shown for subjective data as well.

I would advocate the use of life-history assessment to replace testing with disadvantaged persons wherever competent professionals are available. An objection to this was offered by someone who felt the disadvantaged are not articulate and therefore cannot report history. I do not believe this is usually a matter of ability but has more to do with trust. The disadvantaged are choosy about those to whom they will reveal personal data.

One could argue for filling key posts in government agencies by the use of life-history data. However, the feasibility is questionable in federal and state employment because by now most such selection decisions are very heavily committed to the use of objective procedures, and Civil Service regulations make it difficult indeed to deviate from traditional methods of assessment. Somewhat the same conclusion must be offered in regard to the reform of the academic marketplace. Decisions about university appointments are largely restricted to appraising the candidates' previous status and his publication list, and the willingness of faculty committees to submit to retraining is indeed dubious. Since the academic marketplace has been mentioned, what about the use of life-history data in college admissions? Consider the case of an admissions office that now appraises the qualifications of applicants purely on the basis of dossiers of grades, aptitude tests, and letters of recommendation. Validities of their predictions of academic performance are high enough that there would probably be great reluctance to change. However, grading systems themselves are in serious question for validity (Hoyt, 1965), and there is much serious discontent with the college grade as a criterion of learning. Hence, there may be a golden opportunity in the next decade for admissions officers to shift to a new selection system, one that examines the previous learning and social history of an applicant for evidence of creativity and other values rather than for conventional achievement in the socialized status system. It would be possible to ask about a black applicant, not how much he has learned or whether he has been exposed to enriching environments, but what have been the peak experiences and the most self-actualizing episodes of his life. Some graduate schools already ask such questions of applicants rather than test them for conventional achievements (Solomon, 1970). Why should this not be done in undergraduate admissions? Such interviewing can be done in groups of applicants, I would estimate, with follow-up in individual interviews. The costs of such interviews would exceed present admission costs, but I would estimate not drastically so.

In general, decisions of crucial importance to the individual (medical, legal, employment, higher education, and parole decisions would certainly be included) or to society (the filling of key posts in the professions, government, industry) are relevant to the data in life histories. But are there situations in which it is not desirable for the person to participate in life-history assessment? Considered narrowly, all employment decisions might be of such a character. There is a risk that if the person tells too much, he will not get the job. On the other hand, it is probably not in the person's interest to get a job at which he would fail or which he would not enjoy. There is always a risk in telling one's story honestly and fully. The question is whether one has more to gain from a valid decision than from an invalid one. Mistrust in the competence of the interviewer, or fears of the confidentiality of the life history would and should lead the person to deny full collaboration; life-history assessment is then impossible. This very limitation is, however, a desirable safe-guard against unwarranted invasions of privacy.

Who should conduct such assessment? Can paraprofessionals and subdoctorates do it? In general, I suspect that persons near the age, sex, and socioeconomic level of the informant can conduct more valid life-history interviews than can advanced professionals. Professional qualifications seem to me more relevant in the assessment process at a later point; the synoptic or integrative stage of multiform assessment would require, I should think, such professional knowledge. I suspect that lawyers, Ph.D.s, and M.D.s have more of the kind of scholarly motivation and patience required for putting a documented case together. Professionals alone can protect data from unwarranted disclosure and loose storage practices. But it has yet to be shown that broad-band predictions are more accurate when made by professionals.

Quite clearly, life-history data collection and interpretation cannot be delegated to persons whose zeal is only for precision and standardization. Clerks and psychometrists would not find life-history assessment congenial and would be unfitted for it.

As to how a person learns to collect and interpret life histories, it must be admitted that little attention is given to this in graduate schools of psychology, and little attention to the *normal* life history in schools of medicine or social work, as far as I know.

The problem of negativism goes much deeper than issues of credentials and medical models. The problem results from setting a judge's view of life into a frame of reference that filters out some human data and prevents balanced data from coming through to him. Rather than attack the myth of mental illness and the superficiality of the medical model (Albee, 1968, 1969), an alternate approach would be to reform the frame of reference of the assessment judge. Until the judge cultivates a sense of life when he assesses another person, he will hold onto a variety of cheapening and superstition-mongering conceptions of human nature. Consider the suggestion made in Chapter Three that a person and his judge each look at the person's future in terms of three scenarios: doomsday, or negative; plausible; and utopian, or positive. Each of these possible futures is a part of life. They are illustrated in Figure 10.

There is a natural inclination to choose one or the other of

Figure 10

Assessment Frames of Reference

(a) Jury prejudiced toward a defendant, or Scheff's court — appointed
examiners (1964). (b) On-the-job trainer working with a disadvantaged
person. (c) Psychotherapist in closing stages of therapy (Rogers, 1961).
(d) Maslow in analyzing his "self-actualizing" cases (Maslow, 1954).

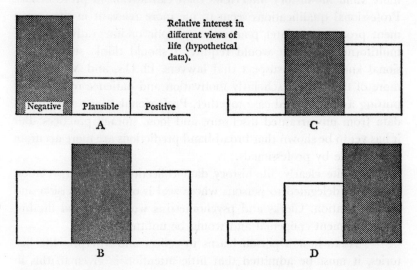

Relative interest in
different views of
life (hypothetical
data).

the three scenarios. One reason for this is belief in determinism,
which implies a single, fixed future. However, even a rigid deter-
minist must not carry this belief too far in looking at his own affairs
and must admit a range of possibilities contingent on his own actions, on those of others, and on luck.

A second factor leading to the belief that one must choose
one scenario is the institutional decision. A person is admitted to a
particular graduate school or not, is declared guilty or innocent by
the jury, marries or not. This reasoning induces us to hire only one
of the three applicants for a job, for example. But how often are
we really limited to such a single gateway? Are there not also con-
ditional admissions, jury recommendations, qualified hospital leaves
—one hesitates to say "qualified marriages," but even this has been
advocated and perhaps it is in fact widely practiced. Qualified
college admissions are perhaps on the increase: at a medical school,
a black applicant who received a poor foundation in chemistry and
biology is judged to be a good prospect to complete medical school

only *if* he receives considerable tutoring. Single forecasts, unqualified by the assumption of extra help, are increasingly inappropriate. The choice can be even more complex. Suppose the choice is between a well-qualified white who wants to practice medicine in rural Georgia and a qualified-admission black who does not?

The point of this example is not how to find a way to arrive at a decision favoring the black. The point is that the phrasing of the scenario is a complex judgment in itself. There are few, if any, simple gateways; rather, the map of the future is more like a maze, with alternative pathways in abundance. But should one not always choose the most plausible scenario? By definition, such scenario is the one that simply extrapolates into the future, under the fewest assumptions. Before answering this question, let us consider why one should make doomsday and utopian forecasts at all. There are situations in which it is far more costly to overlook a disaster, even if it is unlikely, than to predict routine events well. Under those conditions, the doomsday forecast is extremely important to include. In a case in which there is depression, we should consider the possibility of suicide even if it is unlikely. There are situations in which the costs are prohibitive if we overlook human potential. The utopian forecast, even though it cannot be very accurate, is extremely important in coping with a variety of problems of disadvantage. For one thing, it provides an incentive to devise aids to fulfillment of the prophecy. A Sioux Indian is admitted to college; the admissions board hopes for his success—and hedges that bet by providing him with aid that most students do not receive. The board would not take such action if it considered its forecast to be plausible rather than utopian.

The assessment judge should deliberately construct three images of the future. Probably the optimistic one should come first. (If negative chances were considered first, assessment might well halt.) In framing his expectations in optimistic terms, the judge is well aware that he has made many assumptions of favorable contingencies in his forecast. In stating these, he outlines the kinds of support that the person ought to receive in his work, family life, or further development. The utopian scenario, in other words, assumes a string of favorable settings in life and a sequence of creative, intelligent actions on the part of the person being assessed. The

judge should next draw up the negative scenario, if only because he
is aware by now of the assumptions he has been making. The doomsday scenario assumes that (1) "all will go wrong that can go
wrong" and (2) the person, at the first sign of disappointment, will
regress to an immature and self-defeating mode of behavior. After
taking these two extreme scenario positions, the judge may be ready
to design a balanced view of the person's life, the scenario that states
both his assets and liabilities. In general, this forecast not only predicts outcomes whose desirability moderates those of the other two
scenarios, but it also makes fewer assumptions. The judge, then,
states his view of the future in terms of probabilities: the most
probable outcome, making minimal assumptions, is the plausible
future. But he considers also the doomsday prospects, which should
cause us to make "standby" defensive plans (for example, buying at
least some life insurance or major-medical insurance). Third, even
for a severely disadvantaged or unqualified person, the judge considers his magnificent possibilities, which, given certain optimistic
assumptions, ought to influence us to make some provision for lend-
ing him resources to bring about that personal and socially valuable
Utopia.

<h2 style="text-align:center">RESEARCH IN SCENARIO WRITING</h2>

The concept of alternative scenarios for the future was explored by obtaining the forecasts of several hundred assessment
judges and officials to the programed case of a disadvantaged nine-
teen-year-old (Chapter Eleven). The case of Richard was administered to a variety of occupational groups, and their responses
provided an opportunity to document how various types of judges
construct a future for a person. The programing of this case presented early life data (family history, school history, and the like)
and then required judges to estimate his life chances and to predict
specific delinquency problems. The youth's record included certain
problems but not others; the accuracy of prediction could thus be
determined by how many actual problems were spotted by a judge
and by how many problems he validly surmised would not occur.
In other words, it was possible to be accurate in both a negative and
a positive sense.

Life-chance estimates were made with regard to whether

Richard could obtain a job, could hold that job if he got it, and could complete a vocational training program if admitted to it. A judge was asked to estimate each life chance by choosing on the following scale of optimism: less than 1 chance in 5, about 50/50, or better than 4 out of 5 chances. Responses to the case's optimism scale were used to measure a judge's frame of reference about Richard's future. Our research question was: Given the facts of Richard's life, what kinds of judges choose which kinds of scenarios for him? A second question was: Do judges choosing doomsday scenarios make more or less accurate predictions of delinquency problems?

It is a simple matter in this case to classify Richard as sick, delinquent, or hopelessly loaded with handicaps and disabilities. Counselors of the disadvantaged are, however, supposed to be trained to find personal strengths as well as weaknesses in such cases. One research question, then, was: Did counselors find strengths as well as weaknesses when compared with others who reviewed the same case? Another group of judges was composed of federal and state officials who supervised the work and programs of the counselors. Our hypothesis was that these officials are more conservative than counselors. There were clearcut differences among the several occupational groups who reviewed the case. In particular, counselors were less negative in their scenarios than were the officials who supervised them (see Table 12). Only a minority of this case's reviewers (including counselors) were able to perceive optimistic scenarios (it must be remembered that this case is profoundly discouraging and difficult). Nevertheless, the research question was: What kinds of judges were able to work through a hopeful scenario anyway? *Working through* is a good term for this process; since judges were asked at two points for their estimates of life chances (or evaluation of Richard's scenarios), it was possible to obtain at least a rough impression of this process. The finding was that the trained counselors became more optimistic as they went through the case while untrained counselors did not shift (see Table 13).

Now consider the problem of realism. Recall that a judge of this case was asked to predict the incidence of various forms of delinquency—getting arrested for drunkenness, and so on. He was

Table 12. EVALUATION OF CHANCES THAT A PARTICULAR DIS-
ADVANTAGED PERSON CAN HOLD A JOB

	Opinion at end of case		
Population of judges	*Negative*	*Rational*	*Optimistic*
Counselors working with the disadvantaged	194	174	75
Counselors formerly working with the dis- advantaged	36	16	10
VISTA workers (in training)	16	7	5
Personnel interns in federal agencies	26	22	8
Officials in agency supervising the counselors	23	4	1

Chi square $= 21.2$; degrees of freedom $= 8$; significance .007

given credit for recognizing problems that did exist (being able to
make accurate inferences about negative or undesirable events),
and the nonexistence of delinquency problems that commonly occur
but of which poor Richard was not guilty (positive inference). The
research showed that these two kinds of realism were related to the
kinds of scenario visualized by a judge. Judges who chose doomsday
scenarios for Richard were able to predict delinquent acts with
accuracy. Judges with utopian scenarios were able to predict somewhat the forms of delinquency that Richard did *not* commit. The
data also showed that the negative-inference accuracy scores were
higher than the positive accuracy scores. As usual, it is easier to
detect what is weak and incompetent about people—cheap assessment—than to recognize what is strong or creative.

This study documented the expectations of several groups
including two that play rather different roles in assessment. Consider
the differences between this agency's officials and the counselors they
supervise. In general, institutional gatekeepers are charged with defending institutions and are provided with credentials assessment as
their principal decision-making tool. They engage in cheap assess-

Table 13. COMPARISON OF EXPECTATIONS OF TRAINED AND
UNTRAINED COUNSELORS

I. Early in Reviewing Case

	Pessimistic	50/50	Optimistic	N
Trained counselors	60	55	41	156
Untrained counselors	46	118	72	236

Chi square = 17.7; degrees of freedom = 2; significant at .001

II. Later in Reviewing Same Case

	Pessimistic	50/50	Optimistic	N
Trained counselors	52	31	73	156
Untrained counselors	52	111	73	236

Chi square = 30.0; degrees of freedom = 2; significant at .001

Shift in expectations[a]	Chi square	d.f.	Sig.
Trained counselors	16.2	2	.001
Untrained counselors	N.S.	—	—

[a] Shift is calculated by comparing trained-counselor estimates or expectations early in the case (I) with their estimates later in the same case (II). The same is done for untrained counselors.

ment because that is their charge. Their negative view of Richard resulted partly from their official positions and especially from orientation to credentials. Richard's credentials, indeed, were exceptionally poor. The computer would tell anyone who did not recognize it that his life chances were at a real low.

While this sample included only twenty-eight officials, the study of which the case was part revealed many similar instances of negativism toward the disadvantaged by other officials. (A research team visited ninety counseling centers for the disadvantaged; the counselors often volunteered their opinion that the hierarchy above them had this negativism [Dailey, Carlson, and McChesney, 1968].) Further, these thirty, while constituting a small group, were thirty of the top three hundred officials of this agency.

It may sound as if one is building a case against officials. Not so. Such officials are "program people"; they have more responsibility for operating a training, welfare, or other program and less responsibility for assessing individuals and feeling what their lives are like. Their role is to protect the programs. They are doing their job. Anyone in this position will necessarily find himself drawn toward a negativistic, nonindividualistic credentials system. Many structural forces promote this attitude: One is the impossibility of reporting very much information to superiors except in statistical form; it is easy for statistics to report data of the credentials type but almost impossible to report subtleties, especially those that concern counselors. The counselor—or any other professional—has responsibility for individuals rather than for programs. He can well afford the luxury of contempt for credentials and statistical analyses. No special virtue lies in this attitude of the counselors; indeed, in this particular government agency, the counselors had compassion for their clients but very little for their supervisors' immense problems in operating the programs.

But the counselor's role is to help individuals realize themselves. He is at least partially in the utopian-scenario business. Different expectations for Richard's life chances are accounted for, in this theory, by the professional versus the official roles in assessment.

The officials and managers of society are not playing a con game. Their responsibility for programs is real. To control access to life chances and to regulate movement through the status system is a necessary responsibility. The con game begins when the standards, credentials, and symptom complexes are taken seriously. Paper is then substituted for behavior as the object of observation; and status, a part of life, is confused with the whole of a person's life. Worse yet—almost fatal for the conception of therapeutic and other systems for human development—the negative scenarios preempt our thinking about human potentiality.

Reforming
Professional Training

☆☆☆☆☆☆☆☆☆☆☆☆☆☆☆☆☆☆☆☆☆

Reform of the national assessment system calls for two massive tasks. One is to devise an assessment system that is both valid and compassionate—that is, just. The other task is to change the professionals and officials who make decisions about life chances. In this chapter, we consider the role that the life history could play in training and educating new professionals and officials and perhaps in retraining the experienced. The urgency of this reform comes from more than its importance in coping with the problem of equal opportunity, as if that problem were not great enough. There is also the internal problem of the organization of behavioral science itself, made intense by the unremitting warfare and obtuse misunderstandings that divide the different disciplines, which should be together constructing a life science of the person. For example, the discontent of some professional psychologists with graduate departments has recently boiled over (Matulef, Pottharst, and Rothenberg, 1970). In other professions concerned with assessment, we find similar internal struggles. For example, there is the long cold war between psychoanalysts and psychiatrists trained on other bases. There is the rise of what some call radical psychiatry or even antipsychiatry (Laing and Cooper, 1964) within that profession; and there are the cri-

143

tiques formulated by Thomas Szasz (1964). On the surface, it would seem that a better hope for reform in assessment might well be the newer and less conflict-ridden professions or disciplines that do assessment, such as personnel administration, counseling, and criminology. However, I assume that the insights of psychiatry and the quantitative disciplines of psychology are desirable foundations for a national assessment system so that reform is inconceivable without the participation of these two fields. This chapter reflects that assumption, although illustrations will be mostly in terms of clinical psychology. However, the training problem exists in every profession and discipline concerned with the systematic determination of life chances. A system of training and retraining would have different content for the different institutions and professions, but the underlying organization or logic would be the same—that is, to teach the judge to make predictions about life histories by working with them.

In general, a distinction is made between education and training. Education requires one to hook up the particular skill with related areas of knowledge and skill. The art and craft of understanding would need, for example, to be related to studies in the behavioral and biological sciences. Training also involves the acquisition of a skill, but the skill is defined in relation to the assessment problems of the particular institution in which the assessment is to be done. In practice, higher education shows less interest in measuring outcomes than does training. Most college and professional-school grading systems are not evaluated against external criteria; medical-school grades turn out, for instance, not to predict physician performance (Taylor, Price, Richards, and Jacobsen, 1965). Rigorous training measures outcomes. Thus the training designer would seem to be more rigorous than the curriculum maker in higher education. While this may be the practice, it is certainly undesirable, and I would join with Wilbur Schramm (1964) and others (note Glaser, 1962) in extending the formulation and measurement of objectives throughout higher education.

Thus one can see no great distinction between the needs of graduate-education and professional-training institutes for procedures such as the programed-case method. The programed case, by measuring its own outcome, would hopefully document the impact of training or higher education alike in cultivating clinical-scientific discipline in the student or practitioner. One need not assume that we have yet programed cases that would do this, in order to foresee systems of programed cases that would.

This way of thinking requires one to be clear upon the objectives of training or education, to design experiences through which the student can move toward those objectives, and then to provide criteria that can be checked periodically to ascertain progress. The principal training objective of the programed case is accuracy in prediction, especially accuracy that exceeds that from simpler means. We have already explained how this accuracy is to be determined. However, this is only the first (if most vital) of the criteria. For intensive assessment, the complete set of criteria (pp. 71ff) are statements, each beginning "The assessment process is well done if": (1) The judge can accurately predict events. (2) The judge can accurately predict events that have special significance in the institutional setting where the assessment is done, for example, suicide in psychiatry. (3) The person himself (as a result of collaborating in the assessment) can anticipate the outcome of his hopes and goals. (4) The person knows how to devise substitute goals and plans when the first ones fail or have to be abandoned. (5) The person recognizes the most significant events of his life and can link them conceptually and emotionally with the rest of his life. (6) The judge can identify the events the person considers significant and also the events toward which the person acts as if they are significant. (7) The judge can describe the current self-impression of the person. (8) The judge can communicate to another professional a valid impression of the person. (9) The judge can communicate to another professional a valid impression stated in institutionally relevant terms. (10) The judge's qualifications can be appraised by accrediting agencies. This means that a series of life histories constructed by the judge, together with his accuracy in prediction, are so written that a panel can appraise his qualifications through them. The student must learn how to write cases so that he may be professionally judged. In medicine and in clinical psychology, this has an important relation to defense against malpractice suits and also to the responsible keeping of hospital records.

Some of these criteria are searching. They go far beyond what can be taught through devices such as programed cases. An

immediate problem which arises is whether criteria 3 through 6
require a therapeutic relationship; these require that the student of
assessment, in collecting data, benefit that person in specific and
measurable ways. That is exactly the point. The suggestion is that
no one fully understands assessment who does not understand
therapy and/or therapeutic counseling. Ideally, therapeutic experience should precede assessment experience. However, there are assessment situations for which we cannot provide prerequisite intensive experiences in therapy. We should find a way for those judges
who cannot or will not do therapy and/or counseling to acquire at
least a rudimentary appreciation of the emotional impact of assessment.

Do not graduate study and professional education already
seek prediction through life-history data? If so, they do it implicitly
and without much effort to verify their own effectiveness. If one
actually reviews the clinical-psychology teaching programs, for example, it would seem that the student is given criticism of his data
collection (especially in the administration of testing and projective
procedures) and in writing reports. I do not think there is usually
emphasis on prediction or on vigorous and systematic follow-up.
Put another way, it would seem that the objectives of graduate
training are procedural and conceptual, not predictive. I have already indicated (Chapter Six) my reservations about conceptual
training. Just as concept formation is not a primary criterion of
assessment training, it will not be emphasized in the training design
to follow.

SAMPLE PROGRAM

Among the problems of the scientist-practitioner model was
the contradiction between these two parts of the model. The scientist was often an experimentalist and rarely was he a clinical scientist—one who learns from cases to formulate clinically relevant
hypotheses. The professional rarely learned to make hypotheses and
verify them within particular idiographic cases. The design of the
programed case is a miniaturized rough approximation to the kind
of detective search in which it seems true clinicians engage. When
Freud presented a case, he involved the reader in the excitement of
a quest; he did not usually lull the reader with the assured dogma-

tisms of completed theory. The brief case is only a pale and abbreviated copy of the more demanding cases written by the great clinicians; but the features of search for meaning, prediction, and confirmation (or disproof) are explicit in its design. In brief, then, a sufficiently long and properly designed series of programed cases should teach the student to be a clinical scientist—a naturalist in personality (Dailey, 1960; Willems and Raush, 1969). In such a training series, life history is the primary material for training. A student collects life-history data, authenticates it, analyzes and interprets it, makes verifiable predictions, and verifies or disproves them. If he is an effective learner, his work will meet many of the criteria presented above. The series of experiences could be the following:

(1) The student reviews a pre-test series of programed cases, to measure a priori prediction ability. (2) The student then prepares his own life history, following systematic self-interrogation procedures like those described in Chapter Four. An instructor or assessment professional could help him in this process. (3) Students under supervision undertake to collect life-history data from one another and interpret it. Actual forecasts can be made in this process, both in real time (predicting events that have not yet occurred physically) and in subjective real time (events that have physically occurred but are not explicitly stated in the data known to the judge). (4) The student undertakes reanalysis of some of the great clinical cases and of published biographies. (5) The student now undertakes the study of lives of representative persons from his own culture. (6) Then he makes an excursion into the lives of representative persons from other cultures: technically advanced, undeveloped societies, and primitive societies. (7) Now, he is ready to study the life histories of atypical persons, especially the kinds of persons who will be clients of the institutions in which the student expects to work. Finally, (8) the student reviews a post-test series of programed cases, to measure the effects of the above experiences.

For graduate and professional students, data collection is taught at steps 2, 3, and 7. For undergraduates, instruction in data collection would be limited to step 2. In this design, programed cases have been presented as measuring instruments. This has been more for purposes of clarity than for logic. The programed case is also a teaching device. Were there cases available in this form, they would be used in steps 4 to 7 also. The ideal program of training would intermingle programed and unprogramed cases. The purpose of using unprogramed cases is to facilitate transfer. Professional experience, in spite of our best efforts to build in prediction and verification, comes to us in erratically programed form. One must learn to make the transition somehow. Were there enough persons available for experimentation, we might be able to establish empirically the best mixture of programed and unprogramed cases both to train and to transfer. Transfer of training must be demonstrated to assure that programed cases teach or, better, to determine what kinds and sequences of cases teach. The conservative recommendation would be to devise better and more representative cases and then to replicate and extend the very preliminary transfer studies reported here. However, the programed case is already more of a measuring instrument than those now used in graduate education. The clinical student is typically evaluated for his knowledge of theory and his ability to produce experimental designs; and he is checked out on procedures. But his ability to predict behavior is not systematically checked. Therefore, our comparison is between a new training system that permits measurement and a conventional one that does not. This is unequal combat indeed: the clinical professor is very likely to prefer to assume valid a method with which he is familiar over trying out one with which he is not.

Thus in this proposal for training, one asks the assessment instructor to consider two shattering possibilities at once: One is that the assessment system he has been teaching is itself inadequate; and the other is that the criteria by which he evaluates his teaching are not enough.

Perhaps the most significant advantage to the use of programed cases, other than the measurement of student progress, would come from the research yield. In effect, the analysis of inferences from programed cases, to the extent that those cases are representative of the original life histories, constitutes a form of exploration into the structure of those lives. If-then relationships, when reliably perceived by students or professionals who make accurate predictions, provide clues to the organization of life history.

I suggested some ways in which these clues can be interpreted in Chapter Six. Thus, the instructor in assessment, through collecting systematic records of predictions made under varying conditions by his students, is able to make original contributions to the literature not only on assessment but also in personality itself. Such a use of programed-case findings necessitates some special assumptions about the nature of personality, of course. For example, one has to assume that a concept or interpretation of fact that facilitates prediction is more likely true than one which does not.

Knowledge of the concepts of psychoanalysis, of diagnostic categories, of the principles established in laboratories of experimental psychology, and of the rest of what we call the body of knowledge in the behavioral sciences, has an unknown relation to programed-case prediction ability. Until more is known of the relation between nomothetic and idiographic knowledge of a person, the most sensible thing to do is merely to suggest including programed-case laboratories as part of graduate and professional instruction. Regarding the relation to competing assessment models, however, we cannot quite have it both ways. The delicate question of the relation of life-history, projective, and objective-test data now needs to be raised. In brief, objective measurements of ability (especially of intellectual ability) provide a context for interpreting life-history data. They are not the criterion for predictions, but they provide a factual supplement to the data that are used to make the predictions. Responses to personality inventories would appear to provide a characterization of the general mood and self-perception of the person at the time a history is elicited. To the extent that this characterization helps interpret the history, it is again a useful supplement to it. However, the prediction of life-history events, purely on the basis of objective tests and personality inventories, is of only academic interest in the life-history assessment system. Projective protocols offer a different kind of integrative problem. They cannot be the criteria for predictions, any more than can the test and inventory findings. But they may suggest useful hypotheses regarding the meaning of the life-history data. The thema found in projective protocols may represent persisting tensions not so clearly visible in the behavioral episodes; a clinician sensitized to looking for them on the basis of review of a projective protocol may find them more visible when he turns to the life history itself. But, again, what is generated by projective data is hypothesis, not conclusion.

While there has been much fulmination here against credentials, some certification is necessary in organized society. Who will be permitted to practice medicine, law, psychology, to offer assessment services? These services should be offered by persons who show that they can and do understand the people they are "practicing on." The completion of graduate or professional study proves only that the professional has had the opportunity to learn. What proves that he has in fact learned? Some concrete demonstration of proficiency in the crafts of these professions is desirable. I would predict that in the long run, some use of programed cases prepared for this purpose should be considered. What is now done using cases is not done systematically. Lacking rigorous, systematic means of measuring assessment proficiency, we rely on the Graduate Record Examination, the knowledge of substantive fields like chemistry in medicine or statistics in psychology to determine who will enter the professions. We do not attempt to use, as admissions or certification criteria, qualities like empathy and judgment, which I think we shall eventually be able to measure through programed cases.

TEACHING AT THE UNDERGRADUATE LEVEL

It is not uncommon to use life-history material at the undergraduate level. In an introductory course on personality, we were looking for methods that would induce the student to see personality concepts in terms of his own life. This was, in part, a response to the weariness of college students with academic teaching. In part, it represented our conviction that no one should practice surgery without knowing pain—no one should learn assessment of others without engaging in assessment of himself. Most of the students involved in these teaching experiments were headed for the professions, where they would eventually be making decisions about the life chances of others—patients, employees, clients in law, or poor people. Some preparation at the undergraduate level to make salient the human aspects of those decisions appeared urgent.

Thomas Baer (1970) devised a method for large-scale instruction of 200 students in preparing their own life histories. In this method, a standardized stimulus is presented in manner analogous to the sentence-completion procedure (Appendix B). Fifty-seven stimulus phrases, such as, "A time when I had a blind date . . ." or "A time when I felt especially turned on in my courses . . ." or "A time when my parents were . . . ," are presented to the student (Appendix B). He chooses the ones to which he can respond. His paragraph about "The time when" is a specific event meeting the criteria for event (defined in Chapter Five). The student responds in this way to at least twenty-five of the stimuli. The fifty-seven stimuli were selected so that a variety of situations at a variety of stages of life are represented. The stimuli also vary in intimacy. One of the purposes of the students' choice of stimuli is to permit him to choose the level of intimacy on which he cares to respond. After responding to the questionnaire, each student is then instructed to choose from among his responses the fifteen episodes that span life, sample many different situations, and seem significant to him. These fifteen episodes are elaborated specifically and reported chronologically. The student is finally asked to interpret this life history as if he were an objective observer forecasting life styles, occupational, and other concrete choices, and to explain where he obtained the forecast. The history comprised a term paper, an experience of which many students spoke with enthusiasm. The literary quality of much of the work produced gave ample evidence of care and fascination with the task.

Two other methods used for preparing undergraduate life histories were the concurrent method and Bernard Haldane's exercise (1966). The concurrent method involved journal keeping by a group of forty students, collaborating with us in an investigation of student quality of life. Each kept a weekly journal for a year. Each week, the student recorded a "high" (an exhilarating or otherwise highly gratifying episode) and a "low" (a very depressing or negative episode). This design reflected Abraham Maslow's (1970) formulation of the importance of peak experiences and his effort to show such self-actualization as of critical importance in higher education. Most students were able to keep this record, although the time limit for remembering weekly episodes seemed to be about six weeks without special aids for recall. Haldane's exercise was de-

signed by him to help disadvantaged persons find areas of their lives
in which they could report competence rather than mere recitations
of failures in the credentials game. Traditional employment-counsel-
ing procedures, Haldane claimed, simply lower the disadvantaged
clients' already low self-esteem. Thomas Martinez (1968) has shown
how such agencies seem to batter the client's esteem so that he will
accept the kinds of work available. Such negative effects are similar
to those of the medical model discussed in Chapter Seven (p. 128).
Using Haldane's exercise with affluent college students, however, I
found some were initially unable to recall instances when they had
felt self-actualized and competent. The problem of self-esteem is
hardly limited to the disadvantaged. I note that Haldane uses his
method with executives, with whom I also have found it effective.

In all these methods of instructing the group to develop a
case of themselves, two safeguards are necessary. One is to be available on request for individual discussion, and the other is to provide
an alternative assignment. In several cases (of the total of 320 students with whom I have used such methods), the student elected
to study the life of another person rather than to write his own. This
option is clinically wise as well as ethically imperative—the procedure otherwise being an invasion of privacy.

For educational purposes, it would be ideal to have a programed-case version of every well-authenticated life of an eminent
person. This massive task is quite beyond present resources. It has
proven feasible, however, to assign this task to advanced undergraduates and graduate students in the following sense. The student
prepares an abbreviated version of the biography by reducing it to
fifteen representative, life-spanning, well-authenticated, and significant episodes. These requirements are sufficiently demanding that
even a 500-page biography may well present no more than thirty or
forty such episodes. Thus the fifteen episodes comprise a large proportion of the usable biography, if not of the original life itself. The
student then does a paired comparison of the episodes (as in Chapter Six), and verifies this graph by obtaining paired comparisons
under controlled conditions from other students. He can study the
structure of the life and learn something of its thema and the implied
possibilities of prediction in it, without actually completing the case
as a quantified task.

Sources for such biographies include political biographies, inventoried by Fred Greenstein (1969), and anthropological life histories (Langness, 1965). Erik Erikson's published biographies (Luther, 1958; Shaw in *Identity*, 1968, p. 142; and Gandhi, 1969) are appropriate for this analysis, though difficult because of his writing style. *Great Cases in Psychoanalysis* (Greenwald, 1959) contains potential cases. Henry Murray's essay on *Moby Dick* (1941), his "Icarus" (1955), and Robert W. White's cases (1960 and 1963), are among those that could be given this treatment. The purpose of such graphing is to sensitize the student to patterns and thema in life history. Whether this sensitization produces increments in idiographic skill in programed cases could be determined experimentally.

✿✿✿✿✿✿✿✿✿ **9** ✿✿✿✿✿✿✿✿✿

Prospects, Paradoxes, and Postulates

✿✿✿✿✿✿✿✿✿✿✿✿✿✿✿✿✿✿✿✿✿✿✿✿

The problem in personality science, and hence in assessment, has been a lack of method. Personality, as the organized property of a life, becomes detectable only in very long runs of longitudinal data. It becomes visible to the judge only when he knows many events from the life history. Excessive reductionism loses the phenomenon of personality. For Pierre Teilhard de Chardin (1966), life becomes visible only after a fairly high degree of "complexification" has been attained. Below that degree, life cannot be perceived by science at all, appearing only to be dead matter: "Life is, in scientific experience . . . a specific effect . . . of complexified matter . . . perceptible to us only where . . . complexity exceeds a certain critical value—below that value we cannot perceive it at all" (p. 24). Likewise with personality, "the red glow of life" cannot appear in individual units, even if each is a meaningful episode. Still less can a person appear alive if these individual units are reduced to their stimulus-response or trait contents. A life history provides a critical mass of events in sufficient number to permit personality to become visible; below that critical mass, personality is lost.

Why does the experimentalist reduce life history to a few

154

units if this destroys the phenomenon? His problem is analogous to that of the early medical scientist learning anatomy only from cadavers. Much useful information was obtained from cadavers. But scientists knew that physiology could never be created by that means. The experimentalist reduces life history to a few constituent units, almost always occurring within very narrow time spans and in a highly controlled environment, quite obviously because he wishes to manipulate variables and learn what causes what to change. One cannot possibly experiment on a total life history, however, any more than one can experiment on such a real-time process as the moon's orbit. (One might shake the moon up, but what would we use for a control?) An alternative is to devise representations of life in various degrees of complexification, submitting them under controlled conditions to judges, to determine what they can predict and what conditions facilitate prediction. What was a two-party system in science, composed of experimenter and subject, must then become a three-party system of experimenter, judge, and subject. The research is thus not on life itself but rather into the conditions under which life can be understood.

We began our inquiry by noting the social crises facing all the institutions that determine life chances on the basis of individual data. In our search for valid humanistic assessment, we turn to models of assessment based on the life history. These models appear initially easy to find, since all the great contributors to personality theory are concerned with the life span. However, they stop short of formulating specific operations for assessing and evaluating such a complex body of data as a life history.

While we cannot suggest a single sovereign method for collecting and interpreting life history for every separate assessment situation (the institutions varying too much in their demands), we do find it possible to outline a set of criteria for evaluating the effectiveness of a life-history procedure as used in a particular case, an experimental method for validating that procedure, and an approach to training (or retraining) assessment judges. In this chapter, we take a look at the prospects for acceptance of these new methods and offer a model for building an assessment system around them. This model has a dual aspect, in the one direction being concerned with the assessment of individual lives, and in the other, with the development of personality science, a science that ought to represent samples of life and not slices of dead matter.

The problem of intuitive life-history assessment is how to make such subjective data achieve objective results. Our solution will satisfy neither the purely objective nor the purely humanistic extremes. On the one hand, the strict behaviorist and objective tester will be suspicious of the kinds of data that are collected—episodes of behavior—and, on the other hand, the intuitionist will resist the disciplines of programing and of prediction. One hopes that there are enough middle-of-the-road investigators around to replicate the findings or to build better programed cases.

While we have said that whatever achieves prediction is objective enough for us, qualifications should be noted. They are that the predictions shall be within the life history. In a way, this is not a restriction at all, since all that the person *does* is part of his life. However, not everything that happens to him is part of it; there are accidents and there are gratuitous opportunities given the person because of previous opportunities. (Indeed, this is the nature of disadvantage.) The desire to rule out these impersonal features from assessment causes us to reject credentials for the most part and also to downgrade the more artificial kinds of assessment data—those reliable nonevents that psychologists so often create in the name of measurement. Nevertheless, objective facts cannot be omitted from rigorous assessment data. If the person has a hearing loss, whether this resulted from trends in his life or not, this fact must be known in order to appreciate the nature of his interpersonal relations. An extremely high or extremely low I.Q., as has been mentioned, is a part of the background of fact without which the kinds of situations facing the individual will not be intelligible to the intuitive judge. Objective facts have a second role in assessment, and that is to limit the excesses of intuition. No doubt, some judges read into a case what they want, especially if they have some compassion. The very process of identification with the person, which I suspect provides the best interviewers an incentive to go on collecting data after other interviewers halt, can also lead to a sentimental overattachment. A way must be found to require some objective predictions during the process of learning to do assessment and perhaps also during the practice of assessment. While there is objective content in every programed case, we did not classify the events by their proportion of objective content. But it is quite conceivable that a subset of highly objective and well-authenticated events can be discovered that are not affected by overidentification with the person but yet are normally correlated with accuracy in predicting the total set of events. When such purely objective accuracy is too low, the prediction accuracy with the remaining more subjectively oriented events would then be discounted as due to mere overidentification.

In the research analysis, we distinguished two other kinds of predictions: the general, or gross, prediction, which is based on simply adding up the accurate predictions made at all stages of assessment, and idiographic prediction, which is the ability to profit from cumulative amounts of information in particular cases. The latter measure was more sensitive to cultural differences and to the effects of education. However, generality was found in gross predictions, indicating a talent for making them. The reliabilities of the measure, plus the interpretability of the findings, gave us sufficient boldness to conclude that prediction of life-history events is possible. Therefore, we can envision the development of a valid life-history assessment system. The training programs that would put such assessment into effect would use the same kind of instrument with which one demonstrates prediction. The completion of several hundred programed cases would theoretically develop assessment judges with a wide-ranging talent for understanding human lives. They would be certificated if sufficiently accurate. Naturally, a massive project of this order is only a speculation, until we should know more precisely the conditions under which transfer of training does occur from case to case. We think it likely that it is idiographic prediction that transfers, not gross prediction, but we do not pretend more than a dim appreciation of the transfer process.

We nevertheless go on to conjecture what it is that idiographic prediction does. It accumulates and integrates data. In view of the failure of other investigators yet to show differences between configural and linear prediction among clinicians, how do we justify this interpretation? I suspect that test and credentials data have been the most convenient kind for assessment research, and that the negative findings have only been with them. Thus the negative findings in configural understanding do not at all tell us about the configural possibilities of life-history data. I will go out on a limb and conjecture that only life-history data have configural meaning and for this reason produce idiographic learning curves.

Our analyses then took us into the area of the structure of cases. Why is it that untrained judges can predict behavior? The explanation offered was in terms of socially shared meanings or, to be more specific, if-then codes specifying the connections between events. This calculus of behavior is presumably acquired during socialization. One cannot function without if-then codes in life any more than he can function without verbal language. In fact, the behavioral codes should be treated as a form of language. The programed-case experimental design is a way of eliciting such codes. Consider a matrix in which each row shows a particular judge's accuracy in a series of inferences in a particular case. Each column then corresponds to an event in that case. Adding the series of predictions across the row of a matrix, we get the gross accuracy of the judge. Adding the predictions down the columns of that matrix (across judges), we get at the predictability of the particular event. This vertical analysis of the data matrix leads us into the study of behavioral meanings. At this point, experimental linguistics helps us with the analogy. If we wish to understand the structure of a sentence, we can provide the reader with the sentence one word at a time and ask him to estimate the next word. After each estimate, he is given feedback and now knows one additional word. As the proportion of the sentence that is known increases, the estimates become less wild, until he can pretty well estimate what will come next. This is the programed-case design, except that events are used instead of words. We therefore set out to learn about the behavioral calculus by analyzing the relations between cues and predictions in cases. The consistently accurate judges' cue networks were different from the networks of consistently inaccurate judges. This method illustrates the possibility that programed cases can tell us about the organized properties of life history. Judges, through the ways in which they group events in order to make accurate predictions, reveal the natural clusters and sequences of episodes in the case. To the extent that such a case represents the whole life history, perhaps we are then learning something about life-history structure. Note that this method is usable with unique persons. Any number of judges can play; there is only one Leonardo, but experimental replications of Leonardo can be constructed by the programed-case method. One judge may reconstruct what happened to such historically interesting personages and then submit the reconstruction to experimental proof by other judges.

A life, then, is conceived as an information network. While this has an esoteric sound, this kind of information is, like language, shared by many judges and is not technical in nature. I do not expect to find that professional assessment judges are better at the molecular matching of particular events. I do expect eventually to find that their superior motivation in working through very large numbers of realism-reinforcing cases will enable them to exceed the powers of judges who lack that motivation and that training.

PROBLEMS OF ACCEPTANCE

Certain assumptions of the method may make it difficult for some behavioral scientists. Aside from their possible doubts about biography and subjectively collected events, many psychologists will consider unnecessary the proposition that there is organization in the whole of life not found in its molecular parts. At the same time, some clinicians who have an intuitive appreciation of the life history may find the programed-case methodology tedious. One psychoanalyst, asked to comment on a programed case that was being used to teach assessment, stated that he found the case's content interesting but could see no valid reason for the "rather compulsive" format. He was put off by the programing in which the case was occasionally halted and the judge requested to predict what would occur next. It is true that programing alters established intuitive patterns of interpretation and breaks up the natural flow of data to which judges are accustomed.

The model poses a third difficulty for the orthodox. The life-history system bases predictive ability and understanding on the intuitive knowledge of a social system rather than on the explicit, formal knowledge of the behavioral sciences. The earnest behavioral-science scholar could easily infer that his scholarship is in large part useless for understanding individual cases. He may reject this bad news, preferring simply to believe that there is no such thing as an individual case. Fortunately, the model provides this scholar some comfort: While nomothetic science is here held largely useless for understanding the vital issues of particular lives, assessment research is itself a nomothetic inquiry. The search is for general principles that facilitate assessment. An example would be the due process of a courtroom: Due process guides but never replaces the jury's deliberation, which is ultimately idiographic. We thus attempt to resolve the apparent contradiction by postulating *levels* of science. The idiographic understanding of a particular case is a task in what Gordon Allport (1961) called "concrete psychology." Life-history assessment research is *about* idiographic understanding, but it uses the tools of nomothetic (or law-formulating) psychology. The science of personality therefore becomes a three-person rather than a two-person inquiry. Involved are the person whose life is to be assessed, the judge who uses whatever idiographic methods he can, and the experimentalist who keeps "box score" on the judge's results and attempts to learn how that judge can function better. From this partnership, a science of personality can develop. The individual personality was entirely too intricate for direct understanding via the rather clumsy methods of nomothetic science; the attempt was rather like trying to repair a watch with a meat axe. Life-history assessment holds that the individual personality can be understood, but only by an instrument of understanding as intricate as the individual personality itself: an intuitive judge. The experimentalist thus should admit that he himself has not the slightest chance of understanding anything as intricate and subtle as the personality; only *another person,* an intuitive judge, can do this task. Yet the intuitive judge has profound weaknesses; for example, he can make predictions, but he does not know when to attempt these nor does he always test their verity unless compelled to do so. The experimentalist's role is like that of trial judge. He arranges to have evidence presented to the jury but (ideally) does not tell the jury what its verdict should be. The "due process" resembles the controlled presentation of a life history in a programed case; the theory of "evidence" is the theory of personality itself.

Perhaps more acceptable is the life-history model's view of assessment as a learning process. Some assessment investigators have stressed cognitive models (as did Bieri, Atkins, Briar, Leaman, Miller, and Tripodi, 1966); others draw on perception models (Tagiuri,

1969). But most of our methodology used a rather simplified learning theory. Learning in life-history assessment has two aspects. First, the individual person is learned. Events are in some way integrated and generalized. This process appears at first glance to assume self-consistency in the life history (see Lecky, 1945). However, the model does not assume that all the events of life are equally revealing or authentic; a judge progressively learns to emphasize some more than others. The graph data in Chapter Six, for example, showed very great differences among events in how impressive (or salient) they were to judges as data bases for further predictions or generalizations. The judge's problem is to decide where the consistencies lie. If he decides this correctly he can make predictions. We do not assume that one can start anywhere and reconstruct the entire personality. The second aspect is case-to-case transfer of learning skill. It seems quite possible that what transfers from case to case is an ability or inclination to *use* information rather than nomothetic generalizations about "what people will do." In other words, a judge learns to do cases rather than acquire biases and rules about what will happen in new cases. Who can deny, of course, that some judges under some conditions do learn to make generalized expectations about future cases? This occurrence, in the life-history model, has been termed *prejudice* in the literal sense of *prejudgment* (any prediction arrived at without individual data). The real question, however, is not whether judges acquire prejudices but whether they maintain them despite strong evidence to the contrary in an individual case.

The data show, at most, that transfer of idiographic skill from case to case can occur if programed cases have been used. It has not been shown that there is transfer among the unprogramed cases of everyday clinical and industrial experience. We cannot yet be sure that the claimed benefits of professional experience are obtained from professional work as presently organized in clinical psychology, psychiatry, social work, personnel work, law, and the other professional disciplines. Nevertheless, our findings are consistent with the professional assumption that cases teach.

POSTULATES

Perhaps the model now needs to be stated in succinct form. Regarding some of the numbered postulates (each grouped under the major axiom which it expresses or on which it rests), preliminary evidence has been presented. It is clear that representative sampling of cases and judges would be required for more than a preliminary statement (Hammond, 1969).

Life History Axiom. Given intelligible life histories, it is possible to develop an assessment system that is both valid and empathic. This was the original hope—and claim—expressed in Chapter One when we faulted the traditional clinical system for lack of validity and the credentials system for lack of empathy. Thus far, we have learned from programed-case research about validity but not about empathy. Nevertheless, the following postulates appear either plausible or warranted by our findings: (1) Most people are able to make valid predictions in life histories. (2) Given a life history, a judge tends to identify himself with the person in it, and this identification is assumed to facilitate assessment. Two reasons for this postulate can be offered. First, a judge is probably motivated to seek more data about people with whom he can identify. Second, when a judge can identify with a person (attempting to see life through that person's eyes), he probably possesses the behavioral codes (semantics) that in life-history theory make predictions possible.

Semantic Axiom. The basis for valid life-history assessment lies in shared social meanings rather than in technical knowledge. This axiom calls for a totally new direction in assessment theory and research. It holds that formal knowledge of psychological and other behavioral-science principles, facts, and procedures does not facilitate assessment. It assumes that a judge already possesses a knowledge of human nature by virtue of having learned the language, norms, and values of a culture. This knowledge facilitates assessment. This semantic or social-meaning axiom was developed through the concept that events are mutually revealing. Life history is seen as a structure of events, a network of semantic relations. Events mean one another in the sense of the cue structure described in the lens model of Kenneth Hammond, Carolyn Hursch, and Frederick Todd (1964). Thus, the ability to predict events is interpreted as reasoning along lines shown in the network of events. This view of the life history is expressed in the following postulates: (1) When judges interpret life histories, they use events as cues to other events. (2) Judges with similar origins, positions, and experience in a social system will tend to agree upon cue structure better than judges with dissimilar origins, positions, and experience. (3) Event (cue) structure is the primary basis for valid prediction in life-history assessment.

What is termed *role* would be a special case of such event structure. A person in a certain role is governed by expectations of his behavior; a judge thus can know what kinds of behavioral events are likely. "Taking the role of the other" means that a judge knows what role expectations the person is probably fulfilling, and hence the judge can predict.

Learning Axiom. Life-history assessment is a learning process in which increments of data lead to increasingly valid inferences and in which a judge's skill is transferred from case to case. While this is a commonsense axiom, the fact is that, empirically, prediction does not indefinitely increase, and we must consider those forces that cause it to level off. One factor is probably the judge's confidence. In a programed case, judges were required to make predictions for which some believe they lack sufficient evidence. Probably they would not have attempted the predictions if the cases did not compel them to do so. However, other investigators have reported that clinicians often have too much confidence in their impressions (that is, confidence unwarranted by their validity). In brief, there is a disparity—it can be in either direction—between confidence and validity. That disparity is involved in the clinical paradox of which Sarbin, Taft, and Bailey (1960, p. 252) speak: "As a thinking, flexible clinician I can sample more occurrences in the ecology than the nonthinking inflexible prediction table or equation, yet the degree of credibility that may be attached to my inferences (as tested through the confirmation of my predictions) is no higher, and frequently lower." I suspect that this paradox results from the clinician's belief in the axiom; he observes that his information about a person has increased and therefore concludes that he *knows* more about that person; his confidence rises with the amount of information he receives. He may be quite shaken to discover that he is in error. In everyday life, a parallel may be drawn to the shock one receives when a couple, close friends for many years, suddenly divorce. The assumption of knowledge from sheer volume of information is very strong. And yet it is impossible to believe that the predictive accuracy of a judge will rise indefinitely. The leveling mechanism suggested is this: The image of the person under assessment would be (ideally) reorganized every time a new fact is obtained. However, as confidence in one's knowledge of another person rises, new data are increasingly ignored (that is, confidence increases). When clinicians or other judges fixate their images very early (Dailey, 1952; Webster, 1964), they resist additional data and thereafter achieve only a modest degree of accuracy. However, the accuracy (versus data) curve may sometimes rise very quickly early in a case, and thus there is some very solid encouragement given to judges who make up their minds quickly. In this way, prejudice is reinforced. This fixation effect could be reduced by disrupting the judge's confidence; in the programed case, we disrupted confidence by immediate notification of errors. Given this process, the judge in the programed case should be able to exemplify the learning axiom (that accuracy results from amount of information) better than a judge using an unprogramed case. This reciprocal relation between confidence and validity is shown in Figure 11; the area below the curve represents the judge's validity of understanding. In addition to this conjecture about confidence as a disruptive factor in interpersonal learning, we also suggest that the reinforcement of valid prediction develops an attitude that is transferred from case to case. We have called this attitude event orientation (the belief that events are important and worth predicting). This attitude is not only scientific but also humanistic because it implies that a judge values knowing what *has* happened to a person and cares what *will* happen to him in the future. We thus find ourselves unable to separate science and humanism in the concrete task of understanding a person's life. The learning axiom is expressed in the following postulates: (1) The more events a judge knows, the more accurate his inferences of unknown events, up to a point. (2) As information increases, an impression of the assessed person develops that resists further modification. This resistance is introspectively felt as confidence. The point at which an impression totally resists further modification marks the beginning of a learning plateau, or cessation of the process described in postulate 1 above. (3) When judges are given feedback, the learning plateau is postponed; without feedback

Figure 11

False Confidence and Validity

Validity is represented by area under the curve. Actual validity is shaded.
Potential validity is shaded area plus area A.

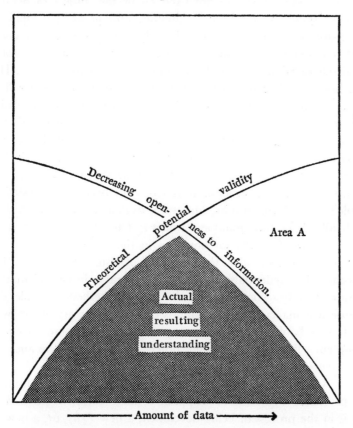

the learning plateau may occur quite early. (4) When judges are given feedback, they become increasingly oriented to knowing events and will generalize this attitude to subsequent life histories. This event orientation is held to facilitate assessment.

FORECAST FOR ASSESSMENT

Ordinarily, issues in assessment theory are kept separate from social and political issues. This separation can no longer be justified. We may anticipate, at best, unremitting pressure to alter such assessment practices, where they are accessible to pressures (for example, college admissions, employment practices, and welfare casework). It would be good—for once—if the *other* points at which assessment is unjust or lacking in empathy could receive our attention even though they are not likely to be the subject of demonstrations, building occupations, lawsuits, and political campaigns. These situations include psychiatric judgment, psychological assessment, counseling of all kinds, the work of parole officials, professional school admissions, and the granting of research money. History, however, does not inspire us with the hope that there will be much reform without pressure. On that basis we can probably anticipate about twenty-five years (until the present generation of decision makers retire) more with traditional systems of clinical and credentials assessment. On the other hand, certain features in life-history assessment encourage more hope than this. One is its greater intrinsic interest. In general, it is easier to become interested in people's lives (in biography, literature, drama) than in the technical details of the traditional assessment systems.

A second reason for hope lies in the current rapid pace of some social change and in the argument of historical necessity. The assessment by credentials has become intolerable in critical matters because it is too conservative; the clinical method is intolerable because it is inaccurate. These faults comprised the arguments with which this book began. They require that some new system of assessment—life history or some other—be developed because the old systems are no longer tolerable.

A third reason for hope of fast reform is the rise of a humanistic psychology. Maslow (1970, p. 29) said: "A new *Weltanschauung* is in the process of being developed, a new *Zeitgeist,* a new set of values and a new way of finding them, and certainly a new image of man. There is a new kind of psychology—presently called the humanistic, existential, third-force psychology—that at this transitional moment is certainly different in many important ways from the Freudian and behavioristic psychologies, which have been the two great comprehensive, dominating psychologies."

However, many humanistic psychologists have placed their interest in the spontaneous here-and-now manifestations of personality such as emerge in sensitivity training or encounter groups; they are correspondingly less interested in research such as ours. This book's perspective lies between the old psychologies and the new; and, like all compromises, life-history assessment may satisfy neither of the extremes it mediates. The experimenter in life-history assessment uses traditional means of measurement, in rigorous designs, to determine whether a judge understands the person being assessed. A judge uses his creative powers to meet standards of both humanistic understanding (or empathic appreciation of a life) and scientific prediction. The assessed person reports his life with the help of an assessment judge. Through the imposition of some discipline on the interaction among these three partners in exploring the possibilities and probabilities of human life, we hope to see new knowledge emerge. Thus assessment science will not mark a complete break with the past, as does humanistic psychology in so many ways, but neither will it be bound by the intolerable restrictions and shortcomings of the old assessment systems.

✿✿✿✿ PART II ✿✿✿✿

PROGRAMED
CASE STUDIES

✿✿✿✿✿✿✿✿✿✿✿✿✿✿✿✿✿✿✿✿✿✿✿✿✿

Several variations upon the programed case methodology are possible. Four are presented in the following chapters. Each model does different things. The news commentator (Chapter Ten) is the form on which we have relied most completely in research. Such a programed case trains and measures. The disadvantaged youth (Chapter Eleven) measures inference-making in a simulated clinical task. It does not train because it does not provide immediate feedback. The Colombian peon (Chapter Twelve) provides immediate feedback, but, as the data are not presented in increments and the inferences are elicited at irregular points, the case cannot yield reliable measurement in its present form. Therefore it is a teaching case. The sales supervisor (Chapter Thirteen) measures inference-making in a simulated personnel task. It provides some feedback but not enough to classify it as a teaching case.

In using such cases to measure inference-making, "zero-level" inferences must be determined. As explained in Chapter Five, this is done by having judges make inferences without any information. Then the case is administered to obtain norms showing how well judges do when they do have various amounts of data beyond the zero level. In practice, we have measured only two levels of

169

*amount—zero level and whatever amount is known in the case up
to the point of inference.*

    *When programed cases containing feedback are adminis-
tered, the obvious caution is to separate the feedback from the inference. The judge makes the inference, and the feedback either is
covered up or is withheld until the next page. For example, in the
news commentator (Chapter Ten), the back of each page is left
blank in reproduction. In the Colombian peon (Chapter Eleven),
pages are usually ended with each inference elicited from the judge.
Then the feedback is given in the immediately following page,
either at the top of the next page or preferably where it cannot be
seen at all.*

    *A variety of scores can be computed from such cases. The
news commentator format yields the most rich variety. The total
score (number right) and the idiographic learning curve (number
right in each third of the case) are the most frequently used statistical results. The disadvantaged youth case yields two kinds of scores
—inference-making (number of correct choices made in predicting
antisocial tendencies) and frame of reference. The theory of frame
of reference is outlined in the discussion of the concept of scenario-
writing in Chapter Seven. Caution should be used in developing
scoring for the Colombian peon case for reasons explained above.
The sales supervisor case is scored by the ratings made identical to
his boss's opinions. We stress that, in the sales supervisor case, the
criteria are only opinions and not facts, as in the other cases. At
this point in personnel research, it is difficult to do without ratings
in appraising performance.*

    *Several problems emerge in using such cases. In general, they
are remarkably self-explanatory; even Korean high school students
were able to respond to the translated version without difficulty.
Some judges believe the facts of the cases are wrong because they
do not appear consistent or logically derived from the preceding
facts. The answer to this is that the judge should rather look to the
validity of his implicit theory, and, in any event, the cases are not
written as self-consistent fiction. Rather, the inevitable discontinu-
ities of life are let stand. A second problem is in recognition of the
person; some judges recognize the news commentator. The answer
may be to do the case anyway but mark it as recognized. Such*

recognition does not always help and the instruction should be given, "Proceed to make the inferences from these data and forget your outside knowledge of the case if possible."

The news commentator case was prepared from many sources. Since Murrow is a public figure, his life is largely a matter of record and to that extent is readily authenticated. The case of the disadvantaged youth was compiled from original interviews confirmed by social and law agency verification. To judges who wonder whether disadvantage can be this severe, I answer that as far as I can tell, this case is not atypical of the ones seen by the U.S. Employment Service. The peon, Alberto, was interviewed in Colombia, but this case was not authenticated; however, I believe him. The sales supervisor's data (and the opinions of his boss) were collected through interviewing by a conscientious investigator under my supervision in a company I know well.

Programed Case: News Commentator

This man is a news commentator. You will be reading a short account of his life. However, instead of reading an ordinary, straight-forward life history, you will follow a special procedure designed to help you see how well you understand him as a human being.

On each page, there are several incidents, lettered A, B and C. Any one of these incidents could plausibly have occurred in his life. Your job is to decide which incident *did* happen.

It is necessary that you not read ahead, and that you make a decision before you go on to each next page. Then at the top of each page, you will be told which of the incidents which you have just reviewed on the preceding page was actually true of the person's life.

As a result of this procedure, you will experience a gradual improvement in understanding this man. However, do not be discouraged if your understanding is inaccurate during the first few pages.

If the procedure is clear to you, please turn the page and begin.

CHOOSE THE TRUE EPISODE:

A₁   When he was five years old, the family recalls, his brothers
      were having their pictures taken in their new go-to-school
      clothes. He dashed into the scene and insisted on being
      in the picture too.

B₁   His earliest memories are of an austere Maine boyhood, when
      he hardly knew his studious father. He remembers splitting
      kindling early in the brisk fall mornings. He observed that
      his mother rose early, worked long hours, uncomplaining,
      loyal, persevering. Today it is difficult for him to sympathize
      with the ignorant or the idle.

C₁   As a sickly eleven-year-old, he showed precocious talent by
      compiling a children's encyclopedia from John Ridpath's
      CYCLOPEDIA OF UNIVERSAL HISTORY. Sample con-
      tents: "All the necessary statistics of the world"; "World
      battleships."

MAKE YOUR CHOICE BEFORE YOU TURN THE PAGE

If You Chose A₁: You were correct. When he was five years old, the family recalls his brothers were having their pictures taken in their new go-to-school clothes. He dashed into the scene and insisted on being in the picture, too.

CHOOSE THE TRUE EPISODE:

A₂   Until he went to college, his mother used to read the family a chapter out of the Bible every night and wanted him to become a preacher. But he had no interest in the ministry.

B₂   Hard circumstances compelled him to leave school in the seventh grade. Thereafter, his education, according to his statement, was gained in the "school of hard knocks." And in his chosen occupation, that proved to be a hard school indeed.

C₂   By the time he was fifteen, his inventive ability had blossomed. One winter morning, he appeared with an elaborate map of the world, the two hemispheres being shown side by side. He had drawn it in ink on paper, then had pasted the paper on linen, and finally had placed it on two varnished rollers. Everyone was astonished.

MAKE YOUR CHOICE BEFORE YOU TURN THE PAGE

If You Chose A₂: You were correct. Until he went to college, his mother used to read the family a chapter out of the Bible every night and wanted him to become a preacher. But he had no interest in the ministry.

CHOOSE THE TRUE EPISODE:

A₃   When he was 19, his home seemed crowded and he felt the call of the West—the mining fields! His mother recognized his restlessness and aided him with money. With a party of about 30, he started overland. Most of the Model-T's broke down, but the husky youth persisted and reached his goal on schedule.

B₃   In high school, he was voted most popular boy and graduated at the head of his class. In college, he was a successful campus politician, a speech major, actor, debater, cadet colonel, and made Phi Beta Kappa.

C₃   At Georgia Tech, he was an all-American quarterback known for his gift of gab and exploits with the campus belles. His classmates and professors remember him as having "a winning personality, a forceful manner, a booming voice," as the college yearbook put it.

MAKE YOUR CHOICE BEFORE YOU TURN THE PAGE

If You Chose B₃: You were correct. In high school he was voted most popular boy and graduated at the head of his class. In college he was a successful campus politician, a speech major, actor, debater, cadet colonel and made Phi Beta Kappa.

CHOOSE THE TRUE EPISODE:

A₄   He was graduated during the dark days of the depression. It was a bitter come-down for the brilliant student—the world did not seem to be waiting for him with an armful of opportunities. He found himself lucky to get a job at the soda counter. With his customary adaptability, he threw himself into hard work, but he didn't much care for the tedious duties and he got out of it as soon as he could.

B₄   His first job after college involved arranging inexpensive European tours for American college students. His second included arranging for international exchanges of graduate students. During this work, he toured Hitler's Germany and was active in a committee that helped several hundred German scholars escape the country.

C₄   After college, he went into newspaper work. Twelve years of work on the City Desk gave him a firsthand acquaintance with fundamentals. It was tedious, and a sharp come-down for a brilliant youngster anxious to make his mark on a waiting world. But he put up with it, on the advice of his elders. Later he admitted, "It was the best discipline I've ever had. Things had always come too easily."

MAKE YOUR CHOICE BEFORE YOU TURN THE PAGE

If You Chose B₄: You were correct. His first job after college involved arranging inexpensive European tours for American college students. His second included arranging for international exchanges of graduate students. During this work, he toured Hitler's Germany and was active in a committee that helped several hundred German scholars escape the country.

CHOOSE THE TRUE EPISODE:

A₅   While stationed in London during the worst of the bombing he insisted that his office be near a building that was a prime target with the result his office was bombed out four times.

B₅   Under the guise of scholarship, he got himself a wartime deferment to do graduate study in political science. While others were fighting, he was studying for his master's degree. When asked about this later, he explained that this was necessary for his contributions in the field of propaganda.

C₅   He conceived a thirst for action and joined the Marines. One of the top men in "boot camp," he was later selected for officers' training. He turned down several opportunities to take an easier war-time job, and made several amphibious landings in the Pacific. He was wounded twice.

MAKE YOUR CHOICE BEFORE YOU TURN THE PAGE

If You Chose A₅: You were correct. While stationed in London during the worst of the bombing, he insisted that his office be near a building that was a prime target with the result his office was bombed out four times.

CHOOSE THE TRUE EPISODE:

A₆   It was not surprising that he became a leading advocate of improved public bomb shelters. He served on a committee to locate suitable underground sites in London, and to persuade the owners to let their property be used.

B₆   When his London dispatches were excessively censored, he resigned and went into a defense industry in New Jersey. He became the top expediter for war materials procurement in the manufacture of torpedoes. He said he was glad to get out of the "writing end" of the war, and into something more tangible for a while. The experience became invaluable to him later, when he served as an investigator of war contracts for a congressional committee.

C₆   During World War II, although his job did not require it, he went on at least 25 bombing missions. His superiors protested his taking such risks as a civilian. One colleague said, "At first I thought he was afraid of being a coward—but it was more complicated than that."

MAKE YOUR CHOICE BEFORE YOU TURN THE PAGE

If You Chose C₆: You were correct. During World War II, although his job did not require it, he went on at least 25 bombing missions. His superiors protested his taking such risks as a civilian. One colleague said, "At first I thought he was afraid of being a coward—but it was more complicated than that."

CHOOSE THE TRUE EPISODE:

A₇   In his career since the war, he has distinguished himself through his services to veterans' organizations. He can't seem to get over the feeling that he should have served in uniform, but didn't.

B₇   In business life since the war, he has become well known for his tact. Hauled before Congressional committees to explain some postwar military contracts, his bearing was notably calm even under the most significant heckling. At one point, practically accused of collusion by the most *acid* of his hecklers, he drew applause from the gallery when he quietly replied, "Senator, we have facts for you to see which will unquestionably change your views."

C₇   Since the war, in his career he has acted with an independence seldom permitted in business. A friend once commented, "He always stands to be counted when the issue is big enough. And he never misses a chance to stand up for the principle of dissent."

MAKE YOUR CHOICE BEFORE YOU TURN THE PAGE

If You Chose C_7: You were correct. Since the war, in his career he has acted with an independence seldom permitted in business. A friend once commented, "He always stands up to be counted when the issue is big enough. And he never misses a chance to stand up for the principle of dissent."

CHOOSE THE TRUE EPISODE:

A_8 During the postwar period when most liberal politicians and commentators were ignoring or minimizing the menace of world Communism, he was a standout for his penetrating and lucid columns exposing the various "front" organizations.

B_8 During the height of Senator Joe McCarthy's power, when even the Army feared him, and no man's career was safe if McCarthy needled him, this man was the first of national prominence to criticize and expose McCarthy's tactics.

C_8 He objected fiercely to the rapid demobilization pushed by Congress right after the war. He called for the occupation of Berlin in force, for stronger military support for China, and for maintaining a posture of strength facing the Communists at every point.

MAKE YOUR CHOICE BEFORE YOU TURN THE PAGE

If You Chose B₈: You were correct. During the height of Senator Joe McCarthy's power, when even the Army feared him and no man's career was safe if McCarthy needled him, this man was the first of national prominence to criticize and expose McCarthy's tactics.

CHOOSE THE TRUE EPISODE:

A₉   In his business transactions, he is brief and to the point. He has the reputation of holding the shortest contract conferences in either Hollywood or New York. His secretary says, "He would rather shave a thousand or two than get into an argument. He thinks it ungentlemanly to debate money matters."

B₉   In business he was known for his penetrating approach to problems and his sharp eye for finances. He had the reputation of being able to look over a complex profit-and-loss statement in a few seconds, and pinpoint the excessive losses which "just didn't look right." The network consulted him regularly, before planning major policy changes or new expensive programing. And he had a sharp "hatchet."

C₉   Of his business activities, he once said, "When other VPs come and say, 'Look, expenses are too high; there's so much going out your spout and not enough coming in,' I answer, 'If that's the way you want to do things, you'd better get yourself another boy.'"

MAKE YOUR CHOICE BEFORE YOU TURN THE PAGE

If You Chose C_9:   You were correct. Of his business activities, he once said, "When other VPs come and say, 'Look, expenses are too high; there's so much coming out your spout and not enough coming in,' I answer, 'If that's the way you want to do things, you'd better get yourself another boy.' "

CHOOSE THE TRUE EPISODE:

A_{10} He likes to play poker, but he refuses to stay in a game if the betting limit goes above a dollar. He plays slowly and frequently delays the game because he cannot make quick decisions.

B_{10} He plays a good game of poker, but late in the game he usually gets impatient and overbets his hands, comes out a big loser. He has been known to bet $2,500 on the turn of a single card.

C_{10} Poker for him is just one more chance to produce some new games from his treasure house of wit. He can't take any game seriously, and in particular, poker. He bets his chips heavily, loses early, and then sits back and talks while the others play.

MAKE YOUR CHOICE BEFORE YOU TURN THE PAGE

If You Chose B$_{10}$:   You were correct. He plays a good game of poker, but late in the game usually gets impatient and overbets his hands, comes out a big loser. He has been known to bet $2,500 on the turn of a single card.

CHOOSE THE TRUE EPISODE:

A$_{11}$ He was noted in the organization for pacing himself. His closest friend said of him, "He seemed to know when and how to roll with every punch. I never knew him to push himself—or anybody else—to excess. Moderation seemed to be the keynote."

B$_{11}$ The key word to describe his approach to work: DRIVE. His department was aptly described as "a beehive of activity." Yet, withal, he always took time for the minor courtesies of business life and insisted that every desk in the department be closed at five.

C$_{11}$ Sometimes he works around the clock for three or four days and nights at a time. The chairman of the board of directors of his company says, "You could almost call it (the tendency to work to exhaustion) a drive to self-destruction. He's never happy unless he's working. When he looks like death, that's when he feels a happy glow."

MAKE YOUR CHOICE BEFORE YOU TURN THE PAGE

If You Chose C_{11}: You were correct. Sometimes he works around the clock for three or four days and nights at a time. The chairman of the board of directors of his company says, "You could almost call it (the tendency to work to exhaustion) a drive to self-destruction. He's never happy unless he's working. When he looks like death, that's when he feels a happy glow."

CHOOSE THE TRUE EPISODE:

A_{12} He constantly worries about the effect of long hours on his health. The worry seems to be justified—he loses about two months a year primarily from respiratory ailments. He believes the respiratory troubles go back to the nights he spent in bomb shelters in London.

B_{12} He is annoyed when anyone asks about the number of hours he puts in. The subject seems to be a sore spot at home, and he would rather not discuss it.

C_{12} In describing his work schedule to a friend, he once wrote, "I hope the foregoing answers your question regarding my health although what it reveals about my sanity may be another question. As far as strenuous work is concerned I can do no better than to quote you a comment made by mother, who said, 'It is better to wear out than to rust out.' "

MAKE YOUR CHOICE BEFORE YOU TURN THE PAGE

If You Chose C$_{12}$:   You were correct. In describing his work schedule to a friend, he once wrote, "I hope the foregoing answers your question regarding my health although what it reveals about my sanity may be another question. As far as strenuous work is concerned, I can do no better than to quote you a comment made by my mother, 'It is better to wear out than to rust out.' "

CHOOSE THE TRUE EPISODE:

A$_{13}$ His modesty and general business deportment are such that he is really well-known only within his own company. But he is one of the ten most powerful men in the country—according to the "insiders." He was asked if this were true. He laughed and said, "I wouldn't know."

B$_{13}$ He rose to the top. His colleagues, exasperated by his sudden world fame and power within his company, organized a "He ain't God Club." He immediately applied for membership.

C$_{13}$ In spite of his earlier reputation, his present semi-retirement has led to a rapid fading from the public scene. Who knows him today? Friends say it is a bit pathetic to see the "great man" drop around to see who will remember him—and the younger people don't look twice at the face which once graced ten million television screens.

MAKE YOUR CHOICE BEFORE YOU TURN THE PAGE

If You Chose B_{13}: You were correct. He rose to the top. His colleagues, exasperated by his sudden world fame and power within his company, organized a "He ain't God Club." He immediately applied for membership.

CHOOSE THE TRUE EPISODE:

A_{14} He hates to hear the word retirement mentioned. He says that he has been busy so long that he would not know how to benefit from leisure.

B_{14} For several years he talked about becoming inactive—about quitting work for six months or a year, "just to keep silent and listen to myself." But few people took him seriously because almost in the next breath he would start outlining some major new project he wanted to get under way. Then he did quit—became semi-retired.

C_{14} In recent years, he has gradually and very sensibly cut down on his work. At the present, he spends six months at Acapulco, three months in the Berkshires in New England, and three months as a consultant in the company.

MAKE YOUR CHOICE BEFORE YOU TURN THE PAGE

If You Chose B₁₄: You were correct. For several years, he talked about becoming inactive—about quitting work for six months or a year, "just to keep silent and listen to myself." But few people took him seriously because almost in the next breath he would start outlining some major new project he wanted to get under way. Then he did quit—became semi-retired.

CHOOSE THE TRUE EPISODE:

A₁₅   He has a mole on his right cheek which he refuses to have removed or disguised—and almost invariably insists on being photographed from his right side. Although he wears expensive suits and shirts custom-made and imported from Saville Row in London, he usually covers his finery with an old raincoat or trenchcoat.

B₁₅   This man is heavy, six feet tall. While his characteristic expression is one of purposefulness and force, the basset hound features break into a grin of delight when he sees something he likes or really admires. This happens about twenty-five times a day; the causes being: pretty girls, a good profit-and-loss statement, or a new job—in that order.

C₁₅   He is smallish, a conservative dresser, and the possessor of a deep bass voice and a dry, often penetrating wit. Unostentatious, he drives to his office in a three-year-old Ford, likes to watch baseball games in season, and bowls when baseball is not in season.

MAKE YOUR CHOICE BEFORE YOU TURN THE PAGE

If You Chose A$_{15}$: You were correct. He has a mole on his right cheek which he refuses to have removed or disguised—and almost invariably insists on being photographed from his right side. Although he wears expensive suits and shirts custom-made and imported from Saville Row in London, he usually covers his finery with an old raincoat or trenchcoat.

This completes the case based on episodes from the life of Edward R. Murrow.

11

Programed Case: Disadvantaged Youth

✿✿✿✿✿✿✿✿✿✿✿✿✿✿✿✿✿✿✿✿✿

The following case is based on authentic data. Although "Richard" gave his permission for the case to be used, and was paid a fee, we have changed the names, dates, and places to protect his identity. However, we believe that none of the essentials of the case have been changed.

We have "programed" the case study in such a way that you can record your analyses and inferences. Then you can later go back and verify or disprove them, in the light of the additional evidence. For full satisfaction to you, then, you will want to follow the programing carefully, avoiding any reading ahead.

Richard's mother says that he pretended to be sick in order to stay out of school. She remembers that once, when Richard was a small boy, she called him repeatedly one day; he would not answer. She found him within easy hearing distance. Before she had a chance to scold him for not answering, he said, "Well, Mother, you know I can't hear you. Why do you call me?"

A memory from early childhood: a laundry truck ran over his dog and killed her and supposedly the puppies she was about to bear. He now says, "Every time I see a laundry truck, I get burned

190

up about it. I get mad. I want to start punching somebody in the mouth and cussing." At other times, he has told his counselor that he gets into fights with laundry truck drivers.

Richard admits playing hooky. Once when he left school, his father happened to be passing by and asked why he was leaving. Richard told him that the teachers kicked him out. His father later checked up, found the story was not true, and whipped him. In recounting this story, Richard says that the real reason he left school was that he was sick and had a temperature of 103°. He never gave that explanation to his father. When asked why not, he shakes his head and does not reply.

He remembers by name several teachers (including coaches) whom he disliked intensely. He says that the coaches would swat him for the "least little thing," such as being a little late or being out of order in class. Richard says that some of his teachers were kind, understanding, and patient. They took time to explain his work to him. He can not remember the names of these teachers.

Richard asked in school to be seated on the front row so that he could see the blackboard. "I got 25 in the right eye and 200 in the left eye. One time I was 400% blind." A report in 1967 from the MD states that his right eye is 20/20 and left eye is 20/200. Richard says the vision in his left eye is all blurred (although he can see color). However, he willingly demonstrated his ability to read the smallest print on a street map, with his right eye.

NOW RECORD YOUR OPINIONS IN REGARD TO THE FOLLOWING INFERENCES:

(1) *about ability to get a job.*

☐ a. The odds are very slight (1 in 5) that he can get a job.
☐ b. The odds are about 50/50 that he can get a job.
☐ c. Very favorable possibilities that he can get a job if counseled properly.

(2) *about ability to hold a job if he gets one* (choose one).

☐ a. The odds are very slight (1 in 5) that he can hold it.
☐ b. The odds are about 50/50 that he will hold it.
☐ c. Very favorable possibilities that he can hold on to some kind of job.

(3) *about his response to a sustained training program* (choose one).

☐ a. The odds are very slight (1 in 5) that he will complete it and learn anything from it.

☐ b. The odds are about 50/50 that he will either get something out of the training or complete it or both.

☐ c. Very favorable possibility that he will stay with it if he gets the breaks.

(4) *about his health:*

CHECK YOUR OPINIONS:

	No	Maybe no	Maybe yes	Yes
a. He is profoundly ill emotionally, and is quite beyond counseling help.	☐	☐	☐	☐
b. He is emotionally ill, but can probably be helped by a counselor.	☐	☐	☐	☐
c. There is definite evidence of a motivation to grow which will enable him to overcome his emotional problems.	☐	☐	☐	☐
d. He has a minor physical defect. If it were corrected, it would make a major difference in his vocational and educational status.	☐	☐	☐	☐
e. His "physical impairments" are largely malingering, and he is using them as an excuse.	☐	☐	☐	☐

(5) *about antisocial tendencies, if any:*

	No	Maybe no	Maybe yes	Yes
a. He is deceitful and dishonest in small things.	☐	☐	☐	☐

	No	Maybe no	Maybe yes	Yes
b. Physical violence toward others.	☐	☐	☐	☐
c. Physical violence toward himself.	☐	☐	☐	☐
d. Plays hooky.	☐	☐	☐	☐
e. Obedient and compliant.	☐	☐	☐	☐
f. Commits sexual offense.	☐	☐	☐	☐
g. Engages in heavy drinking under conditions leading to arrest (drinking, fighting, etc.).	☐	☐	☐	☐
h. Is accident prone.	☐	☐	☐	☐
i. Runs away from home.	☐	☐	☐	☐

Richard took an R.O.T.C. examination while in high school. He recalls, "There was about four or five of us privates and I was in there beatin' my brains out trying to pass the test. [Later] when I was in there in the office I looked at my record and there was a big mark there: PASSED. My brother, he got a higher grade than I did, so he got the stripe [Private, first class]. Everybody got the rank but me."

Richard was in classes for slow learners and was moved up on the basis of age rather than accomplishment. He dropped out of high school early in 1964, at the age of 16. He started to another high school, but dropped out there, early in 1965. Tests indicate that at age 19 his educational level is that of a second grader.

Richard tells the counselors that his parents are his best friends and do everything they can to help him. However, he then goes on to blame them for not defending him against the criticisms of an uncle. The uncle asks Richard if he thinks he is "too good to get out and go to work?"

According to the counselors, Richard's relationship to his

father is stormy. Mr. Huntley has on several occasions threatened to kick Richard out of the home. Usually the explosion comes over Richard's failure to find and keep a job.

Richard's father has had a wide assortment of jobs. During World War II, he was an auto mechanic in the Army. At times he has attempted to operate his own garage. The last such venture ended in bankruptcy about a year ago. At other times, he has worked at a bottling plant, a canning factory, and on labor crews. At the present he changes filters in air conditioning systems. He is barely literate.

Richard's relation to his mother is close. She appears to try to understand his problems. She encourages him to find employment and stick to it. However, she says that he pretends to be sick in order to avoid looking for a job.

You have just reviewed a number of facts about Richard's life history. You will, from this, have some impression of the social relationships in his life. By making the following Sociometric analysis, you can register that impression.

SOCIOMETRIC

On the diagram [Figure 12], write in the names of the individuals who are important to this person. These might also be broadened to indicate groups of individuals. Let the solid connecting lines on the diagram represent a hostile or rejecting relationship (if any); and the dotted lies, an affectionate relationship (if any). On each such line, write a word or phrase that appears to you to characterize the relationship. Add any other lines or remarks that appear to you to clarify the immediate social world of this person. There may be unlabelled lines when you are finished (those on which you do not feel you have any evidence).

Among the persons who are sometimes significant to a youth might be any or all of the following:

—mother	—celebrity or hero
—father	—teacher(s)
—brother(s)	—professor
—sister(s)	—boss(es)
	—priest, rabbi, minister
—physician(s)	—friend (opposite sex)

Figure 12

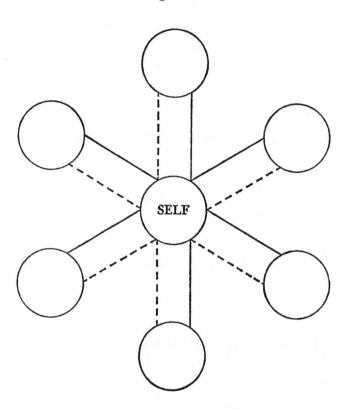

—pet or toy   —others unique in the case
—club or group or friend   —imaginaries

APPRAISAL

What do you now think of this person? What does he want out of life or work? What is he willing to give? What risks will he take? What are his chances? In the following two columns, list his principal assets or strengths and his principal liabilities or weaknesses. Please number them for convenience in later reference.

Strengths   *Weaknesses*

1. ....   1. ....
2. ....   2. ....
   ....

--   --
--   --
--   --

Which of these strengths do you believe that this person is aware of? #............. Which of his weaknesses do you think he is aware of? #..............

PROGNOSIS

Can this person, at the age of 19, be effectively counseled?

☐   a. Definitely not.

☐   b. There is a 50/50 chance to help him, provided

....
....
....

☐   c. There is *some* chance to help him, provided

....
....

Please write here any special definition of counseling you think it necessary to offer, if you believe your prognosis might be otherwise misunderstood: ....
....
....

NOW RECORD YOUR OPINIONS IN REGARD TO THE FOLLOWING INFERENCES:

(1) *about ability to get a job* (choose one)
    ☐   a. The odds are very slight (1 in 5) that he can get a job.
    ☐   b. The odds are about 50/50 that he can get a job.
    ☐   c. Very favorable possibilities that he can get a job if counseled properly.

(2) *about ability to hold a job if he gets one* (choose one)
    ☐   a. The odds are very slight (1 in 5) that he can hold it.
    ☐   b. The odds are about 50/50 that he will hold it.
    ☐   c. Very favorable possibilities that he can hold on to some kind of job.

(3) *about his response to a sustained training program* (choose one)
- ☐ a. The odds are very slight (1 in 5) that he will complete it and learn anything from it.
- ☐ b. The odds are about 50/50 that he will either get something out of the training or complete it or both.
- ☐ c. Very favorable possibility that he will stay with it if he gets the breaks.

CHECK YOUR OPINIONS:

(4) *about his health*

	No	Maybe no	Maybe yes	Yes
a. He is profoundly ill emotionally, and is quite beyond counseling help.	☐	☐	☐	☐
b. He is emotionally ill but can probably be helped by a counselor.	☐	☐	☐	☐
c. There is definite evidence of a motivation to grow which will enable him to overcome his emotional problems.	☐	☐	☐	☐
d. He has a minor physical defect. If it were corrected, it would make a major difference in his vocational and educational status.	☐	☐	☐	☐
e. His "physical impairments" are largely malingering, and he is using them as an excuse.	☐	☐	☐	☐

(5) *about antisocial tendencies, if any:*

	No	Maybe no	Maybe yes	Yes
a. He is deceitful and dishonest in small things.	☐	☐	☐	☐

	No	Maybe no	Maybe yes	Yes
b. Physical violence toward others.	□	□	□	□
c. Physical violence toward self.	□	□	□	□
d. Plays hooky.	□	□	□	□
e. Obedient and compliant.	□	□	□	□
f. Commits sexual offense.	□	□	□	□
g. Engages in heavy drinking under conditions leading to arrest (drinking, fighting, etc.).	□	□	□	□
h. Is accident prone.	□	□	□	□
i. Runs away from home.	□	□	□	□

His job history is roughly as follows. When his father had a garage and parking lot, Richard was his helper and washed cars. Then he was a dishwasher at a hotel. His boss there rode him—"said I wasn't fast enough. . . . I almost broke half the dishes going fast as I could." He worked then at a cafeteria, but lasted only a half day. One of the kitchen employees there said, "Richard wasn't a bad kid, but he seemed afraid, hesitant, and unable to wash dishes and do other work. He took a lot of time and even then the work wasn't half done. The boss told Richard he didn't need to come back."

Richard got a job at a food processing plant, but did not last the day. He suffered a severe sprain of his hand when he got it caught in a conveyor. He worked for a week as a bus boy at the restaurant of a large department store. Richard's account is that he told his boss he would not empty the garbage because it contained glass. They got into a heated argument. Finally, the boss emptied the garbage and fired Richard.

Once he worked in a grocery store for a childless couple who treated him as if he were their own son, as he recalls. He says that his work there was considered good and that he left only because the couple went out of business. He cannot give their name, location of the store, or describe the work he did for them.

At the Job Corps Center, the counselor wrote, "Richard has made no effort to participate in class activities. He has attended vocational class once, academic class once, and never has attended P.E." Richard says that he went to reading, electrical maintenance, and mathematics classes regularly. He admits that he did not attend "P.G." (he means P.E., or Physical Education).

Richard went to the H. Job Corps Center late in 1965. After his first month there, he asked to quit. The counselor talked to him, took his statement and then arranged for him to sign the following statement. "I just can't take this kind of living. I stuck it out for the 30 days like everybody asked me to, but I just don't like it." On the Job Corps Counselor's urging, Richard stayed for another month, but was homesick and permitted to leave at the end of the second month.

Richard tells of fights he has had with his brother, boys in the neighborhood, other students. His mother says, "Richard has a temper but he has arguments, not fights." The records of the local police say nothing about Richard except that he ran away from home once. This is a high crime rate area.

Richard often talks to his counselors about weapons. He has a young friend who works nights at a funeral home. He says the friend is under instructions to check the nine doors of the funeral home regularly, and to draw his .38 revolver each time before he opens the door.

He says that he was a junior deputy sheriff when in the Job Corps, and carried a billy club and a .38. He says he used the club in helping break up a riot at the camp.

He often talks about drums. In the Job Corps, he says he helped organize a band. Richard was the drummer and leader. He says the band played at dances and once for President Johnson. He and the other musicians got to shake the President's hand and he gave them a picnic at which they ate and ate and ate.

Richard claims that he has 13 girl friends. He can easily

strike up a conversation with a girl he does not know. In sharp contrast, Richard implies, his brother is terribly timid and cannot talk
to girls. When questioned for specifics, Richard names one girl
friend. She is a patient at the mental hospital.

The counselor has referred Richard to numerous employers.
However, he reports, "Richard sometimes lies to me. He tells me he
tries to get the jobs but does not. He fakes illness a lot."

Richard's hopes for the future include: becoming a glider
pilot; soldier in Vietnam; enrolling in a Federal program for farm
labor trainees (he can't get in until he can read and write at a
higher level); becoming a security guard. He talks most often about
the Guard and about the .38 revolvers guards carry. He would
rather be a policeman like one of his uncles, but he cannot because
he does not have a high school diploma.

Richard says that he wants a night job. That is when all of
the exciting things happen. He also likes the idea of then being able
to sleep days.

When Richard was flying home from the Job Corps Center,
according to his account, a woman passenger on the plane gave birth
to twins. The stewardess went into hysterics and Richard took over
and delivered the twins. In another account, Richard says that it
was triplets.

On the flight home from the Job Corps Center, Richard
says that an uncle (an employee of the airline) took him to the
pilot's cabin. There Richard sat in the co-pilot's seat while the co-
pilot got coffee for the crew. During this time, there was a birth on
the plane, and Richard says that he helped the stewardess with the
delivery.

The counselor believes that Richard uses rather than respects
or loves him. He believes that Richard feels the counselor is trying
to break up the "vicious circle of failure" and that therefore the
counselor is a threat to Richard. Failure is comforting to Richard.
He predicts it. He controls the situation that way. He acts as if it
were going to happen and helps to bring it about.

APPRAISAL

What do you now think of this person? What does he want
out of life or work? What is he willing to give? What risks will he
take? What are his chances? In the following two columns, list his

principal assets or strengths and his principal liabilities or weaknesses. Please number them for convenience in later reference.

Strengths	*Weaknesses*
1.	1. ....
2.	2. ....
....	....
....	....
....	....
....	....

Which of these strengths do you believe that this person is aware of? #............. Which of his weaknesses do you think he is aware of? #.............

PROGNOSIS

Can this person, at the age of 19, be effectively counseled?

☐ a. Definitely not.

☐ b. There is a 50/50 change to help him, provided

....

....

☐ c. There is *some* chance to help him, provided

....

....

Please write here any special definition of counseling you think it necessary to offer, if you believe your prognosis might otherwise be misunderstood: ....

....

....

....

FINAL NOTE

We appreciate your effort in thinking about what most people would consider to be a very difficult case. We would like to ask your opinion as to its difficulty in comparison with other cases you see; please check one of the following:

The case of Richard is:

☐   a. far more difficult than any I have ever seen.

☐   b. more difficult than most cases I have seen.

☐   c. about the same as most cases I have seen.

☐   d. not relevant to my work (i.e., I can't answer any of
        the above).

Is this type of case instructive? Bearing in mind the limitations of your time and the possible inadvisability of a longer case,
what other kind of data would you have preferred to have? ....

....

....

....

....

....

....

Would it be interesting to you to know how others respond to
this case?

☐   a. Yes

☐   b. No: it is too far removed from my work, not suffi-
        ciently instructive, etc.

Programed Case: Colombian Peon

Alberto was born in 1934 in Trujillo, the second son of a very poor family. His father was a laborer. Alberto does not remember much about those early years, but he knows it was a struggle. He did not see his father more than a few times during his first few years of life. "He could not really support us," Alberto says, "and I only remember his coming to visit us a few times. But I do remember him as a friendly, patient, helpful person."

Alberto's mother had a sharp temper. While he used to blame his father for their troubles, Alberto came to understand why the father left them. "She was a stubborn woman, could hardly read or write." When Alberto was six, his father came back to move the children to Cali. "He must have been a fine man, to do that." Cali in those days was many times smaller than now.

Unable to find regular work in Cali, the father had to put the children up for adoption. Thus the four children, separated first from their mother, now were separated from one another and from their father. His foster father, Juan P., was an industrious man. He and the foster mother, Maritza, living together in a common law marriage (not unusual in that area), operated a small business, selling trinkets. They worked hard and did well. Juan wanted

Alberto in school, and he started at age eight. Alberto says that Juan "wanted to help me." Alberto probably saw Juan more often than he saw his own father. He remembers Juan with gratitude, and without comment upon his heavy drinking. Alberto once saw Juan kill a man (shot him with a pistol), and the drinking killed Juan within three years.

Maritza, the foster mother, was, according to Alberto, "a typical Indian type"—high cheekbones, dark, unable to read or write, interested only in her own home. She had lived in Cali all her life, but was so limited in outside contacts that she got lost when she attempted to go out into the city. Alberto did not care much for Maritza.

Alberto saw his father twice after this—"He couldn't stay away, without seeing us." But the last time, Juan got angry, said, "You are not supposed to see these kids." It scared him off for good. The mother tried to visit the children. The foster parents would get upset. They were afraid she would take Alberto away.

1. *What does Alberto appear at this point to want from life, to admire most strongly, and to disparage or reject?* In answering this question, first note the things or people he mentioned favorably and then those he mentions unfavorably, among the following list. Mark favorable objects with a check; unfavorable with an X.

☐ His original father   ☐ Laboring people
☐ Money   ☐ Indians
☐ His original mother   ☐ Having a family to be-
☐ His foster father   long to
☐ His foster mother   ☐ Violence

He mentioned his two fathers favorably and the two women and Indians unfavorably. It is less certain at this point what he really thinks of violence and money.

The point of these questions is to bring out the early identifications and values of Alberto, and the significance of his outlook will become more apparent as the case goes on.

Before you read on, what is your reaction to the following proposition: "Since Alberto grew up in extremely modest background, he would readily accept a position as a menial, a servant." What are the pro's and con's?

What impressed Alberto most about his foster parents was their little business. "I have always wanted my own business—this goes all the way back to when I was about nine, I guess."

At Juan's death, Maritza took another husband. The new husband wanted Alberto to quit school immediately. Alberto left them, got a job as a servant, kept himself in school. He was then eleven.

2. *What bothered Alberto the most about his impoverished condition?*

☐ the food   ☐ money—the cause
☐ the lack of good clothes   of arguments with his
☐ nothing—he accepted it   foster mother
☐ the humiliation

It seems likely that his low social status is what Alberto could not accept—the humiliation was too much for him. The dream of having a small business, of being independent, perhaps is related to this desire to rise from the low status.

Of his life as a servant, Alberto recalls, "The pay was pitiful. They gave us room and board and ten pesos a month (about a dollar). They wanted us to work for nothing." For Christmas, his employers gave him old clothes.

What could he look ahead to? "I was the lowest thing, but if I worked there for enough years, I could become the top houseboy at thirty pesos a month."

"It was humiliating," he says. "They were bossy. They have to show, what you call—lordship? There's always somebody higher than you." They would slap or whip him when they saw him sitting around. He was one of the "backside people"—his place was to live back in the kitchen.

But it was better than living with Maritza, the foster mother. "However," Alberto now says, "I feel sorry for her now. She's old, needs help. She squandered the money her first husband left her."

"There are some generous people in Colombia. She was a godmother (sic) at this man's wedding when he was poor. He was a miner. He is prosperous today, and he has given her thousands of pesos. Her second husband spent it all."

Alberto got tired of being a houseboy and quit. Sometimes,

after that, he would go back to live with Maritza—when she was in
a good mood. Then when she became angry, whipped him, he would
leave. The main issue was—"She wanted me to be a helper. Once
when I bought shoes, she got upset because I didn't bring her the
money."

On the occasion of a friend's funeral, Maritza gave Alberto
money for the priest and flowers. On the way, Alberto was tempted
by a movie, and spent all the money. Alberto talked in his sleep
about it that night, Maritza heard, and was furious.

3. *Did receiving gifts from his employers make Alberto
grateful? If not, how do you account for it? Was he not grateful to
his original father and his foster father for what they did for him?
Was he grateful to Maritza?*

....

....

....

....

Note: Alberto was not grateful to the persons who employed
him as a servant for giving him what had no value to themselves. He
was not grateful to Maritza, possibly, because she was, to his thinking, an ingrate—squandered what her first husband left her. He was
grateful to his fathers because, he felt, their giving was selfless. The
meaning of *gifts* is a subtle question, but a key question in learning
to deal with the impoverished person and in the underdeveloped
country.

Was it hard to live alone, as he sometimes had to? No, the
food was cheap. He could get by. But those years gave him a longing
to own, to have "something nice." He still has that longing.

Over this five-year period, he did various odd jobs—construction labor, theatre doorman, office boy. He would from time to
time live in a community housing area, where 40 families stayed.
They did not understand his constant efforts to get an education.
They made fun of him, saying, "You should get a shovel, dig the
ground, like the rest of us."

"They feel the carpenter should stick to his tools, and that
physical work is what counts. If you use your mind to find an easier
way, that makes you lazy. Colombia doesn't have many inventors."

4. *Alberto is evidently able to resist the "social pressure" of the other members of the laboring class. Education is manifestly for him a tool to lift himself by his bootstraps. What is it in his background which makes him different?*

☐ He is stubborn, as was his mother

☐ He has had some encounter with people who live differently.

☐ He is more intelligent

☐ He has more initiative

☐ He is more moral and conscientious

Before we discuss these answers, we want to ask you an additional question.

5. *In Alberto's efforts to get an education, he takes up the study of English at one point. What kind of a student do you think he will be?*

☐ *Excellent*—he has a burning desire to move up and sees education as a tool for advancement

☐ *Good*— he could be better, but the pressures of work make it impractical for him to concentrate as much as he should

☐ *Poor*—while he is eager, he has no patience and persistence with studies

"But I wanted to get away. Why? Maybe, because I was stubborn—like my mother."

He studied English eagerly. But his grades were poor. He was extremely impatient, would get frustrated when a subject was slow. He still has this trouble, he says: later, when he wanted to take up the guitar, his teacher insisted that he learn classical work before getting into popular music, so he quit.

Did he like Cali? Summing up Cali, he says, "I loved the environment, but not the economy." It was warm, but never hot. He did not have to wear a coat. The town was of very modest construction—the most characteristic materials he remembers were the clay roofs, and the walls composed of successive layers of local materials, first the bamboo structure, then the horse manure, and then white paint.

The people were gay, frank. When he visited the United States, he found the people proper and strait-laced. He missed the fiestas—many a year. There were lots of saints and political dates, and each merited a fiesta. There was a lot of drinking and dancing. Alberto had his first drink at 14.

For companions he would run with a particular group of boys, but not if Maritza could help it. She held him back, wouldn't let him go to the school picnics—she said it was the money. He had to learn to swim himself.

6. *What do you anticipate his attitude might be toward the Roman Catholic Church?*

☐ It was like a Mother to him—warm, comforting, and re-assuring

☐ It was like a Father to him—encouraging him to get an education, having ambitions for him

☐ It was like neither, and he eventually became quite negative toward the Church

What did he think of the Church? As a boy, he had wanted to become a priest. In his teens, he says, "My eyes opened; I saw they were not as holy as they are supposed to be."

He feels that the Church there "keeps people ignorant by not telling them the whole story."

7. *What attitudes will Alberto form toward persons in social classes above his own?*

☐ He will want to become one of them

☐ He will attack them, every chance he gets, at one point joining the Communist Party out of hatred of the upper classes

☐ He will not admit anyone has a social class higher than his own

His studies began to center upon English. This goes back many years, as an ambition. When he was a small boy, he always wanted to be someone else than who he was—"I wanted to be the person next to me." So that when he found himself in school competing with persons with more education, he wanted to be one of them—"one of those people who were above me."

In his housing area, where they ridiculed him for studying English ("You should get a shovel"), he found that the children hated to use complex words because it would appear that they were showing off.

He found that other Colombians resisted learning something new because of the zeal for perfection. If a Colombian cannot do something perfectly, he hesitates to attempt to do it at all—for fear of ridicule. The Colombian himself ridicules others who fail, according to Alberto.

In contrast, when he visited the United States later he felt the people had initiative—"get up and go." On further thought, he added, "the young people have. The older people are just critical."

8. *How will Alberto act, in the presence of middle-class people? In his early twenties, he gets a job at an Institute in Cali which teaches English, and thus is in the presence of the middle-class students at that Institute.*

    ☐ He feels their equal, because he himself already knows English (which they are learning), and behaves with poise
    ☐ He is hostile and avoids them
    ☐ He is shy and lacking in words

He got a job at an American Institute which taught English in Cali. He found himself, at the beginning, like other "lower-class" people in the presence of the middle class: shy, lacking in words. Why is this? He blames the middle-class person, who wants to be "his Lordship" over the lower class.

Alberto helped at the Institute for several years, to pay for his classes. He helped enroll students, did some proctoring of exams, Spanish tutoring.

He found himself studying English with college people, better dressed than he. Then, when his fellow Colombians realized he was employed at the Institute, the only Colombian employee there, they began to respect him more. "Some of them decided I was from Puerto Rico," he says, "and at any rate I passed the Middle Class Barrier."

9. *When Alberto gets a little money ahead and a steady job, what will be his attitude toward his family—his original father and mother and brothers and sisters?*

    ☐ He will try to find them, to "recapture his childhood" so to speak, which he never had

☐ He will pretend he never had them—cut himself off entirely
from that life

☐ He will send them money, feeling, "We have grown apart,
but I have obligations anyway."

When Alberto could afford it, he began to look for his
family. "I was like a detective, asking everywhere," he recalls. Why
did he do this? "I never had a childhood. It is one of my ambitions
to have all my family in one town." He also dreams of having a
house, having a business of his own.

Later, Alberto was to go back to try to find his father. But
no one seemed to have heard of him. Finally, someone said that his
father had been killed. They told Alberto the same thing about his
mother, too, but years later, Alberto was to find her again.

Now 31, Alberto is well on his way to these things. But he
has times when he is acutely impatient—31 seems late to him—and
he has trouble eating and sleeping in his concern.

He has left the Roman Catholic Church. He felt that the
Church had led him to think of Protestants as atheists, and he has
not found them as frightening as he expected. He now attends
"various churches," but does not apparently feel rooted in any one.

In regard to his ambitions, he says, "Sometimes I hate myself because I am not doing things soon enough. I have been able to
have a car. But I don't yet have a house, and I am already 31."

10. *How do you account for Alberto's intense feelings about
wanting a house? His feelings that he is not doing things soon
enough? What, in short, is he searching for?*

....

....

....

....

....

....

....

We believe that Alberto has a suppressed nostalgia for the
old days in Cali. The life history does not emphasize this, and you
are entitled to conclude that we are reading between the lines, but

we are very much impressed with the comparison he made between Colombia, the country of the past and of his past, and the United States on his visit: Colombia: "The people were gay, frank. He missed the fiestas. . . . There was a lot of drinking and dancing." United States (and middle-class culture in general): "The people were proper and strait-laced . . . while the young people here show much 'get up and go,' the older people are critical. . . ."

One of the reasons we believe in the suppressed nostalgia interpretation is Alberto's ambition: he has a vague, unrealized ambition to learn music. We think he has an intense, and largely unrecognized, longing for the gayer style of life he left.

The search for his family, which he pursued with great expense and vigor, was in many ways an attempt to recapture his lost childhood, and this interpretation is Alberto's own view of what that search meant.

Here is a man, then, between two cultures and perhaps hating himself for it. He is in no doubt that he must "move up" in the world, but he is dimly aware that he has lost something, left something of himself behind.

Programed Case: Sales Supervisor

NAME: Sam Grant

AGE: 34

FAMILY: Married, have two adopted children.

EXPERIENCE: Employed by this company for seven years—three years on a bread route and four years as sales supervisor. Before that, route salesman for a competitor in another city. Before that, route salesman for a dairy for two years, which I left when they split the route.

EDUCATION: High School graduate—in upper 10% of a class of 300. Favorite subjects were English, history, science. Am now taking (and have almost completed) a management correspondence course. In addition, my training as a hospital corpsman during the war was the equivalent of about a year of college or medical school.

EXTRACURRICULAR ACTIVITIES: (none listed)

WHAT KIND OF CAREER ARE YOU LOOKING FOR? I intend to advance as high and as fast as I can.

HEIGHT: 5'8"

WEIGHT: 160

HEALTH: Normal

WHAT ARE YOUR QUALIFICATIONS FOR PROMOTION? My experience as a supervisor and as a route salesman. By the reports and morale of the people under me, I know that I have talent for handling men. Strong point: contacting the customer.

EVERYONE HAS A FEW SHORTCOMINGS. WHAT ARE YOURS? Need additional training in consumer contact.

MILITARY SERVICE: Most of my time was spent in the hospital corpsman school. This was the equivalent of a year of college.

FAMILY LIFE: Father was a dairy route salesman. My family moved often. Mother has an administrative job. My sister is a medical technician, one brother is a uniform salesman, and the other brother is a management trainee with an oil company. Married 11 years. My wife doesn't work. We have two adopted children. I give a lot of time to my young son. I belong to no organizations.

TEST FINDINGS

1. Intelligence at about the 80th percentile.
2. Temperament test—within usual limits except for one trait—he is more depressive (sad, melancholy, etc.) than about 85% of the people who have taken the test.

Prediction: Performance as a sales supervisor:

☐ 1. consistently a top-notch performer
☐ 2. does an average or above average job
☐ 3. can handle the job with extra help from the boss and training
☐ 4. does not belong on this job

We are not going to give you the feedback at this point. Instead, we'll go on to the next part of the case.

INTERVIEW INFORMATION

Sam wanted to go to college, but didn't have enough money. He says that his parents could have sent him and his younger brother as well. But they didn't, and Sam put his younger brother through the state university.

At one point, Sam mentioned that his father had once been a policeman in St. Louis. The interviewer noted, "Sam made this statement sarcastically with a smirk on his face."

How would you describe Sam's attitude toward his father?

Why do you have this opinion? ....
....
....
....

What attitude toward his boss would you expect Sam to have? ....
....

Why do you have this opinion? ....
....
....
....

Do you see any evidence that Sam would be a good father and spend time with his children? ....
....
....
....

Does the preceding question have any bearing on Sam's on-the-job performance?
☐ Yes
☐ No

When questioned in more detail about his frank opinion of his own strengths and weaknesses, Sam said that he was self-confident, determined, flexible, straight-forward, honest with himself, and clean. He especially stressed this last point. He said that he was probably too demanding of his men on cleanliness. He also admitted that he was irritable and intolerant.

What is there in Sam's background that might lead him to stress cleanliness more than anything else? How do you think his men would react to Sam's strong emphasis on cleanliness? ....
....

Is Sam now giving the same image of himself in the interview—that he gave on the temperament test?
☐ Yes
☐ No

The interviewer noted that Sam had written this on the application blank under the heading of spare-time activities: "Working at home in yard and around the house. I like art and reading. Also help out with Little League baseball."

The interviewer asked him more about his spare-time activities. Sam said that he subscribed to True, Electrical Journal, Hi-Fi, and Stereo, and had a set of Encyclopaedia Britannica. He called himself a thorough reader—"from cover to cover." ("Thorough reader"—of the magazines. We don't think he meant cover-to-cover reading of the encyclopaedia.)

Why does this man study management? (You remember that he is taking a course in business administration by correspondence.)

....

....

....

Please review your comments on this case in the preceding parts. It is all right to change your mind on any of them since now you have a great deal more information about Sam.

Predictions:

☐ 1. consistently a top-notch performer
☐ 2. does an average or above average job
☐ 3. can handle the job with extra help from the boss and training
☐ 4. does not belong on this job

Which of the following statements do you think his boss, the sales manager, made about Sam?

☐ A. Sam is hard-driving as a leader—expects and gets results from all the men in his group.
☐ B. Sam needs a great deal of pushing—has lacked enthusiasm and aggressiveness.
☐ C. Sam has the ability, but he has just not applied himself.
☐ D. Sam would be a top-notch supervisor, but I have found him drinking on the job.

The Facts: The sales manager rated Sam this way:

☐ "can handle the job with extra help from the boss and training"

He made this statement:

☐ "Sam needs a great deal of pushing—has lacked enthusiasm and aggressiveness."

ANALYSIS

How would you describe Sam's attitude toward his father? The history brought out that Sam's attitude might be called disre-

spectful, hostile, or resentful. Sam says he wanted to go to college
and that his parents could have sent him, but that they didn't. He
shows his disrespect by smirking when mentioning that his father
was once a policeman.

*What attitude toward his boss would you expect Sam to
have?* Uncomfortable—not necessarily hostile or disrespectful, but
perhaps a milder form of those two attitudes.

Why? The case brought out that Sam's attitude toward his
father was a poor one. While a man's boss is not necessarily like a
father to him, early experiences in the home may condition many of
his later relationships to people in authority. Remember, Sam smirked
at the idea of his father being a policeman. A policeman is one of
the most common symbols of authority. A man's boss is another one.

*Do you see any evidence that Sam would be a good father
and spend time with his children?* Yes, there is plenty of evidence
on this point. Sam began playing the role of a good father by paying
for his younger brother's college expenses. You might even go so far
as to say that probably Sam feels that he became a foster father to
the younger brother because their father wouldn't do his duty. It's
easy to see why such a man would be happy to adopt children. He is
probably being accurate when he says he spends time with his children and helps the Little League baseball program. This "helping
attitude" is also consistent with the job of hospital corpsman.

What bearing has this personal trait on his job performance?
Sam seems to consider it one of his main duties in life to play
"father" to persons he considers neglected or abandoned. We wonder if his present job is consistent with such an outlook.

*What is there in Sam's background that might lead him to
stress cleanliness more than anything else?* Sam was a hospital corpsman in the Navy. If you have never heard about the Navy's stress
on cleanliness, ask any sailor. And as a hospital corpsman, Sam
certainly must have been given a thorough indoctrination about the
need for cleanliness. In that work, the stress was logical. But would
it necessarily be logical in another job?

*How do you think his men would react to Sam's strong
emphasis on cleanliness?* They might consider it exaggerated. As a
matter of fact, some of them do call Sam "picky." They think he
gives too much attention to a "minor" requirement of their work and

too little thought to "more important" aspects, such as sales problems. But these men are handling food! Perhaps Sam is the ideal person for this job.

Why does this man study management? In his application, he said, "I intend to advance as high and as fast as I can." In the interview, his smirking reference to the police job indicated that he didn't think his father went very high. Sam may be a fellow who thinks that a person is no good if he doesn't go up the ladder.

LONG RANGE FORECASTS

The sales manager thinks Sam has the intelligence required for top management. He arrived at that opinion without knowing the results of the intelligence test. Sam must have done some things that have caught the manager's eye. But the manager considers him indifferent and lacking in enthusiasm. He may have gotten that impression because Sam is ill at ease when with persons of authority.

What can be done about this? Well, think of it this way. Sam Grant is 34 years old. He has taken more than three decades to get the way he is. A great deal can be done through simple, patient supervision of Sam Grant. But it will take months, even years, because Sam's attitudes are long-standing.

Is there any cause for optimism? The sales manager has told us that Sam has improved lately, with some added attention he has received. Should this surprise us? Sam actually has some desire for close human relationships. Remember, he put his younger brother through college and, also, he and his wife have adopted two children. Sam really wants to get along and to have close, satisfying relationships with people.

But his off-duty relaxation—hi-fi, heavy reading, work around the house—is not the type which would make a person outgoing. Sam is doing little on his own to cultivate the personality required in sales work.

Know what? We think Sam is in the wrong field. Why not plant maintenance engineering? There are many arguments in favor of his going into a technical field. He is smart, likes technical subjects, completed the tough hospital corpsman's school. Why keep him in a field for which he is not well suited, temperamentally or socially?

Incidentally, why is Sam in sales?

✥✥ **Appendix A** ✥✥

Interpersonal
Checklist

✥✥✥✥✥✥✥✥✥✥✥✥✥✥✥✥✥✥✥✥✥✥

Adapted from Leary's Interpersonal Checklist (1957).

--------- Well thought of P1

--------- Able to give orders A3

--------- Forceful A4

--------- Self-respecting B5

--------- Independent B6

--------- Able to take care of self C7

--------- Can be strict D9

--------- Firm but just D10

--------- Frank and honest E11

--------- Complains if necessary F13

--------- Often gloomy F14

--------- Frequently disappointed G16

--------- Able to criticize self H17

--------- Apologetic H18

----------- Wants everyone to like him L58

----------- Sociable and neighborly M59

----------- Kind and reassuring N61

----------- Tender and soft-hearted N62

----------- Enjoys taking care of others O63

✧✧ Appendix B ✧✧

Biographic
Questionnaire

✧✧✧✧✧✧✧✧✧✧✧✧✧✧✧✧✧✧✧✧✧✧✧✧

Instruction. Please respond to at least 25 of the following 57 statements by recording an episode. Give the place, year of your life, circumstances, and your own behavior and feelings at the time. Limit your response to 150 words if possible.

I. Parental family. Please respond to both the first two.
1. A time you felt strong emotions toward your father.
2. A time you felt strong emotions toward your mother.
3. If you had brothers and sisters, describe an episode involving you and one or all of them.
4. If you have no brother or sisters, describe either an episode in which you wished you did, or one in which you were especially happy that you did not have any.
5. A time when you were especially proud or embarrassed by the physical appearance of your parents.
6. A time you felt that one or both your parents acted in particularly bad taste or good taste.
7. An episode when you were being punished for some misbehavior or rewarded for some accomplishment.
8. An incident involving you and a favorite aunt, uncle, grandmother, grandfather, or other similar relative.

222

II. School and work.   Respond to at least two of the following.
   9. An episode involving your favorite teacher.
   10. If you had difficulty with a certain subject, tell about an episode in which that difficulty was especially painful, or in which you overcame that difficulty.
   11. A time when you did especially well in your studies or activities at school and how you were rewarded.
   12. A time when you got in trouble in school.
   13. The first time you ever applied for a job.
   14. A time when you were especially satisfied or dissatisfied with the work you did on a job, and if your employer recognized your work as good or bad.
   15. A time when you worked with your hands or muscles.
   16. A time when you were embarrassed by something a teacher or employer said to you.

III. Religion.   Respond to at least one of the following.
   17. An occasion when you prayed.
   18. A time when you felt especially strong belief in God, or a time when you felt especially certain that God did not exist.
   19. An experience in a religious institution; or, if you have never attended, a time when you wished you did or were glad you didn't.
   20. A time when you felt especially different from another person due to differing religious beliefs; or a time when you felt especially close to someone due to a common religious belief.

IV. Interests, hobbies, habits.   Respond to at least three of the following.
   21. A time when you read something you enjoyed.
   22. A time you ate or drank something you especially liked or disliked.
   23. A time when you engaged in an athletic event of some sort and were successful or unsuccessful.
   24. A time when you were engaged in discussing a particularly interesting subject.
   25. Some adventure or strange thing that has happened to you.

26. A time during which you traveled away from home and during which you were particularly happy or unhappy.

27. A time during which you were occupied with your favorite hobby.

28. An episode involving a favorite pet.

V. Physical appearance and condition. Respond to at least two of the following.

29. A time you felt that you were in especially good or bad shape.

30. A time you dressed in a way that you were especially proud or ashamed of.

31. A time when you thought you were particularly handsome or unattractive.

32. A time when you were especially worried or pleased about your health.

VI. Emotions and feelings. Respond to at least two of the following.

33. A time you cried.

34. A time you felt lonely.

35. A time you felt quarrelsome, resentful, or impatient with someone.

36. A time you had a fist fight.

37. A time you felt pressured, or a time you felt exalted, a sense of exhilaration.

38. A time when someone severely criticized you, with or without cause.

VII. Love, dating, sex. Respond to at least three of the following.

39. A blind date.

40. A time you thought a particular girl looked "lovely," "sexy," or "cheap."

41. The worst date you ever had.

42. A time when you had sexual relations with someone.

43. The best date you ever had.

44. A time when you felt especially sexually attracted to someone.

45. A time when you said something special or failed to do

the right thing to make yourself attractive to someone whom you liked.

46. A time you felt that someone else handled himself extremely well or extremely poorly in a sexual matter, or in speaking about it.

VIII. Relationships with other people. Respond to at least three of the following.

47. A time you particularly enjoyed or disliked a group activity.

48. A time when you especially wanted to be with a particular person, or when you especially did not want to be with a particular person.

49. A time when you felt that friendship was the most important thing on earth, or a time when you felt that true friendship was impossible to achieve.

50. A time when you were or were not the "leader" of a group, and if you were happy or unhappy in that position.

51. A time when you told someone off or were told off by another person.

IX. Money and property. Respond to at least two of the following.

52. A time when you felt especially that money was or was not important.

53. A time when you saw another person begging on the street and how you felt.

54. A time when you stole something, or a time when you resisted the temptation to steal.

55. A time when you borrowed or loaned money or property to someone.

56. The time you made best use of your allowance.

57. A time when you dreamed about all you would do if you had a lot of money.

Bibliography

ADLER, A. "The Practice and Theory of Individual Psychology" (1914). In *Individual Psychology* (Trans. P. Radin). Totowa, N.J.: Littlefield, Adams, 1969.

ALBEE, G. W. "Models, Myths and Manpower." *Mental Hygiene*, 1968, *52* (2), 168–180.

ALBEE, G. W. "Emerging Concepts of Mental Illness and Models of Treatments: The Psychological Point of View." *American Journal of Psychiatry*, 1969, *125* (7), 870–876.

ALLPORT, G. W. *Personal Documents in Psychological Science*, bulletin 49. New York: Social Science Research Council, 1942.

ALLPORT, G. W., VERNON, P. E., AND LINDZEY, G. *A Study in Values*. Boston: Houghton Mifflin, 1960.

ALLPORT, G. W. *Pattern and Growth in Personality*. New York: Holt, Rinehart and Winston, 1961.

ANSBACHER, H. L., AND ANSBACHER, R. R. *The Individual Psychology of Alfred Adler*. New York: Harper & Row, 1956.

BAER, T. A. Unpublished paper, Office of Institutional Research, Dartmouth College, 1970.

BALDWIN, A. L. "Personal Structure Analysis: A Statistical Method for Investigating the Single Personality." *Journal of Abnormal and Social Psychology*, 1942, *37*, 163–183.

BARITZ, L. *The Servants of Power*. Middletown, Conn.: Wesleyan University Press, 1960.

BARKER, R. G. "Psychology's Third Estate." Paper read at Meeting of the Greater Kansas City Psychological Association, Kansas City, Mo. Sp. (unpublished paper), 1964. In Willems, E. P., and Rausch, H. L. *Naturalistic Viewpoint in Psychological Research*. New York: Holt, Rinehart and Winston, 1969, 122–146.

BARKER, R. G., AND WRIGHT, H. F. *One Boy's Day*. New York: Harper & Row, 1951.

BELLAK, L. "Somerset Maugham: A Thematic Analysis of Ten Short Stories." In White, R. W. *Study of Lives*. New York: Atherton, 1963, 143–159.

BENDIX, R. *Max Weber: An Intellectual Portrait*. Garden City, N.Y.: Doubleday, 1960.

BENTZ, V. J. "The Sears Experience in the Investigation, Description and Prediction of Executive Behavior." In Myers, J. A., Jr. (ed.). *Predicting Managerial Success*. Ann Arbor, Mich.: Foundation for Research on Human Behavior, 1968.

BIERI, J. A., ATKINS, A. L., BRIAR, S., LEAMAN, R. L., MILLER, H., AND TRIPODI, T. *Clinical and Social Judgment*. New York: Wiley, 1966.

BLOCK, J. *The Q-Sort Method in Personality Assessment and Psychiatric Research*. Springfield, Ill.: Thomas, 1961.

BROWN, R. *Social Psychology*. New York: Free Press, 1965.

BRONFENBRENNER, U., HARDING, J., AND GALLWEY, M. "The Measurement of Skill and Social Perception." In *Talent and Society*. Princeton, N.J.: Van Nostrand, 1958, 29–111.

BÜHLER, C. *Der Menschliche Lebenslauf als Psychologisches Problem*. Leipzig: S. Hirzel, 1933.

BÜHLER, C. "The General Structure of the Human Life Cycle." In Bühler, C., and Massarik, F. *The Course of Human Lives*. New York: Springer, 1968, 24–25.

BÜHLER, C., AND MARSCHAK, M. "Basic Tendencies of Human Life." In Bühler, C., and Massarik, F. *The Course of Human Life*. New York: Springer, 1968, 92–101.

BÜHLER, C., AND MASSARIK, F. *The Course of Human Life*. New York: Springer, 1968.

BUROS, O. K. *The Mental Measurements Yearbook*. Highland Park, N.J.: Gryphon, 1965.

CAIN, L. D. "Life Course and Social Structure." In Faris, R. E. L. (ed.). *Handbook of Modern Sociology*. Chicago: Rand McNally, 1964, 272–309.

CANNELL, C. F., AND KAHN, R. L. "Interviewing." In *Handbook of Social Psychology* (2nd ed.). Vol. 2. Reading, Mass.: Addison-Wesley, 1968, 562–595.

CASEY, R. L., MASUDA, M., AND HOLMES, T. H. "Quantitative Study of Recall of Life Events." *Journal of Psychomatic Research*, 1967, *11*, 239–247.

CATTELL, R. *Personality and Motivation Structure and Measurements*. New York: Harcourt, Brace & World, 1957.

CLINE, V. B. "Ability to Judge Personality Assessed with a Stress Interview and Sound Film Technique." *Journal of Abnormal and Social Psychology*, 1955, *50*, 183–187.

CLINE, V. B., AND RICHARDS, J. M., JR. "Accuracy of Interpersonal Perception—A General Trait?" *Journal of Abnormal and Social Psychology*, 1960, *60*, 1–7.

COMFORT, A. *The Biology of Senescence*. New York: Holt, Rinehart and Winston, 1956.

CRONBACH, L. J., AND GLESER, G. C. *Psychological Tests and Personnel Decisions*. Urbana: University of Illinois Press, 1965.

DAILEY, C. A. "The Effects of Premature Conclusion on the Acquisition of Understanding of a Person." *Journal of Psychology*, 1952, *33*, 133–152.

DAILEY, C. A. "The Practical Utility of the Clinical Report." *Journal of Consulting Psychology*, 1953, *17* (4), 297–302.

DAILEY, C. A. "The Natural Structure of the Life History." *Vita Humana*, 1959a, *2* (1).

DAILEY, C. A. "Graph Theory and the Analysis of Personal Documents." *Human Relations*, 1959b, *12* (1), 65–74.

DAILEY, C. A. "Natural History and Phenomenology." *Journal of Individual Psychology*, 1960, *16*, 36–44.

DAILEY, C. A. "The Experimental Study of Clinical Guessing." *Journal of Individual Psychology*, 1966a, *22*, 65–79.

DAILEY, C. A. "Prejudice and Decision Making." *Personnel Administration*, 1966b, Sept./Oct., 6–13.

DAILEY, C. A., CARLSON, G. H., AND MC CHESNEY, M. R. "The Projects CAUSE: An Evaluation." Washington, D.C.: U.S. Department of Labor, 1968.

DE CHARDIN, P. T. *Man's Place in Nature*. New York: Harper & Row, 1966.

DE FINETTI, B. "Foresight: Its Logical Laws, Its Subjective Sources." In Kyburg, H. E., Jr., and Smokler, H. E. *Studies in Subjective Probability*. New York: Wiley, 1964, 93–158.

DE WAELE, J. P. *La méthode des cas programmés en psychologie de la personnalité et en criminologie*. Brussels: Dessart, 1971.

DOLLARD, J. "Criteria for the Life History—with Analysis of Six Notable Documents." New Haven, Conn.: Yale University Press, 1935.

EDEL, L. *Literary Biography*. Garden City, N.Y.: Anchor Books, Doubleday, 1959.

EDWARDS, W., AND TVERSKY, A. *Decision Making*. Baltimore: Penguin Books, 1967.

ERIKSON, E. *Young Man Luther*. New York: W. W. Norton, 1958.

ERIKSON, E. *Identity: Youth and Crisis*. New York: W. W. Norton, 1968.

ERIKSON, E. *Gandhi's Truth*. New York: W. W. Norton, 1969.

EYSENCK, H. J. *The Scientific Study of Personality.* London: Routledge & Kegan Paul, 1952.

FANCHER, R. E. "Explicit Personality Theories and Accuracy in Person Perception." *Journal of Personality,* 1966, *34* (2), 252–261.

FANCHER, R. E. "Accuracy Versus Validity in Person Perception." *Journal of Consulting Psychology,* 1967, *31* (3), 264–269.

FISHER, J. "The Twisted Pear and the Prediction of Behavior." *Journal of Consulting Psychology,* 1959, *23,* 400–405.

FRANK, J. *Courts on Trial.* New York: Atheneum, 1963. Originally published by Princeton University Press, 1949.

FRENCH, R. L. "The Motorola Case." *The Industrial Psychologist,* 1965, *2,* 29–50.

FRENKEL, E. "Studies in Biographical Psychology." *Character and Personality,* 1936, *5,* 1–34.

FREUD, S. *Leonardo da Vinci* (Trans. A. A. Brill). New York: Random House, 1947.

FRIEDENBERG, E. Z. "Social Consequences of Educational Measurement." *Proceedings of the 1969 Invitational Conference on Testing Problems.* Princeton, N.J.: Educational Testing Service, 23–30.

GAGNE, R. M. *The Conditions of Learning.* New York: Holt, Rinehart and Winston, 1965.

GARDNER, J. *Excellence: Can We Be Equal and Excellent Too?* New York: Harper & Row, 1961.

GARRATY, J. A. *The Nature of Biography.* New York: Vintage Books, Random House, 1957.

GENDLIN, E. T., AND RYCHLAK, J. F. "Psychotherapeutic Processes." *Annual Review of Psychology,* 1970, *21,* 155.

GLASER, R. *Training Research and Education.* New York: Wiley, 1962.

GOFFMAN, E. *The Presentation of Self in Everyday Life.* Garden City, N.Y.: Doubleday, 1959.

GOFFMAN, E. *Asylums.* Garden City, N.Y.: Anchor Books, Doubleday, 1961.

GOFFMAN, E. *Interaction Ritual.* Chicago: Aldine, 1967.

GOLDBERG, L. R. "The Effectiveness of Clinician's Judgments: The Diagnosis of Organic Brain Damage from the Bender-Gestalt Test." *Journal of Consulting Psychology,* 1959, 25–33.

GOLDBERG, L. R. "Simple Models or Simple Process? Some Research on Clinical Judgments." *American Psychologist,* 1968, *23* (7), 483–496.

GOTTSCHALK, L., KLUCKHOHN, C., AND ANGELL, R. "The Use of Personal Documents in History, Anthropology, and Sociology." *Social Science Research Council Bulletin,* 1945, *53.*

GOUGH, H. "Some Reflections on the Meaning of Psychodiagnosis." *American Psychologist,* 1971, *26* (2), 160–167.

GREENBERG, D. S. "Basement Science: What Happens When a Do-It-Yourself Scientist Looks to Washington for Support." *Science,* 1964, *164,* Oct. 30, 621–623.

GREENSTEIN, F. I. *Personality in Politics.* Chicago: Markham, 1969.

GREENWALD, H. *Great Cases in Psychoanalysis.* New York: Ballantine Books, 1959.

GRIGG, A. E. "Experience of Clinicians and Speech Characteristics and Statements of Clients as Variables in Clinical Judgment." *Journal of Consulting Psychology,* 1958, *22,* 315–319.

HALDANE, B. J. "Focus on Success Instead of Failure." *National Education Association Journal,* 1966, *55* (32).

HAMMOND, K. R. Personal Communication, 1969.

HAMMOND, K. R., HURSCH, C. J., AND TODD, F. J. "Analyzing the Components of Clinical Inference." *Psychological Review,* 1964, *71,* 438–456.

HARARY, F., NORMAN, R. Z., AND CARTWRIGHT, D. *Structural Models: An Introduction to the Theory of Directed Graphs.* New York: Wiley, 1965.

HOLMES, T. H., AND MASUDA, M. "The Social Readjustment Rating Scale: A Cross-Cultural Study of Japanese and Americans." *Journal of Psychosomatic Research,* 1967, *11,* 227–237.

HOLMES, T. H., AND RAHE, R. H. "The Social Readjustment Rating Scale." *Journal of Psychosomatic Research,* 1967, *11,* 213–218.

HOLSOPPLE, J. Q., AND PHELAN, J. G. "The Skills of Clinicians in Analysis of Projective Tests." *Journal of Clinical Psychology,* 1954, *10,* 307–320.

HOYT, D. P. "The Relationship between College Grades and Adult Achievement: A Review of the Literature." *Research Reports,* American College Testing Program, 1965, *7.*

INHELDER, B. "Criteria of the Stages of Mental Development." In J. M. Tanner and B. Inhelder (Eds.), *Discussions on Child Development: A Consideration of the Biological, Psychological, and Cultural Approaches to the Understanding of Human Development and Behavior.* The Proceedings of the First Meeting of World Health Organization Study Group on Psychological Development of the Child. Vol. 1. Geneva, N.Y.: International University Press, 1953, 75–96.

JEFFREY, R. C. *The Logic of Decision.* New York: McGraw-Hill, 1965.

KELLY, E. L. "Consistency of the Adult Personality." *The American Psychologist,* 1955, *10,* 659–681.

KELLY, E. L., AND FISKE, D. W. *The Prediction of Performance in Clinical Psychology.* Ann Arbor: University of Michigan Press, 1951.

KIRKPATRICK, J. J., EWEN, R. B., BARRETT, R. S., AND KATZELL, R. *Testing and Fair Employment*. New York: New York University Press, 1968.

KLUCKHOHN, C. "Cultural Anthropology and Psychology." In *Proceedings of the 15th International Congress of Psychology. Brussels, 1957*. Amsterdam: North Holland Publishing Co., 1957, 63–75.

KORZYBSKI, A. *Manhood of Humanity*. New York: E. P. Dutton, 1921.

KORZYBSKI, A. *Science and Sanity*. Lancaster, Pa.: New York: The International Non-Artistotelian Library Publishing Co., The Science Press Printing Co., distributors, 1941.

KOSTLAN, A. "A Method for the Empirical Study of Psychodiagnosis." *Journal of Consulting Psychology*, 1954, *18*, 83–88.

KUTNER, L. "The Illusion of Due Process in Commitment Proceedings." *Northwestern University Law Review*, 1962, *57*, 383–399.

LAING, R. D., AND COOPER, D. G. *Reason and Violence*. New York: Basic Books, 1964.

LANGNESS, L. I. *The Life History in Anthropological Science*. New York: Holt, Rinehart and Winston, 1965.

LEARY, T. *Interpersonal Diagnosis of Personality*. New York: Ronald Press, 1957.

LECKY, P. *Self-Consistency, A Theory of Personality*. New York: Island Press, 1945.

LEWIN, K. *Principles of Topological Psychology*. New York: McGraw-Hill, 1936.

LIEF, A. (ed.). *The Commonsense Psychiatry of Dr. Adolf Meyer*. New York: McGraw-Hill, 1948.

MARTINEZ, T. M. "Why Employment Agency Counselors Lower Their Clients' Self-Esteem." *Trans-Action*, 1968, *5* (4), 20–25.

MASLOW, A. H. *Motivation and Personality*. New York: Harper & Row, 1954.

MASLOW, A. *Toward a Psychology of Being*. Princeton, N.J.: Van Nostrand, 1962.

MASLOW, A. "Peak Experience in Education and Art." *The Humanist*, 1970, Sept./Oct., 29–31.

MASUDA, M., AND HOLMES, T. H. "Magnitude Estimations of Social Readjustments." *Journal of Psychosomatic Research*, 1967, *11*, 219–225.

MATARAZZO, J. D. "The Interview." In Wolman, B. J. (ed.). *Handbook of Clinical Psychology*. New York: McGraw-Hill, 1965, 403–540.

MATULEF, N. J., POTTHARST, K. E., AND ROTHENBERG, P. J. *The Revolution in Professional Training*. National Council on Graduate Education in Psychology with the Cooperation of the E & T/

BPA Ad Hoc Committee on Professional Training of the American Psychological Association, 1970.

MEEHL, P. *Clinical Versus Statistical Prediction*. Minneapolis: Minnesota University Press, 1954.

MEEHL, P. "Some Ruminations of the Validation of Clinical Procedures." *Canadian Journal of Psychology*, 1959, *13*, 102–128.

MEEHL, P. "The Cognitive Activity of the Clinician." *American Psychologist*, 1960, *15*, 19–27.

MILGRAM, S. "Behavioral Study of Obedience." *Journal of Abnormal and Social Psychology*, 1963, *67*, 371–378.

MILLER, S. M. "The Credentials Society." *The Public Interest*, 1967, Fall (9), 127–128.

MISCHEL, W. *Personality and Assessment*. New York: Wiley, 1968, 106–145.

MURRAY, H. A. *Explorations in Personality*. New York: Oxford University Press, 1938.

MURRAY, H. A. "In Nomine Diaboli." *New England Quarterly*, 1941, *24*, 435–452.

MURRAY, H. A. "American Icarus." In *Clinical Studies of Personality*. Vol. 2. New York: Harper & Row, 1955.

MURRAY, H. A. "Preparations for the Scaffold of a Comprehensive System." In S. Koch (Ed.), *Psychology: A Study of a Science*. Vol. 3. *Formulations of the Person and the Social Context*. New York: McGraw-Hill, 1959.

MYERS, J. K., AND BEAN, L. L. *A Decade Later: A Follow-Up of Social Class and Mental Illness*. New York: Wiley, 1968.

OSKAMP, S. "Overconfidence in Case-Study Judgments." *Journal of Consulting Psychology*, 1965, *29*, 261–265.

PETERSON, D. R. *The Clinical Study of Social Behavior*. New York: Appleton-Century-Crofts, 1968.

PHILLIPS, D. J. "The Will To Live." *Trans-Action*, 1971, *8* (3), 16.

RAHE, R. H., MC KEAN, J. D., AND ARTHUR, R. J. "A Longitudinal Study of Life—Change and Illness Patterns." *Journal of Psychosomatic Research*, 1967, *10*, 355–366.

RAUSH, H. L. "Naturalistic Method and the Clinical Approach." In Willems, E. P., and Raush, H. L. (eds.). *Naturalistic Viewpoints in Psychological Research*. New York: Holt, Rinehart and Winston, 1969, 122–146.

ROGERS, C. R. *On Becoming a Person*. Boston: Houghton Mifflin, 1961.

ROTH, J. A. *Timetables*. Indianapolis: Bobbs-Merrill, 1963.

SANFORD, N. "The Freeing and Acting Out of Impulse in Late Adolescence: Evidence from Two Cases." In White, R. W. *Study of Lives*. New York: Atherton, 1963, 4–39.

SARBIN, T. R., TAFT, R., AND BAILEY, D. E. *Clinical Inference and Cognitive Theory.* New York: Holt, Rinehart and Winston, 1960.

SCHEFF, T. J. "The Social Reaction to Deviance: Ascriptive Elements in the Psychiatric Screening of Mental Patients in a Mid Western State Hospital." *Social Problems,* 1964, *11,* 401–413.

SCHRAMM, W. "The Challenge of Curriculum." In A. de Grazia and D. A. Sohn (Eds.), *Programs, Teachers, and Machines.* New York: Bantam, 1964, 3–15.

SELYE, H. *The Stress of Life.* New York: McGraw-Hill, 1956.

SHERWOOD, M. *The Logic of Explanation in Psychoanalysis.* New York: Academic Press, 1969, 73, 261.

SKINNER, B. F. "The Science of Learning and the Art of Teaching." *Harvard Educational Review,* 1954, *24,* 86–97.

SNOW, C. P. *The Two Cultures and the Scientific Revolution.* Cambridge (Eng.): University Press, 1959.

SNOW, C. P. *The Two Cultures and a Second Look.* Cambridge (Eng.): University Press, 1964.

SOLOMON, L. N. "Specific Philosophy of Program of U.S. International University." In N. J. Matulef, K. E. Pottharst, and P. J. Rothenberg (Eds.), *The Revolution in Professional Training.* National Council on Graduate Education in Psychology, 1970, 60–63.

SOSKIN, W. F. "Bias in Postdiction from Projective Tests." *Journal of Abnormal and Social Psychology,* 1954, *49,* 69–74.

SPRADLEY, J. P. "The Moral Career of a Bum." *Trans-Action,* 1970, *7* (7), 16–29.

STERN, G. G., STEIN, M. I., AND BLOOM, B. S. *Methods in Personality Assessment.* New York: Free Press, 1963.

SZASZ, T. *Myth of Mental Illness.* New York: Hoeber-Harper, 1964.

TAGIURI, R. "Person Perception." In Lindzey, G., and Aronson, E. *The Handbook of Social Psychology.* (2nd Ed.) Reading, Mass.: Addison-Wesley, 1969, 395–449.

TAYLOR, C. W., PRICE, P. B., RICHARDS, J. M., JR., AND JACOBSEN, T. L. "An Investigation of the Criterion Problem for a Group of Medical General Practitioners." *Journal of Applied Psychology,* 1965, *49* (6), 399–406.

THOMAS, W. I., AND ZNANIECKI, F. *The Polish Peasant in Europe and America.* New York: Knopf (2-vol. ed.), 1927.

TOULMIN, S. *Foresight and Understanding.* New York: Harper & Row, 1961.

VAN GENNEP, A. *The Rites of Passage* (Trans. M. B. Vizedom and G. L. Coffee). Chicago: University of Chicago Press, 1960.

WEBSTER, E. C. *Decision Making in the Employment Interview.* Montreal: Industrial Relations Center, McGill University, 1964.

WESSMAN, A. E. (ed.). *Harvard Psychological Clinic—1927–1957.* Cambridge, Mass., 1957.

WHITE, R. W. *Lives in Progress.* New York: Holt, Rinehart and Winston, 1960.

WHITE, R. W. (ed.). *The Study of Lives.* New York: Atherton, 1963.

WIGMORE, J. H. *The Principles of Judicial Proof* (2nd ed.). Boston: Little, Brown, 1931.

WILLEMS, E. P., AND RAUSH, H. L. *Naturalistic Viewpoints in Psychological Research.* New York: Holt, Rinehart and Winston, 1969.

WYLER, A. R., MASUDA, M., AND HOLMES, T. H. "Seriousness in Illness Rating Scale." *Journal of Psychosomatic Research,* 1968, *11*, 363–374.

Index

A

Ability, tests of, 5
Accuracy. *See* Prediction
Actuarial assessment, 59–60
ADLER, A., 22, 39, 42, 44, 45
Age status, 34, 43, 57
ALBEE, G. W., 135
ALLPORT, G. W., 24, 39, 51, 88, 160
ANGELL, R., 47, 50
ANSBACHER, H. L., 36, 42
ANSBACHER, R. R., 36, 42
Anthropology. *See* Life history
ARTHUR, R. J., 32–34, 84
Assessment: in academic institutions, 133–134; in bureaucratic organizations, 9, 13–14; criteria of, 15, 71–75; of the disadvantaged person, 136–142, 152, 190–211; in law, 24, 30–31, 134; as learning, 102, 160–161, 163–165; multiform, 18, 42; research on, 21–23; by self, 45; therapy-oriented, 21; use of behavioral codes in, 158–160, 162. *See also* Life history, Validity
ATKINS, A. L., 160
Authentication: of credentials, 51; external, 51–52, 69; internal, 52–53; of programed cases, 78–79; use of behavioral laws in, 52–53. *See also* **Validity**

B

BAER, T. A., 85, 150–151
BAILEY, D. E., 20, 23, 102, 163
BALDWIN, A. L., 28
BARITZ, L., 10
BARKER, R. G., 49, 50, 84
BARRETT, R. S., 5
Behavioral code, 44–45, 59, 158
Behavioral data, 21, 49, 52, 120
Belgian judges, 90, 97
BELLAK, L., 55
BENDIX, R., 15
BENTZ, V. J., 133
Bias, 49. *See also* Disadvantaged persons
BIERI, J. A., 160
BLOCK, J., 74, 103
BLOOM, B. S., 42
BRIAR, S., 160
Broadband utility, 133
BRONFENBRENNER, U., 59
BROWN, R., 60
BUHLER, C., 30, 35, 38–39, 42, 43, 45, 56
Bureaucratic assessment, 9, 13–14. *See also* Civil Service
BUROS, O. K., 76

C

CAIN, L. D., 34

237

72
74
75
76
79
80
83
86
88